John Foxe and the Elizabethan Church

John Foxe
and the
Elizabethan Church

V. NORSKOV OLSEN

University of California Press
Berkeley, Los Angeles, London
1973

University of California Press
Berkeley and Los Angeles, California
University of California Press, Ltd.
London, England
Copyright © 1973 by The Regents of the University of California
ISBN: 0–520–02075–8
Library of Congress Catalog Card Number: 70–165231
Designed by Jean Peters
Printed in the United States of America

TO MY WIFE

Acknowledgments

$\mathcal{F}$OR THE CONCEPTION and execution of this work I am first and foremost indebted for invaluable help and scholarly guidance to Professor Patrick Collinson, my mentor, because this book grew out of a doctoral dissertation presented to the Faculty of Theology and the Department of Ecclesiastical History, King's College, University of London. I also wish to express my appreciation to the Reverend C. W. Dugmore, Professor of Ecclesiastical History in the University of London, and A. G. Dickens, Professor of History and Director of the Institute of Historical Research at the University of London, for their valuable suggestions and their encouragement to pursue this study of John Foxe. None of these scholars, of course, are in any way responsible for the justice of the interpretations given in this book, for which I alone am responsible.

A significant debt of gratitude I wish to express to Norman V. Hope, Archibald Alexander Professor of Church History, Princeton Theological Seminary, who first guided me into Reformation studies and from whom I learned to admire the Protestant Reformers while employing their analytical and critical capacities to the utmost.

Clyde L. Manschreck, Director of the Center for Reformation and Free Church Studies at the Chicago Theological Seminary, was most gracious to rea dthe final draft of the manuscript. I wish to acknowledge his suggestions and comments with thanks.

Help has been given unstintingly by many libraries. I am pleased for the opportunity to mention the following: the British Museum, the Institute of Historical Research, the Lambeth Palace, the Public Record Office—all of London; the Cambridge University Library and the Bodleian Library, Oxford. I am especially grateful to the Librarians of the Doctor William's Library, London, who allowed me to borrow rare books and keep them beyond stated periods.

The research facilities of the University of Basel and my two years' sojourn in that city did much to broaden my understanding of the Marian exiles and John Foxe especially. I am most thankful to the University of Basel for the hospitality extended to me.

After taking up residence in California, I found a new haven in the Huntington Library. The research facilities here surpass one's expectation; and for one whose special interest is the Elizabethan era, this library has made California the Golden West.

The book was long in writing. Now that it is ready to go to press, I wish to express my appreciation to Alain L. Hénon, Associate Editor at the University of California Press, with whom all the dealings for the publication of this book have been most cordial. The publishers deserve sincere gratitude.

The debt to my wife remains, as always, beyond evaluation. During the many years of graduate studies and research, she was always at my side. Unselfishly she laid aside her own pursuits and buried her own talents (for shorter and longer periods) in order to make her husband's objectives her own. Only by her unfailing help and inspiration were his objectives realized. The book is also hers.

V. N. O.

Contents

Abbreviations

AM (1554)   *Commentarii Rervm in Ecclesia ... Liber Primus.* Strassburg, 1554.

AM (1559)   *Rervm in Ecclesia . . . Commentarii.* Basel, 1559.

AM (1563)   *Actes and Monuments.* London, 1563.

AM (1570)   *Actes and Monumentes.* London, 1570. 2 vols.

AM (1576)   *Acts and Monumentes.* London, 1576. 2 vols.

AM (1583)   *Actes and Monuments.* 4th ed. London, 1583. 2 vols.

AM (1641)   *Acts and Monuments.* 8th ed. London, 1641. 3 vols.

AM   *The Acts and Monuments of John Foxe.* Ed. Josiah Pratt. London, 1853–1870.

Adul.   *De non Plectendis Morte Adulteris Consultatio.* London, 1548.

Apoc.   *Eicasmi sev Meditationes in Sacram Apocalypsin.* London, 1587.

CC   *A Sermon of Christ Crucified.* London, 1831.

Cong.   "To the True and Faithfull Congregation, of Christes Vniuersall Church," preface to *AM* (1570).

CT   *Christus Triumphans, Comoedia Apocalyptica,* Ed. T[homas] C[omber]. London, 1672.

Exc.   *De Censvra sive Excommvnicatione Ecclesiastica.* London, 1551.

FCCP   "Foure Considerations Geuen out to Christian Protestantes, Professours of the Gospell," preface to *AM* (1583).

FJ   *Of Free Justification by Christ.* London, 1694.

FQP   "To All the Professed Frendes and Folowers of the Popes Proceedinges, Foure Questions Propounded," preface to *AM* (1576).

FW   A Letter of John Foxe to Archbishop Whitgift. Lambeth Palace Library MS, no. 2010, fols. 117–121 v. N.d.

Nob.   *Ad Inclytos ac Praepotantes Angliae Proceres, Ordines, & Status, totamque eius gentis Nobilitatem, pro Afflictis Fratribus Svoplicatio.* Basel, 1557.

OT   *A Sermon Preached at the Christening of a certain Jew.* Trans. James Bell. London, 1578. Reprinted in *British Reformers*, Vol. XII (London, 1831).

PGT   "To the Persecutors of Gods Truth, Commonlye Called Papistes," preface to *AM* (1563).

Pratt   First part of *AM*, I, containing Pratt's biography of John Foxe, as well as some of Foxe's minor works, letters, and prefaces.

QE (1563)   "To the Qvene's Most Excellent Maiestie, Quene Elizabeth," preface to *AM* (1563).

QE (1570)   "To the Right Vertvovs, Most Excellent, and Noble Princess, Quene Elizabeth," preface to *AM* (1570).

Syl.   *Syllogisticon.* London, 1560–1564?

UPH   "A Declaration Concerning the Utilitie and Profite of Thys History," preface to *AM* (1563).

LJF   "The Life of John Foxe," by Simeon Foxe, preface to *AM* (1641), II.

Prolegomena

*T*HE LIFE of John Foxe, 1517–1577, spans the formative and formulative period of the English Reformation, and he himself is counted as one of its prominent figures and most prolific writers. Foxe's influence and the high esteem in which he was held, not only in the reign of Queen Elizabeth I but also during the centuries following, are generally recognized by the great value placed upon his signal work, the *Acts and Monuments*, commonly called the "Book of Martyrs." During its early history it was considered second only to the Bible. Together with the Holy Scriptures and Bishop Jewel's *Defence of the Apology of the Church of England*, it was placed in some convenient place in the parish churches so that the people could read it before or after the services.[1] The last (ninth) edition appeared in 1684. The continued interest in this work is seen in the great number of editions printed through the centuries. The British Museum catalogue lists thirty-five complete versions, not including the ancient editions, and more than fifty abridgments and extracts, some of which have been published within recent years.

The story of the life and work of the man will be unfolded as this study proceeds, but some biographical data should be

---

[1] John Strype, *Annals of the Reformation* (Oxford, 1824), Vol. III, pt. 1, p. 738.

mentioned here. His father died when he was very young, so his boyhood was spent in the home of his mother's second husband, Richard Melton. Friends who recognized his talents sent him to Oxford about 1534, and here he was educated at Brasenose and Magdalen colleges. The latter college nominated him a fellow in 1538, and he held this fellowship for the next seven years. He obtained his M.A. in 1544, but declined ordination for which he was due in 1545. His intimate friends and correspondents at this time included Alexander Nowell, Hugh Latimer, and William Tyndale, and he shared their Protestant convictions. Together with five of his colleagues he resigned his fellowship in 1545, and we find him for a short while vicar and then tutor near Stratford-on-Avon. In February 1547, he married Agnes Randall, a member of the William Lucy household, where Foxe had the post of a tutor. Next we find Foxe teaching in the London residence of the widowed duchess of Richmond. Here he taught her son Thomas, the future Duke of Norfolk and loyal patron of Foxe; and the daughter Jane, who became countess of Westmoreland; as well as the boy Charles Howard, the later Lord Howard and commander of the English fleet against the Armada. While a tutor in London, Foxe composed his earliest writings and became more intimately associated with the church. He was ordained deacon by Bishop Ridley of London in 1550.

During the reign of Mary, Foxe went abroad into exile. Leaving in the spring of 1554, he stayed for a short period first in Strassburg and then in Frankfurt, later settling in Basel, where he was closely associated with John Bale, Laurence Humphrey, and Edmund Grindal. Foxe returned to England in the autumn of 1559 after having published the Latin edition of the *Acts and Monuments* (1559). This edition is generally considered to be the first in view of the smallness of the Strassburg edition (1554).

After his return to England, Foxe was ordained a priest in January 1560 by his friend Grindal, bishop of London. The success of the first English edition of the *Acts and Monuments* (1563) at once made Foxe an important public figure, yet personally he was very modest and self-effacing. His son Simeon, who practiced medicine in London for nearly forty years and died in 1642, tells us in his biography of John Foxe, printed in the 1641 edition of the *Acts and Monuments*, that his father lived "a life passed over without noise, of modesty at home, and abroad, of continuance, charity, contempt of the world, and thirst after heavenly things: of unwearied labours, and all actions so performed, as might be exemplary, or beneficiall to others."[2] Relating the death and funeral of his father, he observes: "Upon the report of his death the whole City lamented, honouring the small Funerall which was made for him, with the concourse of a great multitude of people, and in no other fashion of mourning, than as if among so many, each man had buried his own father, or his own brother."[3]

Foxe felt himself called to be a promoter of peace and concord, and his own personality equipped him to take on such a role. In his earliest work, a tract against the death penalty for adultery, he tells the reader in the opening paragraph: "I have always by nature been most averse to controversy, preferring rather even to concede than to enter into contention with others. So I cannot at all desert the cause of sinners, for whom so willingly Christ died. Rather, with the Samaritan I would help the wounded and half-dead [traveller] with oil and necessities." He adds disapprovingly: "There are many who think we all should be more ready to condemn than to pardon."[4] Simeon testifies to the charitable nature of his father when he writes: "Master Fox was by nature so ignorant in requiting injuries, that he would many times with much adoe confesse himself wronged, even then, when he had in his hands ability to revenge."[5]

Apparently Foxe's own gentle nature influences him to write about the gentleness of others. Speaking about Constantine, whom he greatly admires, he mentions the "singular gentle nature of this meek and religious Constantine." Furthermore, he continues, all princes should learn from him "how gently to govern."[6] Christ is referred to as "the meek King of glory" and readers are warned how "dangerous a thing it is to refuse the gospel of God, when it is so gently offered."[7] During the Marian persecution he writes to the nobility of England, asking: "Where is the Pauline equity; where is your clemency?" Foxe admon-

[2] *LJF*, sig. B1v.
[3] *LJF*, sig. B2r.
[4] *Adul.*, sig. Aiir-v.
[5] *LJF*, sig. A5r.
[6] *AM*, I, 298.
[7] *AM*, I, 89.

ishes them to act in a "moderate way, worthy of a theologian."[8]
In another connection he urges: "Be controlled by the Spirit of
gentleness,"[9] and make use of "the kindness of the gospel."[10]
Foxe's gentle nature, considerate disposition, and moderate attitude toward various controversial issues will be noticed on a
number of occasions. The same qualities made him well-disposed
to toleration, a topic to which special attention is given in chapter vi.

Foxe's personality and outlook were, to some degree, influenced by Christian Humanism. Henry VIII patronized the
Humanists, and while Foxe was at Oxford, an Erasmian climate
pervaded the university. Here Foxe was engaged not only in
theological but also in literary, historical, and philosophical pursuits, and the many references in his writings to Greek and
Roman classics point out that his humanistic studies had not been
in vain. He shared the hope of the Christian Humanists that the
new learning would bring a new age of enlightenment which
would advance the preaching of the Gospel. Dealing with the
significance of the invention of printing, he points out some of
its benefits for the advancement of Christian Humanism: "As
printing of books ministered matter of reading, so reading
brought learning, learning showed light, by the brightness
whereof blind ignorance was suppressed, error detected, and
finally, God's glory, with truth of his word, advanced."[11]

Foxe was an admirer of Erasmus. When he arrived on the
Continent in the spring of 1554, he went first to Rotterdam to
see the house in which Erasmus was born. Thence he journeyed
to Frankfurt, because he had heard that Froben, the renowned
printer from Basel, was there. Foxe later tells us that they "had
conversed about Erasmus."[12]

---

[8] *Nob.*, pp. 15, 51.   [9] *Adul.*, sig. Ciii*r*.

[10] *Pratt*, App. XIII, p. 31.

[11] *AM*, III, 721–722. Foxe's discussion of this subject was later extracted
and printed as a small tract, *The benefit and invention of printing; by J. F.,
that famous martyrologist. Extracted out of his "Acts and Monuments"*
(London, 1704).

[12] Harleian MS, no. 417, fol. 118.

The influence of Erasmus and other Christian Humanists was no doubt made relevant to Foxe during his stay in Basel as a Marian exile from September 1555 to September 1559. Erasmus had lived in Basel during several periods of his life and there he died in 1536. The two famous printing and publishing houses of Froben and Oporinus had a great share in making Basel a center of Christian Humanism. Erasmus had worked in the first, and when he returned in 1535 was warmly welcomed by the latter. Oporinus retired from his professorship at the university in 1542 in order to dedicate his life to publishing. When Foxe arrived in Basel, took up his work as proofreader with Froben and Oporinus, and, in the following year, matriculated at the university, he was placed in surroundings that could not but be conducive to his ideals of Christian Humanism. Erasmus's practical concern, his anticeremonial attitude, and his emphasis on spiritual religion were fully shared by Foxe, as were his moderation and his plea for toleration. Foxe vigorously defended Erasmus and his *Paraphrases* on the New Testament, which was required to be available in the churches not only under Edward but also under Elizabeth. This work and the "Book of Martyrs" found their place together and thus identified a relationship between the two men. In the endeavors of the Christian Humanists for a return to original sources and to the pure and primitive church, Foxe was actively engaged. This aspect of Foxe, the Erasmian, leads us to another, the Puritan.

John Foxe has often been referred to as a Puritan, but this term, perhaps more than any other from the Elizabethan and Stuart periods, has been subject to distortion. When, therefore, Foxe is called a Puritan, we must determine what is meant by this appellation. Puritans are commonly apprehended as a homogeneous group who began a protest movement during the reign of Elizabeth I. This protest developed into the Civil War and the exodus to the New England states by some, and placed its religious stamp on life and society in the English-speaking world. By definition, Puritanism means different things, not only when applied to various stages but also to diverse men and groups within the same period. The dilemma of definition has remained with us to the present time.[13] The term has been applied to English Protestants at large by the Roman Catholics, to Nonconformists by the Anglicans, to those who remained within the religious settlement and to those who fled abroad, to those who were strongly Calvinistic in theology and to those who opposed it, to Anabaptists, Presbyterians, and Congregationalists; Puritans are distinguished as Puritans in religion, Puritans in state, Puritans in church policy, and Puritans in morality; they are defined as Episcopalian Puritans, Presbyterians Puritans, and Congregationalist Puritans, as well as Puritans of the church type and Puritans of the sect type. The term came to symbolize various negative aspects within church and society as did the words "Jew" and "popery"; thus it became loaded with emotional explosiveness.

In spite of the difficulty in giving a precise meaning to the word—a problem that has been increased rather than simplified by the unnecessary generalizations of later historians, novelists, playwrights, economists, and poets—it is possible to draw a concrete picture of the Puritanism represented by John Foxe.

The word "Puritan" may have its roots partly in the endeavors of the Christian Humanists to bring Christianity back to the purity of the New Testament and the early church. Among the Christian Humanists, "pure" came to symbolize the quest of the Renaissance for a return to original sources and the attempt to renew many aspects of life and doctrine within the church which the Papacy had defiled and polluted. Words like "pure," "purify," "purity," "pure doctrine," "pure church," "pure faith," "pure Gospel," and synonyms were used on the Continent by the Reformers and in England during the reign of Edward VI by visiting professors such as Bucer and Martyr and returning exiles such as Hooper and Coverdale, as well as by the Marian exiles both on the Continent and at their return to England in the beginning of Elizabeth's reign.[14]

[13] For attempts to define Puritanism, see Christopher Hill, *Society and Puritanism in Pre-Revolutionary England* (London, 1966), pp. 13–29; Basil Hall, "Puritanism: the Problem of Definition," in *Studies in Church History*, Vol. II, ed. G. J. Cuming (London, 1965), pp. 283–296.

[14] Leonard J. Trinterud, ed., *Elizabethan Puritanism* (New York, 1971), pp. 3–6.

The word "Puritan" seems to have been coined in the 1560s. John Stowe refers to Puritans when he writes, in 1567, that there were "many congregations of the Anabaptysts in London, who cawlyd themselvs Puritans or Unspottyd Lambs of the Lord." He tells us the various places where they worshiped and in this connection mentions that for some time they worshiped "ny Wolle Key in Thamse strete, wher only the goodman of the howse and the preachar, whose name was Brown (and his awditory wer cawlyd the Browyngs), were comyttyd to ward."[15] Most likely Stowe makes use of the term "Puritan" as a name that had recently been applied to the nonconformity he opposes. Patrick Collinson thinks that these designations "would almost certainly be opprobrious labels attached to them, not what they called themselves."[16] The Spanish ambassador, De Silva, may have had these Anabaptists in mind, as well as other separatist groups in London, when he wrote under the date February 16, 1568: "About a week ago they discovered here a newly invented sect, called by those who belong to it 'the pure or stainless religion.' They met to the number of 150 in a house where their preacher used a half a tub for a pulpit, and was girded with a white cloth. Each one brought with him whatever food he had at home to eat, and the leaders divided money amongst those who were poorer, saying that they imitated the life of the apostles and refused to enter the temples to partake of the Lord's supper as it was a papistical ceremony." In another letter, written on March 14, we find these lines: "Orders have been given to release the people who call themselves members of the pure or apostolic religion, on condition that within 20 days they conform to the religion of the State or leave the country." Three months later, on June 26, he states: "In spite of the threats made to the sect called the Puritans, to prevent their meeting together, I am informed that recently as many as 400 of them met near here, and, although a list of their names was taken, only six of

[15] John Stowe, *Three Fifteenth-Century Chronicles, with Historical Memoranda*, ed. James Gairdner, Camden Society, new series, Vol. XXVIII (London, 1880), p. 143.
[16] Patrick Collinson, *The Elizabethan Puritan Movement* (London, 1967), p. 86.

them were arrested, in order to avoid scandal and also because they have their influential abettors."[17]

It has been suggested that the designation "Puritan" originated with the Catholics.[18] For example, Thomas Stapleton, a Catholic controversialist who left for the Continent soon after the accession of Elizabeth, refers indirectly to the English Reformers as Puritans in his written attack of 1565.[19] Thomas Harding, who during the reign of Edward VI upheld the reformed religion but subscribed to the required declaration on the accession of Mary and left England when Elizabeth became Queen, made the first attack on Foxe, the historiographer, after the publication of the first English edition of the *Acts and Monuments* in 1563. He refers two years later to this major work of Foxe as "that huge dongehill of your stinking martyrs, which ye haue intituled Actes and monumentes."[20] Harding's work is directed against Bishop Jewel's *Apology of the Church of England* of 1562. The controversy with Jewel began in 1564 when he answered Jewel's sermon preached against the Catholics at St. Paul's Cross, 1559. Jewel published a *Defence* (1568), and in Harding's reply in the same year he scornfully makes use of the expressions "vnspotted Congregation" and "Puritanes."[21]

It is somewhat ironical that the term "Puritan," used by the Catholics against Archbishop Parker and his associates, was used in turn by these gentlemen when their critics published *An Admonition to the Parliament* (1572).

Thomas Fuller gives the following description of the beginning of Puritanism:

> The English Bishops, conceiving themselves empowered by their canons, began to shew their authority in urging the clergy of

[17] *Calendar of Letters and State Papers relating to English Affairs*, Vol. II (Elizabeth, 1568–1579), ed. Martin A. S. Hume (London, 1894), pp. 7, 12, 43.

[18] See Trinterud, *op. cit.*, pp. 6–8.

[19] Thomas Stapleton, *A Fortresse of the Faith* (Antwerp, 1565), sig. 32r–46v.

[20] Thomas Harding, *A Confvtation of a Booke Intitvled An Apologie of the Chvrch of England* (Antwerp, 1565), sig. 14r.

[21] Thomas Harding, *A detection of sundrie foule errours...by M. Jewell* (n.p., 1568), fol. 332r.

their diocese to subscribe to the liturgy, ceremonies, and discipline of the church; and such as refused the same were branded with the odious name of puritans.

A name which in this notion first began in this year [1564], and the grief had not been great if it had ended in the same. The philosopher banisheth the term, (which is *polysaemon*,) that is subject to several senses out of the predicaments, as affording too much covert for cavil by the latitude thereof. On the same account could I wish that the word *puritan* were banished common discourse, because so various in the acceptions thereof. We need not speak of the ancient *cathari*, or primitive puritans, sufficiently known by their heretical opinions. *Puritan* here was taken for the opposers of the hierarchy and church-service, as resenting of superstition. But profane mouths quickly improved this nickname, therewith on every occasion to abuse pious people, some of them so far from opposing the liturgy that they endeavoured (according to the instructions thereof in the preparative to the confession) to accompany the minister with a *pure* heart, and laboured (as it is in the absolution) for a life *pure* and holy. We will therefore decline the word, to prevent exceptions, which, if casually slipping from our pen, the reader knoweth that only nonconformists are thereby intended.

These, in this age, were divided into two ranks: some mild and moderate, contented only to enjoy their own conscience; others fierce and fiery, to the disturbance of church and state.[22]

The event that is the historical background for Fuller's description will be dealt with in connection with a discussion of Foxe's part in the Vestiarian Controversy. Here it suffices to say that in March 1564, some of the clergy petitioned Archbishop Parker for indulgence toward their refusal to wear vestments. John Foxe was one of the twenty who signed this formal request. Fuller speaks about two types of Puritanism, "the fierce and fiery" and the "mild and moderate," and places Foxe among the latter.

Fuller gives 1564 as the year when the term "Puritan" was in use by Elizabethan Divines. This fact does not necessarily contradict the assertion that it was first used by the Catholics. When

[22] Thomas Fuller, *The Church History of Britain* (Oxford, 1845), IV, 327–328.

the Catholic writers used the term, its usage would most likely antedate the writings already quoted. Whether or not the term "Puritan" was first used by the Catholics, it is certain that it was coined during the 1560s. Leonard J. Trinterud has pointed out that, in the writings of Parker and his colleagues, the word "Puritan" was first used against their critics after the Admonition Controversy.[23] When the high officials within the Elizabethan Church applied the term to these critics after 1572, they surely knew that the Catholics had already used it against themselves. Basil Hall, who makes Stowe's and Fuller's statements the historical beginning of the term, does not refer to its Catholic origin as Trinterud does, but states that from 1570 to 1640 the position is clear:

> Puritan is the regular word for those clergymen and laymen of the established Church of England whose attitude ranged from the tolerably conformable to the downright obstreperous, and to those who sought to presbyterianise that Church from within. Whereas Brownist, Separatist, Barrowist, and Anabaptist are the appropriate terms (each, it will be remembered, carrying a point of differentiation for those who refused to accept the principle that Christ's Church could be conterminous with the Tudor or Stuart state.[24]

This definition seems to be supported by Richard Baxter who, at the beginning of the Civil War in 1642, writes:

> Any man that was for a spiritual, serious way of worship (though he were for moderate Episcopacy and liturgy), and that lived according to his profession, was called commonly a Presbyterian, as formerly he was called a Puritan, unless he joined himself to Independents, Anabaptists, or some other sect which might afford him a more odious name.[25]

Hall finds that contemporary sources do not apply the term "to those who deliberately removed themselves" from the established Church, for they "were given the names appropriate to their particular views."[26]

[23] Trinterud, *op. cit.*, p. 8.   [24] Hall, *op. cit.*, p. 294.
[25] J. M. Lloyd Thomas, ed., *The Autobiography of Richard Baxter*, abridged from the *Reliquiae Baxterianae*, 1696 (London, 1925), p. 154.
[26] Hall, *op. cit.*, p. 290.

A homogeneous view of Puritanism, which in turn makes it difficult to define the term, was partly created by eighteenth-century historians for whom "Puritanism became an ancestral banner under which a dissenter, after the death of Queen Anne, could sink party feelings and struggle against the established Church." Another factor has been called "an historical fixation on Puritanism." From this point of view modern America began with Puritanism, and anyone who can be counted as a contributor to this phase of American history finds place among the Puritans. The loss of the word's original meaning was also furthered by

> . . . those historians who after 1662, whether writing from the point of view of Roman Catholicism, of Anglicanism, or of nineteenth-century liberalism, have accepted the principle of herding into one pound all those of protestant convictions who troubled, or strayed from, the fold established by the Act of Uniformity of 1559, and calling it Puritanism have thus masked the emphases of Puritanism, indicated its incoherence, and regarded it with sorrow if not anger as a byword for negations and moral repressions occasionally illumined by genuine piety and moral integrity; or, writing from the point of view of sociology, regard 'Puritanism,' however diverse, as a useful springboard for economic and political discussion without regard to its primarily and intensely religious signficance.[27]

However distorted the concept of Puritanism may be in the public mind, the term still expresses an acknowledgment of qualities essential to the Puritan character. The Puritans have been described as "elect spirits, segregated from the mass of mankind by an experience of conversion, fired by the sense that God was using them to revolutionize human history, and committed to the execution of his Will."[28] G. G. Coulton and Gerald R. Owst have brought to our attention the link between Puritanism and the Middle Ages. Owst states:

> Further, all that that unpopular word "Puritanism" has ever stood for, to the minutest detail, shall be found advocated unceas-

[27] *Ibid.*, pp. 286–287.
[28] Alan Simpson, *Puritanism in Old and New England* (Chicago, 1961), p. 39.

ingly in the preaching of the pre-Reformation Church. The long face, the plain diet, the plainer attire, the abstention from sports and amusements in company, the contempt of the arts, the rigid Sabbatarianism, the silence at meals, the long household prayers, the stern disciplining of wife and children, the fear of hell, the heavy mood of "wanhope," are typical of the message of the faithful friar.[29]

M. M. Knappen confirms the plausibility of the suggested medieval ties:

> Puritanism was a transitional movement linking the medieval with the modern. Only recently have students begun to notice the strength and importance of its medieval ties. Puritan asceticism is seen to be directly related to Roman Catholic asceticism; Puritan economic doctrine, to the social teachings of the scholastics.[30]

Recently, Irvonwy Morgan has convincingly shown that the Puritan preachers were successors of the Preaching Friars.[31] In seeking to define Foxe, the Puritan, we should notice that he characterizes himself as a Preaching Friar. The description is found in a letter written in 1561 to his friend and colleague, Laurence Humphrey, who, after his return from exile, had become president of Magdalen College in Oxford. The letter furnishes an interesting insight into Foxe's concept of his own calling:

> What do I hear? you to be president of Magdalen? I am glad for your sake and that of the college. "But why do I trifle thus and congratulate you, when I ought to reproach you? Come now, tell me, my friend, have you really deserted your flock and order? Are you not ashamed to be a runaway, a renegade? You should have taken from me an example of greater constancy; for I remain still in the same rags and filth (*pannis et sordibus*) in which England received me on my return from Germany. I change not my degree nor order, which is that of the mendicant brothers, or if

[29] Gerald R. Owst, *Preaching in Medieval England* (Cambridge, 1926), p. 94. See also G. G. Coulton, *Ten Medieval Studies* (Boston, 1959), chap. 4.

[30] M. M. Knappen, *Tudor Puritanism* (Chicago, 1965), p. ix.

[31] Irvonwy Morgan, *The Godly Preachers of the Elizabethan Church* (London, 1965).

you will, the preaching brothers. You too were in this order, and perhaps were to be a good partner with us. But now you have left our company and gone up higher, riding as they say, in a white chariot." Yet while I congratulate Magdalen, I fear I shall suffer; I may lose my good comrade. While we were on the same plane, we met as equals, and spoke frankly and familiarly. But now I must bid farewell to my old fellow-soldier: for what he will be like raised to the presidency, I cannot tell. Yet even as I write, your letter arrives, and shows me that my old Laurence still lives unchanged.[32]

Twenty years later Foxe makes another comparison with the monks. In 1581 his son Samuel was dismissed from Magdalen College, Oxford. It seems that the extreme Puritans had initiated his dismissal. The father refers to them as "these factious puritans" who are "worse than the old monks, and would reduce all to Judaean servitude."[33] This statement is made at a time when the division between the moderate and more fierce Puritans of the early 1560s had widened greatly. Foxe could not agree with the Mosaic legalism that developed among the "factious puritans."

It has been affirmed that casuistry is the moving force behind Puritanism.[34]

The mainspring of the Puritan's mechanism was his moral consciousness. The beautiful and the true were to him only the handmaidens of the good. . . .

The Puritan moral standard was formidable in the extreme. It was all inclusive and absolute. All acts were moral. At no moment was one exempt from ethical considerations. There would be an accounting for every idle word, and about the criterion there was no relativity or shadow of turning.[35]

Edward Dering, whom Patrick Collinson has called "a mirror of Elizabethan Puritanism,"[36] stresses that all acts must be con-

---

[32] Quoted by J. F. Mozley, *John Foxe and His Book* (London, 1940), p. 66.

[33] *Ibid.*, pp. 111–112.   [34] Hall, *op. cit.*, p. 296.

[35] Knappen, *op. cit.*, pp. 341, 342.

[36] Patrick Collinson, *A Mirror of Elizabethan Puritanism: The Life and Letters of 'Godly Master Dering'* (London, 1964).

sidered from a moral point of view which is theocentric. "If I seeme curious, or to stande vpon light poyntes (beside that in the worshipp of God ther is nothing light) so the cōscience of man is exceding tender that it will neither be troubled nor touched in the least title, contrarie to a perswasiō of trueth. The waight of sinne is not in substance of matter, but in the Maiestie of god, that is offended. And be the thing neuer so litle, yet the breach of his cōmaundement, deserueth death."[37] This in turn meant that, within the fellowship of the saints, preaching and instruction aimed at a high standard of conduct and private and public discipline had to be exercised in case of any fault.

It has been suggested that "at the heart of the difficulties in so much discussion of Puritanism" lies the fact "that many of those who work on the literature and history of the sixteenth and seventeenth centuries in England do not always have the time or the interest to study the theology of these protestants, whereas it is here largely that the distinctions and lines of development can be determined without falling back on the practice of generalisations and qualifications so often resorted to." Basil Hall therefore suggests that it "is particularly in their doctrine of the Church (including ministry, ordination, discipline of morals, and the sacraments) that the differences among those commonly called Puritans can be determined."[38] That the question of the nature of the church and its ministry is of great significance in determining the differences among those called Puritans is implied by A. G. Dickens when he, with his historical insight, speaks about "Episcopalian, Presbyterian and Congregationalist Puritans."[39] Leonard Trinterud classifies the Puritans within a framework of theology and ecclesiology, dividing them into four groups: (1) The Original, Anti-vestment Party; (2) The Passive-Resistance Party; (3) The Presbyterian Party; (4) The Separatist Party. He makes John Foxe one of his two representatives of the original anti-vestment party.[40] While Foxe did oppose the vestment, he was not an extremist as were many

---

[37] *A parte of a register* (Middleburg, 1593), p. 81.
[38] Hall, *op. cit.*, pp. 295–296.
[39] A. G. Dickens, *The English Reformation* (London, 1964), p. 318.
[40] Trinterud, *op. cit.*, pp. 10–16.

others within this group. Foxe, who died in 1587, could easily have been a moderate representative of the passive resistance party. (This suggestion is made to place Foxe in a rightfully broader context, not to criticize, since Trinterud himself acknowledges a certain agreement between groups one and two.)

As the present study, to a very large degree, deals with Foxe as a theologian with special reference to his ecclesiology, it is hoped that Foxe, the Puritan, may emerge. There are good reasons to propose that he be named an Anglican Puritan; and in the light of the results of my study, a few preliminary and qualifying observations should be made regarding this suggestion. The basic qualities that have emerged as characteristic of Puritanism seem to be personified in Foxe. The relationship between Christian Humanism and Puritanism is most evident in his life and work, as is the tie between Puritanism and the medieval preaching friars.

Most biographical sketches of Foxe, in discussing why he did not accept any preferment within the Church of England, give as the reason his opposition to the wearing of the vestment. While there may be some truth to this, it is doubtful that this alone would have held him back. I believe Foxe himself gave his reason when he wrote to Humphrey that he considered himself a preaching friar. His ministry bore witness to the fact that he wished to be free to do the work of a "Gospeller."

The faithful friar was moved by a spiritual religion. He desired to convert men and women and to lead them to sanctity. It is a credit to Foxe that he acknowledged these positive aspects of the life and work of the friars. Irvonwy Morgan has pointed out that if "there is one fact more than another which gave rise to the growth and extension of the Puritan movement it was the corruption of the Preaching Friars and Monastic Brotherhoods and their eventual dissolution in the days of Henry VIII."[41] Foxe, the Puritan, stepped into this vacuum. The godly friars had felt that they could best achieve their objectives of a spiritual religion by establishing a brotherhood within the church, as did the Pietists later in the *collegia pietatis*. It was within the framework of an *ecclesiola in ecclesia* that Foxe saw the opportunity

[41] Morgan, *op. cit.*, p. 2.

to work for the English Church as a whole. This aspect of Puritanism is described by Basil Hall when he, after various attempts to define Puritanism, concludes that "Puritanism was essentially the earlier and English form of that mutation from the protestantism of the Reformation which on the Continent is called Pietism."[42]

The concern with "casuistry" finds, as would be expected, a prominent place in the life of Foxe. One of his earliest works dealt with excommunication. Mosaic legalism, however, which characterized much of Monasticism and Puritanism, was opposed by Foxe; he called the extreme Puritans the "new monks." Knappen has stated that among English Puritans is found "a surprising lack of Christological thought."[43] Cautiously A. G. Dickens comments: "These are hard misgivings which every reader of Puritan literature must sometimes have felt, but the final word should perhaps await a still fuller investigation of the theological content of Puritan writings."[44] We can accurately state that Foxe's life and ministry were Christocentric. That the dynamics of Luther's *sola fide* and *sola gratia* were the essence of his religion is richly illustrated in his writings.

When we qualify Foxe's Puritanism with the term "Anglican," we mean that his Puritanism sought to find its realization within the episcopal structure of the Church of England in close relationship with the ruling monarch and the Parliament. In view of the fact that John Foxe during his own lifetime was respected and honored by both Anglicans and Puritans, it is justifiable to suggest that he embodied some of the basic characteristics of the English Reformers and personified some of their main aspirations. His life was a *via media* between the Anglicans and the Puritans after the Admonition Controversy, in 1572, until his death 1587. It is safe to say that Foxe was a mirror of Elizabethan Anglican Puritanism.

The theology of the English reformers has often been analyzed in order to see how far they were influenced by the men of Wittenberg, Zürich, or Geneva, in other words, to classify them within one of the groups of the Continental Reformers. Foxe

[42] Hall, *op. cit.*, p. 296.
[43] Knappen, *op. cit.*, p. 376
[44] Dickens, *op. cit.*, p. 321.

had a fundamental knowledge of Lutheran and Reformed theology and was influenced by both, but at the same time he had his roots in the religious soil of his own country. He recognized his debt to the basic principle of the Continental Reformation, justification by faith; however, his relationship to Luther deserves special mention. William A. Clebsch asserted in his article, "The Elizabethans on Luther,"[45] that all the editions and expansions of the *Acts and Monuments* presented "a unified, well-constructed story, at the heart of which stood Luther.... By placement and by attention he was skillfully made *the* hero."[46] Before examining this assertion we should mention that Foxe's first publication, about 1547, was a translation of one of Luther's sermons, but the following year two other translations came from his pen: a sermon of Oecolampadius and a catechism of Urbanus Regius. Full twenty years later he again dealt with a specific work of Luther when he edited and prefaced Henry Bull's English translation of Luther's *Commentarie vpon the Fiftene Psalmes.* The following year, 1578, he wrote a preface to a collection of some of Luther's sermons, but the same year he wrote a preface to a sermon by Regius and the next year he reprinted with slight revision a tract also by Regius.

In the *Acts and Monuments* Foxe pays tribute to the historical significance of the Lutheran Reformation: "When was this glorious reformation of the church ever true or like to be true, if it be not true now, in this marvellous alteration of the church in these our latter days? or when was there any such conversion of christian people in all countries ever heard of, since the apostles' time, as hath been since the preaching of Martin Luther?"[47] Foxe also recognized that while many "had somewhat broken the way" for the German Reformation, Luther himself "gave the stroke, and plucked down the foundation, and all by opening one vein, long hid before, wherein lieth the touchstone of all truth and doctrine, as the only principal origin of our salvation, which is, our free justifying by faith only, in

---

[45] William A. Clebsch, "The Elizabethans on Luther," in *Interpreters of Luther*, ed. Jaroslav Pelikan (Philadelphia, 1968), pp. 97 ff.
[46] *Ibid.*, p. 109.
[47] *AM*, IV, 256.

Christ the Son of God."[48] Clebsch is certainly correct in con-
cluding from such statements that Foxe had a "quite clear understanding of Luther's christocentrism" and perceived "precisely
what the modern Luther renaissance rediscovered, that the Reformer's overriding significance lay in the fact that his religion
centered on God and his theology centered on Christ." In this
respect Foxe is a follower of Luther; the present study has already mentioned and will further confirm that Christology was
the center of Foxe's theology. But while recognizing Foxe's debt
to Luther, it is quite another thing to make Luther his hero, or
to claim that "always, Foxe built his story around Luther as
the man who opened a new epoch of church history." Clebsch
refers to William Haller's statement that Foxe "gave Englishmen
their 'first comprehensive printed account of Luther and the
German reformers,' "[49] and, being eager to make Luther the
hero of Foxe, he makes the categorical assertion already referred
to, that at the heart of the *Acts and Monuments* stands Luther.

First it should be noticed that Haller's statement is not about
Luther in particular but about the Continental Reformation at
large, for in full it reads: "Drawing upon Luther, Melancthon
[*sic*], Sleidan, Flacius, Crespin, Pantaleon and similar sources, he
supplied the English public with its first comprehensive printed
account of Luther and the German reformers, Zwingli and his
successors at Zürich, the reformers and martyrs of the Rhineland
and Switzerland, including—though briefly—Geneva, and of
France, Piedmont and Italy.... [Foxe] brought his readers up
to date concerning the state of the Protestant cause on the Continent."[50] Second, it is most pertinent to notice that Haller presents the rightful place of Luther in the scheme of the *Acts and
Monuments* when he points out that "Foxe was as certain as
Aylmer that Wyclif begot Huss, Huss begot Luther and Luther
begot truth, but it did not occur to him that England should wait
for truth to come to her from Germany. It had come to England

---

[48] *AM*, IV, 259.

[49] Clebsch, *op. cit.*, pp. 115, 107, 109.

[50] William Haller, *Foxe's Book of Martyrs and the Elect Nation* (London, 1963), p. 174.

straight from the apostles and had remained there ever since through all vicissitudes."[51]

Foxe's life and work had many facets: he was Foxe, the Historiographer, the Martyrologist, the Humanist, the Erasmian, the Puritan, the Anglican, the Elizabethan Eusebius, the Gospeller, the Ecclesiologist, the Erastian, the precursor of Elizabethan nationalism, the Lutheran, and so on. If any of these are enlarged at the expense of the others, or if any single one is considered with no reference to the rest, then the true picture of him is distorted. His greatness is that many were his mentors but he was the disciple of none. He was able to absorb and learn without becoming a replica of this one or that one. The writings of Foxe reveal that he was an independent thinker in his relationship both to the Continental Reformers and to the Elizabethan Divines.

Having already inquired into some aspects of Foxe's life and work, it becomes appropriate to consider Foxe, the Historiographer and Martyrologist. The English version of the *Acts and Monuments* appeared in nine ancient editions, published respectively in 1563, 1570, 1576, 1583, 1596, 1610, 1632, 1641, and 1684. The first English edition of the *Acts and Monuments* (1563) contains a dedicatory address to Queen Elizabeth I and "A Declaration Concerning the Utilitie and Profite of Thys History," as well as two Latin prefaces, one of thanksgiving to Jesus Christ and another to the learned reader. Foxe also writes a special message "To the Persecutors of God's Truth, Commonlye Called Papistes."[52] In the 1570 edition a new dedicatory preface to the Queen replaces the old, and two new addresses are printed, one "To the True and Faithfull Congregation, of Christes Vniuersall Church," and the other "To All the Professed Frendes and Folowers of the Popes Proceedinges." The latter was no doubt written on account of the pope's bull against Queen Elizabeth I and the northern rebellion. This edition also contains a lengthy comparison between the primitive and latter churches of Rome. In 1576 and again in 1583, the 1570 edition

---

[51] *Ibid.*, p. 165.

[52] The various prefaces of the *Acts and Monuments* are listed separately in the bibliography.

was reprinted with only minor changes. In the 1583 edition, however, a new preface was added dealing with "Foure Considerations Geuen out to Christian Protestantes." A most valuable biography of John Foxe written by his youngest son, Simeon, was printed in both Latin and English in the 1641 edition of the *Acts and Monuments*.[53]

The *Acts and Monuments* should be placed within the context of Protestant historiography of the sixteenth century. Thomas Brightman, a transitional figure between Foxe and seventeenth-century historiographers, gives credit to three authors for placing the church in a unified historical perspective. He first refers to "that worthy worke of the Centuries at Maidenbrough" by Flacius, and then he speaks about "our Cuntryman Iohn Foxe, and Iohn Sleidan."[54]

Matthias Flacius of Illyria (1520–1575) studied in Venice, but as he was sympathetic to the Protestant Reformation, he went to Basel and from there to Tübingen. About 1544 he became professor at the University of Wittenberg. After Moritz of Saxony enforced the Leipzig Interim of 1548 (a modification of the Augsburg Interim by Emperor Charles V), which asserted justification by faith alone but reestablished much of Roman usage, Flacius went to Magdeburg, which had not accepted the Interim. Here he worked on the *Catalogues Testium Veritatis* ("Catalogue of Witnesses for the Truth"), which was a collection of testimonies by martyrs and other Protestant sympathizers against the Papacy. It was published in Basel in 1556 by Oporinus at the time Foxe worked for him as proofreader, so Foxe would be well-acquainted with this work; he may even have proofread parts of it. The same year Oporinus also published Foxe's apocalyptic drama *Christus Triumphans*.

The first Protestant church history was edited by Flacius under the title *Ecclesiasticae Historiae*, better known as "The Magdeburg Centuries." It was published in thirteen volumes during the years 1561–1574, also in Basel. This work presents

---

[53] That Simeon is the author has been proved conclusively by J. F. Mozley, *op. cit.*, pp. 1–11.

[54] Thomas Brightman, *A Revelation of the Reuelation* (Amsterdam, 1615), p. 397.

history as a great controversy between Christ and Antichrist, represented respectively by the church of the elect and the Papacy. In the true church—often existing as the hidden church —is found an unbroken succession of true doctrines as opposed to the institutional religion based on the succession of popes. Flacius expressed a Protestant theological view of history in which God intervenes on behalf of the church of the elect, through whom He also works out His objectives of salvation. The forces of history are evaluated theologically as moving in an ellipse around two foci: the first and second Advents of Christ. Because the Bible was the inspired record of salvation-history, it became a lesson book by which the elect could evaluate God's intervention both in past and present history; even the sacrifices and sufferings of the martyrs had not been in vain for God overrules history after His grand design. Thus the Bible also became the guarantee that the historical future was on their side. This concept of the Bible and salvation-history led to the belief that the church antedated New Testament times; a point about which more will be said later. It should be kept in mind that the work of Flacius was a synthesis of the Protestant Reformers' view of church history; when John Foxe adopted the subject matters and objectives of Flacius's "Witnesses for the Truth" and "Church History" in his own work, he placed himself in the mainstream of Protestant martyrology and historiography. English historiography, as related to the work of Foxe, is noted later in connection with some observations regarding Foxe's contributions to the writing of English Protestant history.

Johannes Sleidanus or Sleidan (1506–1556) was appointed historiographer by Philip of Hesse in 1544 under the influence of Martin Bucer. Invited by Archbishop Cranmer, he went to England in 1551, but returned later to Germany and was appointed professor of law at Strassburg in 1544. In 1540 he began to write about the Reformation,[55] and finally wrote his book about the state of religion and commonwealth during the reign

---

[55] See preface: "The Life of the Learned John Sleidan," in John Sleidan, *The General History of the Reformation of the Church* (London, 1689), sig. A2r.

of the emperor Charles V (1555).[56] This work was translated and printed in English in 1560.[57] Sleidan places his history within an apocalyptic framework, especially the four monarchies of the book of Daniel.[58] This apocalyptic view of history is also expounded in another work translated into English in 1563.[59]

The reference to Sleidan's apocalyptic view of history, which Flacius shared, leads us to mention the often neglected fact that the Reformation view of church history was shaped and sustained by a historical application of biblical apocalyptic imageries and time periodizations, to a large degree inherited from the medieval church. It is difficult for the twentieth-century theologian and historian to realize that chiliasm and apocalyptic eschatology were more than a phenomenon seen in Radical enthusiasts at the time of Luther or by the Fifth Monarchy men in England during the Civil War. The validity of the Reformers' exegesis and historical application of biblical apocalyptic literature is not the issue in this connection. The vital point is that in order to estimate correctly their view of church history, we must acknowledge that there were a "normal" millennialism and a "normal" apocalyptic eschatology which were not alien to, but played a prominent role in, the Reformers' total involvement in the life of church and society.

Before considering the general principles and significant features of the "normal" apocalyptic outlook, it will be profitable to turn to Eusebius of Caesarea (ca. 260–340), who praised Constantine for bringing relief and peace to the Christian church in his *Life* and *Eulogy* of the emperor. He also wrote a smaller book on the martyrs of Palestine in the Diocletian persecution. It is his *Ecclesiastical History* that is most significant to our study. Containing the story of the early church from the time of Christ to the victory of Constantine over Licenius in 324, it is written as a *sacra historia* depicting the suffering of the elect

---

[56] John Sleidan, *De Statv Religionis et Reipvblicae, Carolo Quinto, Caesare, Commentarii* (n.p., 1555).

[57] John Sleidan, *A Famouse Cronicle of Oure Time* (n.p., 1560).

[58] *Ibid.*, sig. Aiiiir.

[59] John Sleidan, *A Briefe Chronicle of the Four Principall Empyres* (London, 1563).

at the hands of the ungodly emperors, the vicars of Satan; yet their steadfastness and martyrdom conquered the world.

John Foxe is the example, par excellence, of how the Protestant historiographers were indebted to Eusebius. His *Acts and Monuments* is comprised of five books. Book I is mainly based on the material of the ten persecutions of the early church as described byEusebius. In fixing his apocalyptic time periods, Foxe made the time period of Revelation, chapter twelve, span the history of the persecuted church until Constantine. With Constantine the millennium began and lasted until Wycliffe, when a new persecuting period began, being made up likewise of ten persecutions. This second persecution period, of the same length as the first, ended with the reign of Elizabeth. It is therefore not surprising that in the two prefaces to the Queen in the *Acts and Monuments*, Foxe speaks as a Eusebian. He likewise hoped that his work would mean the same to the English Church as Eusebius's history did to the Post-Nicene church. Eusebius had said: "We regard it as one of our most urgent duties to hand down, for the knowledge of those that come after us, the events of our own day, which are worthy of no casual record."[60] Foxe expressed the same objective:

> ... when I weighed with myself what memorable acts and famous doings this latter age of the church hath ministered unto us by the patient sufferings of the worthy martyrs, I thought it not to be neglected, that so precious monuments of so many matters, meet to be recorded and registered in books, should lie buried by my default, under darkness of oblivion.... nothing did so much stir me forward hereunto, as the diligent consideration and special regard of the common utility which every man plentifully may receive by the reading of these our "Monuments" or Martyrology.

Foxe likewise compared the martyrs of the early church with those of his own time:

> ... if martyrs are to be compared with martyrs, I see no cause why the martyrs of our time deserve any less commendation than

[60] Eusebius, *The Ecclesiastical History*, trans. J. E. L. Oulton (Cambridge, 1953) (VIII, int.) II, 251.

the others in the primitive church; which assuredly are inferior unto them in no point of praise, whether we view the number of them that suffered, or greatness of their torments, or their constancy in dying, or also consider the fruit that they brought, to the amendment of posterity, and increase of the gospel. They did water with their blood the truth that was newly springing up; so these, by their deaths, restored it again, being sore decayed and fallen down.

... seeing we have found so famous martyrs in this our age, let us not fail then in publishing and setting forth their doings; lest, in that point, we seem more unkind to them, than the writers of the primitive church were unto theirs.[61]

Eusebius's detailed description of nearly 150 martyrs of which nearly 100 are mentioned by name, as well as his attack on heretical groups and nearly fifty individual heretics, left their mark upon Foxe's detailed narrative of persons, whether martyrs or enemies. Each martyr was a paradigm of the history of the church, for the church was in war against evil, and the church of the elect was persecuted by the apostate church. God's retribution against those who persecuted His people was carefully noticed and illustrated by both men. Foxe can with good reason be named the Elizabethan Eusebius, even though he differed from Eusebius in his eschatological outlook.

In the history of the interpretation of the many imageries found in the books of Daniel and Revelation, a few were considered of basic importance as symbolic prophecy conveying the predicted course and the divine vindication of history. They can be summarized very briefly together with some of their basic historical applications. In the book of Daniel, chapter 2, a great statue is described whose "head was of fine gold, his breast and his arms of silver, his belly and his thighs of brass, his legs of iron, his feet part of iron and part of clay" (vv. 32–33). In Jewish literature from the time of Josephus and in Christian writings since the days of Irenaeus, Tertullian, and Hippolytus, the four different metals represented four great empires beginning with Babylon and ending with Rome. That his feet were "part of iron and part of clay" represented the division of the Roman empire. The climax of the story reads: "Thou sawest till that a

---

[61] *Pratt*, pp. xxv, xxvi, xxvii.

stone was cut out without hands, which smote the image upon his feet that were of iron and clay, and brake them to pieces. Then was the iron, the clay, the brass, the silver, and the gold, broken to pieces together, and became like the chaff of the summer threshingfloors; and the wind carried them away, that no place was found for them: and the stone that smote the image became a great mountain, and filled the whole earth" (vv. 34–35). Here the Judeo-Christian *telos* of history was expressed: "The God of heaven [shall] set up a kingdom, which shall never be destroyed." In chapter 7 a parallel description is given of the four empires in the form of four beasts, one succeeding the other. The fourth beast develops into a number of kingdoms represented by its ten horns. Among these horns an eleventh appears, and, since the writings of Hippolytus, who wrote the first complete commentary on the book of Daniel, this eleventh (or "little") horn was said to represent Antichrist, for "he shall speak great words against the most High, and shall wear out the saints of the most High, and think to change times and laws: and they shall be given into his hand until a time and times and the dividing of time" (v. 25). But when he has appeared "the judgment shall sit, and they shall take away his dominion, to consume and to destroy it unto the end. And the kingdom and dominion, and the greatness of the kingdom under the whole heaven, shall be given to the people of the saints of the most High, whose kingdom is an everlasting kingdom, and all dominions shall serve and obey him" (vv. 26–27). From the time of the Ante-Nicene Fathers these two chapters described prophetically and historically the linear concept of time and the one-directed movement of history toward the kingdom of God.

In the book of Revelation three chapters should be noticed. In chapter 12 the drama between God and Satan, good and evil, the elect and Antichrist, is placed in a cosmic setting. A beautiful woman "clothed with the sun, and the moon under her feet" gives birth to "a man child, who was to rule all nations with a rod of iron: and her child was caught up unto God, and to his throne" (v. 5). The dragon was cast to the earth, and persecuted the woman who "fled into the wilderness." From the time of Tertullian, Christian expositors made the woman symbolize the church who gave "birth" to Christ. The elect of the true church were objects for persecution and often hid from the eye of man. In chapter 13 an apocalyptic beast is described, an amalgamation of the four described in chapter 7 of the book of Daniel. Likewise since the time of Irenaeus and Tertullian this beast was said to symbolize Antichrist. In Daniel 7 and Revelation 12 and 13, the length of Antichrist's rule and the persecution of the elect is synchronized by the expression "a time and times and the dividing of time" or "forty and two months" (Rev. 12:6, 17; 13:5). This time period of 1260 days or three and a half years plays a most significant role in the various schemes of time periodization proposed through the centuries. During the Christian era and specifically during the Reformation period, the imageries of these chapters were reproduced in paintings and statues, sculpted in walls of churches and other buildings, woven into tapestries and printed as woodcuts in Bibles and other religious works, not least in Protestant and antipapal literature.

Chapter 20 of the book of Revelation has inspired the two words "chiliasm" and "millennialism," derived respectively from the Greek and Latin words for thousand. In the Bible the thousand year period is mentioned only in this chapter. The apocalyptic language portrays an angel throwing the Devil into a bottomless pit and then chaining him for "a thousand years," but the elect "lived and reigned with Christ a thousand years." The period was marked with one resurrection at the beginning and another at the close. The millennial idea, conceived differently by various men during diverse periods, has nevertheless been the focal point in any periodization of church history. Some interpreters assume that the Second Advent of Christ will precede the millennium; others maintain that it will follow the millennium. The former is named the premillennial and the latter the postmillennial concept. In order to evaluate, as best as possible, Foxe's periodization of church history, fixed as it is within an apocalyptic framework, it will be necessary to give a "bird's-eye" view of the history of apocalyptic interpretation with special reference to the millennial idea.

Eschatological urgency characterized the proclamation of the disciples of Christ, and the Apostolic and Ante-Nicene Fathers continued to express the confidence of the Apostolic church in the nearness of the Second Advent, the last judgment, the end of the world, and the kingdom of Christ. The Fathers, however, framed this Apostolic eschatology within millennialism. The Ante-Nicene premillennial view was expressed in the middle of the second century by the great apologist of the Christian faith, Justin Martyr. In his *Apology*, addressed to the emperor Antonius, and the *Dialogue*, a defense of his Christian faith against Trypho the Jew, Justin speaks about the glorious advent of Christ and the millennium marked off by the resurrection of the godly at its beginning and the resurrection of the ungodly at its termination. During the thousand years Christ will dwell in Jerusalem which will be rebuilt and enlarged according to the Old Testament prophets.[62] Irenaeus, bishop of Gaul during the last quarter of the second century, asserted that, at the Second Advent of Christ, the saints would rule over the earth.[63] Likewise Tertullian[64] and Hippolytus,[65] in the early part of the third century, and Lactantius,[66] in the first part of the fourth century, held to the premillennial view and a more or less defined concept of a glorious reign with Christ on this earth preceding the eternity of heaven.

Constantine's acceptance of Christianity and his forming a Christian society by elevating Christianity as the only true religion of the empire profoundly altered the chiliastic idea of the Ante-Nicene church. In his *Life of Constantine* Eusebius refers to Constantine's erection of a new church in Jerusalem as "a monument to the Saviour's victory over death, with rich and lavish magnificence." He adds: "And it may be that this was that second and new Jerusalem spoken of in the predictions of the prophets, concerning which such abundant testimony is

---

[62] Justin Martyr, *First Apology*, chap. 52 in *The Anti-Nicene Fathers* (hereafter referred to as *ANF*), I, 180; *Dialogue With Trypho*, chaps. 31, 52, 80, 81 in *ANF*, I, 209, 221, 239–240.

[63] Irenaeus, *Against Heresies*, book 5, chaps. 34 and 35 in *ANF*, I, 563–566.

[64] Tertullian, *On the Resurrection of the Flesh*, chaps. 22, 25, and 27 in *ANF*, III, 560–561, 563, 564–565; *Against Marcion*, book 3, chap. 25 in *ANF*, III, 342–343.

[65] Hippolytus, *Treatise on Christ and Antichrist*, sect. 65 in *ANF*, V, 218.

[66] Lactantius, *The Epitome of the Divine Institutes*, chap. 72 in *ANF*, VII, 254.

given in the divinely inspired records."[67] This is apparently a reference to Revelation 21. The erection of churches in other places occasioned similar remarks; for example, in his address to Bishop Paulinus of Tyre upon the completion of a new church there, Eusebius proclaimed it to be "a new and far goodlier Jerusalem," fulfilling the prophecies of Psalm 46 and Isaiah 35.[68] In his eulogy of Constantine, Eusebius compares the feast of the bishops (held after the Council of Nicea) to the beginning of the kingdom of Christ,[69] thus setting forth the idea of a golden age of the church beginning with the rule of Constantine.

The movement away from a premillennial concept had already begun with Origen, who contended the belief in the actual resurrection of the body allegorized the Second Advent of Christ, making it a symbol of the Christian's existential experience with Christ. It is therefore not surprising that he condemned millennialism.[70]

The Jewish people produced a large amount of apocalyptic literature, both during the last century and a half before the Christian era and in connection with the Jewish revolts against the Romans in the early Christian period. The influence of this literature together with pagan apocalyptic worship led to types of Christian chiliasm expressing itself in fanatic and extreme religious utopianism, which made the Post-Nicene church discredit millennialism. This trend was also furthered by the fact that the imminent *parousia* of Christ as preached by the Apostolic church had not come to pass.

The new concept of the millennium, which became the accepted Christian philosophy of history for the next thousand years, was presented by Augustine in his work *De Civite Dei*, although first outlined by Tichonius, a little-known writer of the late fourth century.[71] The first resurrection which should

---

[67] Eusebius, *The Life of Constantine*, book 3, chap. 33 in *A Select Library of Nicene and Post-Nicene Fathers of the Christian Church* (hereafter referred to as *NPNF*), 2d ser. I, 529.

[68] Eusebius, *The Ecclesiastical History* (X. ii. 4), II, 399.

[69] Eusebius, *The Life of Constantine*, book 3, chap. 15 in *NPNF*, 2d ser. I, 524.

[70] Origen, *De Principiis*, book 2, chap. 10; book 3, chap. 6; book 2, chap. 11, sect. 2 in *ANF*, IV, 293–296, 344–348, 297.

[71] Tichonius, *The Book of Rules of Tychonius*, ed. F. C. Burkitt, Vol.

inaugurate the millennium, according to Revelation 20, is interpreted spiritually, allowing the thousand year period to begin with the incarnation of Christ and to synchronize with the Christian dispensation until the end of the world. Thus the number was figurative; however, he expected the end in less than a thousand years.[72] It is most significant to notice that the Christian church is understood to be the kingdom of Christ. Likewise the promise of the New Jerusalem is realized in the church. The progress of the church is assured by the fact that Satan is bound for a thousand years.[73]

In Augustine's periodization of history are found seven epochs: (1) Adam to the Flood, (2) Noah to Abraham, (3) Abraham to King David, (4) King David to the Babylonian captivity of the Jews, (5) The Babylonian captivity to the incarnation of Christ, (6) Christ to the end of the world or the Second Advent of Christ, (7) The eternal Sabbath rest.[74] This periodization is based upon the world week theory or the millennial typology of the Genesis creation week (*Septem dies, et septem aetates mundi*), each creation day representing a thousand years (Psalm 90:4; 2 Peter 3:8 supplied the biblical foundation) or an epoch. This scheme was inherited from early Judeo-Christian apocalyptic writings. However, the dream of a future glorious age was also a widespread pagan concept. The Etruscans held the belief that the present condition of mankind would remain for only six thousand years. There also seem to be some similarities between Parsiism and Jewish eschatology.[75]

In Jewish apocalyptic writing such as the *Slavonic Enoch*, also called *Second Enoch* and the *Secrets of Enoch* (probably edited

---

III in *Texts and Studies: contributions to Biblical and Patristic literature*, ed. J. A. Robinson, 1st ser. (Cambridge, 1894).

[72] Augustine, *The City of God*, book 20, chaps. 5–10 in *NPNF*, 1st ser., II, 425–428; book 18, chap. 53 in *NPNF*, 1st ser., II, p. 394.

[73] *Ibid.*, pp. 427–428.

[74] Augustine, *De Genesi Consti Manichaeos*, book 1, chap. 23 in Migne, *Patrologia Latina* (hereafter referred to as *PL*), Vol. XXXIV, cols. 190–193.

[75] William Sherwood Fox, *Greek and Roman Mythology*, Vol. I in *The Mythology of All Races*, ed. Louis Herbert Gray (Boston, 1916), p. 289. J. A. MacCulloch, "Eschatology," in *Encyclopaedia of Religon and Ethics*, ed. James Hastings (New York, 1925), V, 376, 381.

in Egypt during the first half of the first century A.D.), the thousand year period is symbolically linked to the Genesis creation week.[76] Barnabas, one of the Apostolic Fathers, writes in a way characteristic of this world week theory:

> The Sabbath is mentioned at the beginning of the creation [thus]: "And God made in six days the works of His hands, and made an end on the seventh day, and rested on it, and sanctified it." Attend, my children, to the meaning of this expression, "He finished in six days." This implieth that the Lord will finish all things in six thousand years, for a day is with Him a thousand years. And He Himself testifieth, saying, "Behold, to-day will be as a thousand years." Therefore, my children, in six days, that is in six thousand years, all things will be finished. "And He rested on the seventh day." This meaneth: when His son, coming [again], shall destroy the time of the wicked man, and judge the ungodly, and change the sun, and the moon, and the stars, then shall He truly rest on the seventh day.[77]

Irenaeus,[78] Hippolytus,[79] and Lactantius,[80] as well as Jerome,[81] agreed with Barnabas. According to the chronology of the Septuagint (the Greek translation of the Hebrew Old Testament), which is several centuries longer than the Hebrew text, the incarnation of Christ took place five thousand and five hundred years after the Creation. Accordingly, these writers expected six thousand years of history to be completed in a not-too-distant future. The basic principles in the scheme adopted by Augustine can be summarized as follows: The premillennial theory is discarded and the millennial hopes are centered in the church; Satan, who was bound at the incarnation of Christ, will be loosed for three and a half years at the end of time and Antichrist will

[76] *Slavonic Enoch* 32:2; 33: 1, 2, in *The Apocrypha and Pseudepigrapha of the Old Testament in English*, ed. R[obert] H[enry] Charles (Oxford, 1913), II, 451.

[77] Barnabas, *The Epistle of Barnabas*, chap. 15 in *ANF*, I, 146.

[78] Irenaeus, *Against Heresies*, book 3, chaps. 28–29, 35 in *ANF*, I, 557–558, 565–566.

[79] Hippolytus, *Fragments From Commentaries*, "On Daniel," fragment 2, chaps. 4–7 in *ANF*, V, 179.

[80] Lactantius, *The Divine Institutes*, book 7, chaps. 14, 25, and 26 in *ANF*, VII, 211–212, 220, 221.

[81] Jerome, *Ad Cyprianum Presbyterum*, in *PL*, Vol. XXII, col. 1172.

appear;[82] this will be followed by the literal second coming of Christ, the resurrection of the dead, the last judgment and the eternal Sabbath rest. These concepts dominated the view of church history for the next thousand years.

Pope Gregory I (590–604), as "the last of the Latin fathers and the first of the popes, connects the ancient with the mediaeval church, the Graeco-Roman with the Romano-Germanic type of Christianity."[83] He also expresses the Augustinian concept: the stone of Daniel chapter 2 or the fifth kingdom is being fulfilled in the church. Satan was "bound" at the beginning of the Christian dispensation and the thousand years represent the whole period of the Christian church. At the time of the end, Satan will be "loosed" and the final judgment will take place.[84]

The Venerable Bede (ca. 673–735), the father of English historiography, furthered the permanent acceptance of Augustine's views through his works *Baedae opera historica* and *The Explanation of the Apocalypse*.[85] Likewise Thomas Aquinas (1225–1274), the Angelic Doctor of the Latin Church, perpetuated the Augustinian historiography as the orthodox version. At the same time he also asserted that the "thousand two hundred sixty days mentioned in the Apocalypse... denote all the time during which the Church endures, and not any definite number of years."[86] This is undoubtedly a criticism of Joachim's periodization of church history.

Joachim of Floris (d. 1202) divided the history of the world into three ages: that of the Father, the Son, and the Holy Ghost. The three epochs were represented by the apostles Peter, Paul, and John and illustrated respectively epochs of law, grace, and more abundant grace. The second period began with Christ and

[82] Augustine, *City of God*, book 20, chap. 8 in *NPNF*, 1st ser. II, 428.

[83] Philip Schaff, *History of the Christian Church* (Grand Rapids, Mich., 1953–1959), IV, 212.

[84] Gregory the Great, *Epistles*, book 5, epistle 43 in *NPNF*, 2d ser. XII, 179; *Moralium*, book 32, chap. 15 in *PL*, Vol. LXXVI, col. 649.

[85] The Venerable Bede, *Baedae opera historica*, trans. J. E. King (London and New York, 1930); *The Explanation of the Apocalypse by Venerable Beda*, trans. Edward Marshall (Oxford and London, 1878).

[86] Thomas Aquinas, *Summa Theologica* (pt. 3, "Supplement," q. 77, arts. 1, 2), trans. Fathers of the English Dominican Province (London, 1932), pp. 141, 143–144.

would end in A.D. 1260, when the age of the Holy Spirit would inaugurate a new spiritual society where men would live by the *imitatio Christi*.

The new feature of Joachim's scheme is that the epoch inaugurated by Christ (the Augustinian millennial concept) is not the final one, but another age could be expected before the final consummation. Further, he brings the 1260 day period into focus by devising the hermeneutical principle that a prophetic day should be counted as a literal year and calls the 1260 days "that great number which contains all these mysteries."[87]

It has already been noticed that Aquinas spoke figuratively about the numerical value of this time period. The medieval church did the same, except for the early Spiritual Franciscans and certain individual writers. However, the significance of the "1260 days," interpreted by various men in varied ways during different periods, will be noticed over and over again in our study, and not least in the writings of John Foxe.

Without going into any details of the Reformers' periodization of church history, it is important to notice that while the periodization of the Christian era might differ with different writers with each using the various imageries of the Revelation to support his own view of history, all believed the present epoch to be the last. The basic principles used by Luther, as a historiographer, may serve as a classical example of Protestant historiography.[88]

The apostle Paul held a triadic pattern of church history: before the law, under the law, and under grace. This became the basis for Luther's three great epochs of history: the Patriarchs, Abraham and the Law of Moses (this period ends with Pentecost), and the Christian dispensation. The latter period is decidedly eschatological as it will culminate in the last judgment. The final phase prior to the Second Advent is marked by a renewal of the Gospel and the appearance of Antichrist. From the vantage point of this struggle, Luther looked back upon history and perceived three major phases in the history of the Christian

---

[87] Joachim, *Liber Concordie Novi ac Veteris Testamenti* (Venetijs, 1519), fol. 12v, fol. 118r.

[88] John M. Headley, *Luther's View of Church History* (New Haven and London, 1963).

church: the ancient church, the development of Antichrist which had its seat within the church in the form of the Papacy, and the last days, the sign of which he saw fulfilled in his own time. The fall of the church or the beginning of the antichristian apostasy he traced from the year 606 when Pope Boniface III accepted the title of universal bishop from the emperor Phocas. On the other hand the beginning of the last days' restoration of the Gospel began with John Huss. However, Luther saw God's working down through the centuries in the mainstream of *corpus christianum* and would not go so far as to deny the Papacy any part in being a church. This view was shared by John Foxe and is dealt with in greater detail in connection with an analysis of his works. In order to place the concepts mentioned above in wider perspective as a background for the study of Foxe, it will be profitable to turn shortly to some of the principles guiding the men within the Radical Reformation since they moved within a different historical framework in their periodization.[89]

The first and fundamental difference between the Magisterial Reformers and Radical Reformers lies in their concept of the millennium. The former held to an Augustinian millennial view in a modified form, while the latter adhered to the premillennial idea of the Ante-Nicene church. The Magisterial Reformers believed that they lived in the last age and that the Second Advent ushering in eternity was imminent. The Radicals expected a new age of a thousand years, during which Satan would be bound, followed by the final judgment and eternity. Accordingly, the fifth kingdom of Daniel was still to be fulfilled in a golden age, and was not, as in the Augustinian view, brought to consummation in the church. In their opposition to the latter view, the eschatology of the Radicals would drive them to break with the *corpus christianum* from the time of Constantine. In their millennialism they considered themselves in perfect harmony with the Apostolic and Ante-Nicene Fathers, who in turn were in accord with the New Testament. Since the Radicals saw themselves as God's chosen instrument to herald the new

[89] See George Huntston Williams, *The Radical Reformation* (London, 1962), esp. pp. 857–861.

millennial age, their task was not a reformation but a restitution of what they believed to be Apostolic Christianity. In their different eschatological concepts the Magisterial and Radical Reformers both recognized that there was a gulf between them which neither was able to bridge. The Radicals' relationship to the state and the magisterial church (as well as their soteriological outlook) were shaped by their eschatology.

There is a definite parallel between the extreme chiliasm in the Ante-Nicene church and the Post-Nicene Fathers' reaction against it, and the events connected with Thomas Müntzer and the Zwickau Prophets and the Reformers' opposition to their apocalypticism. While extensive research into the sources of the Radical Reformation has definitely substantiated that it is not justifiable to classify the Radical Reformers as a whole with Müntzer and the Zwickau Prophets, the facts still remain that they all moved within the same millennial framework. Likewise, the Puritans of the seventeenth century were not all Fifth Monarchy men; yet to a very large degree the Puritan historiographers during the period of the Civil Wars held basically the same millennial view as the former, and differ from the Elizabethan Divines—whether they be Anglicans or Puritans—who stood in the Augustinian tradition.

Michael Servetus, who on account of his anti-Trinitarian views was arrested and put to death by the city council of Geneva in 1553 under the direction of Calvin and with the approval of most other Reformers, exemplifies that shift in the application of the 1260 day period of Revelation 12, which reflects the Radicals' view of the fall of the church.[90]

Servetus's main theological work is his *Christianismi Restitutio*, in which he claims to be a restorer of Christianity, no doubt in opposition to Calvin's *Institutes of the Christian Religion*. Like Joachim of Floris, he considered the 1260 days as actual years, but covering a period during which the true church of God's elect were found not in, but outside, *corpus christianum*. The period began with Constantine and the Council of Nicea. Here the doctrines of the Trinity and infant baptism were endorsed; church and state were molded into one entity, resulting

---

[90] Schaff, *op. cit.*, VIII, 732–757.

in the establishment of the Papacy under Pope Sylvester. The age of Antichrist was thus calculated from 325 to 1585; consequently, it could only be expected that the Protestant magisterial churches were considered within the antichristian domain. In this connection it should be noticed that there seems to be a coherence between the Radicals' apocalyptic periodization and Arian tendencies. The underlying philosophy is that because the fall of the church took place at the time of Constantine, the trinitarian doctrine endorsed by the apostate church must be heretical. Their apocalyptic view of the fall of the church thus had its share in shaping an anti-Trinitarian theology. In England, the distinctive feature of the Radical Reformation "was the close interrelationship of Libertinism, anti-Trinitarianism, Anabaptism of the Melchiorite strain, and Spiritualism."[91] Foxe's records of the public hearings of the Anabaptists, and his own pleading with them, reveal that they did not seem able to present or substantiate an orthodox view of the incarnation and the nature of Christ. This phenomenon has often appeared within extreme apocalyptic movements; the present-day sect of Jehovah's Witnesses is a typical example.

Since the termination of the 1260 years was near, so was the end of Antichrist's reign. Joachim's concept of the age of the Holy Spirit at the end of 1260 years was never forgotten. Further, already in the middle of the second century, Montanus had reacted against the formalism of the church by proclaiming himself an instrument of the Holy Spirit for the inauguration of its new dispensation. The Radicals were also able to refer to Tertullian as one who had joined the Montanists. Accordingly an apocalyptic expectation of the Holy Spirit was anticipated in connection with the final phase of the great controversy between Christ and Satan—or the elect and Antichrist—and the ushering in of the new millennial age.

We have already noticed that in England the Venerable Bede firmly established the Augustinian philosophy of history, which would make its followers oppose any moderate or fanatic chiliastic concept of the Ante-Nicene church. John Wycliffe, in so many respects important to Foxe, expressed his belief that

[91] Williams, *op. cit.*, p. 778.

the present age was the last in his short treatise, *The Last Age of the Churche*, in 1356.[92] The two Lollard treatises of the fourteenth century, *The praier and complaynte of the ploweman vnto Christe*[93] and *The Lanterne of Light*,[94] spoke about the struggle with the Papacy, which to them was Antichrist, stressing that this struggle would culminate in the Second Advent of Christ and the final judgment. Foxe recorded the first work, not "changing any thing of the matter."[95]

William Tyndale and John Bale stood within the Augustinian tradition, believing the present age to be the last. This concept remained with Foxe throughout his life, even though he modified the traditional view of the thousand year period. Later, in the evaluation of Foxe's detailed periodization of history, his views will be compared with those of other Elizabethan historiographers, and theirs in turn with representative opinions among midseventeenth-century Puritans. Here it suffices to state that the differences in eschatological outlook between these two groups cannot be emphasized strongly enough when evaluating the apocalypticism of Foxe. In this connection reference must be made to the thesis of William Haller's book, *Foxe's Book of Martyrs and the Elect Nation*. According to Haller, and others who follow him, Foxe was largely responsible for the widespread conviction that England was God's elect nation and Elizabeth his appointed servant to turn the nation into a new Israel; Haller thus makes Foxe an ancestor of the apocalyptic nationalism of the seventeenth century.

Whatever Foxe's influence may have been in the creation of a national faith in the fight for national independence, it seems to me that Haller's emphasis does not present a balanced view of his objectives. In his introduction to one of Foxe's minor works, T. H. L. Parker gives his opinion on Foxe's intent:

---

92 If Wycliffe is not the author, as Lechler thinks (see Gotthard Lechler, *John Wycliffe and his English Precursors* [London, 1884], p. 63), the tract no doubt reflects his views.

93 *The praier and complaynte of the ploweman vnto Christe* (Antwerp, 1531).

94 Ed. Lilian M. Swinburn (London, 1917).

95 *AM*, II, 727.

A word in passing may be said against Professor Haller's thesis that the *Actes and Monuments* is a religionationalistic book designed to give Englishmen the belief that England was a nation chosen by God above all others to do his will. Foxe was no Rosenberg, with his Nazi blood and folk ideology. There is this much truth in it, that he was influenced by the nationalistic surges of his age and by the relative prosperity and popular pride that marked Elizabeth's reign. But he knew very well that the Kingdom of God was not to be equated with the realm ruled by Queen Elizabeth. The kingdom to which his book bears witness is the Kingdom of Christ. The Reformation that he recounts is a step, probably the final step, on the course of God's plan from the Creation to the Second Coming. It was this robust and joyful hope that provided the sinews in the faith of the 'Gospellers' and imparted such an urgency to their lives.[96]

The present study fully confirms Parker's assertion. Further, there may even be found some degree of difference between the influence of the *Acts and Monuments* and Foxes own objectives; therefore, the former ought not to color one's perception of the latter.

The Magisterial Reformers sought to establish the validity of the Protestant Reformation in the light of a Protestant view of church history. Having modified the Augustinian millennial view with the eschatology of Christ and Paul, they saw the Protestant revival of the Gospel, as opposed to Antichrist's teachings, as a sign of the end. Not only the Reformers' actual relationship to the state, but also their view of history, entitled them to be called Magisterial Reformers: Constantine and later emperors who supported the church were, from their viewpoint, with good reason called Christian emperors.

Rome had become Antichrist by usurping the power of the Christian emperor, but the Reformation sought to restore the godly prince to his former Christian responsibility and authority, which should be used in a positive way to advance the evangelical church. That the godly ruler should become a second Josiah or Constantine was a necessary part of the struggle against Antichrist. For example, Luther and others considered Frederick the

[96] T. H. L. Parker, ed., *English Reformers*, Vol. XXVI in the Library of Christian Classics (London, 1966), p. 68.

Wise to be the eschatological emperor,[97] and Wittenberg itself was elected to be God's chosen city as Jerusalem had been in former days. But any national self-consciousness which emerged as a result of the religious leadership of the godly prince was framed within the eschatological view of the end, and included neither the chiliastic concepts of the early church, nor the millennial views of the Radical Reformers and the Puritans of the Civil War years.

Turning to England we find, as would be expected, the creation of a Protestant historiography with a distinctive English emphasis. John Wycliffe, accepted as the Morning Star of the Reformation, had set the stage for some of the basic views found in English Protestant historiography, especially the belief that God's elect will be persecuted at the hands of the Papal Antichrist. Accordingly, the historiographers were eager to collect material dealing with the Lollards, and in Foxe's chronology, Wycliffe was a focal point. The murmur against the Papacy in the fourteenth century was closely related to the quest for national independence from its jurisdiction. Wycliffe became a spokesman against the foreign rule which had held the English people in its yoke since the reign of William the Conqueror. The national independence movement was in fact part and parcel of the Magisterial Reformation: it played a vital role in the Reformation in Switzerland, in Germany, and during the reign of Henry VIII; and John Foxe significantly helped to create a national faith that was shared by the English Reformers at large.

Tudor Protestant historiography began with William Tyndale. For him, history moved toward the Second Advent of Christ, a literal resurrection, and the eternal kingdom. With Luther he believed that the origin of the papal apostasy began at the time of Boniface III and Emperor Phocas. He gradually developed the great controversy between Christ and Satan (in the three works: *The Parable of the Wicked Mammon, The Obedience of a Christian Man*, and *The Practice of Prelates*) until, with the help of biblical apocalyptic imagery, the Papacy was clearly identified as Antichrist. In Tyndale's particular re-

---

[97] *D. Martin Luthers Werke. Kritische Gesamtausgabe*, ed. J. F. K. Knaake et al. (Weimar, 1883), VIII, 475–476.

interpretation of English history, several aspects appear significant.[98] In Medieval England the archbishops of Canterbury
from Anselm and Becket to Thomas Wolsey had been part of
an international conspiracy led by Antichrist disguised as the
pope, seeking to make the English kings their submissive servants. During this period the original Christianity which had
been planted in England early in the Christian era had gradually
been corrupted. In spite of the force of Antichrist, God had re-
peatedly sent "prophets" to rebuke and warn the people as well
as to lead them back to the Scriptures as the true foundation of
truth. The lesson to be drawn from the war between the elect
and the apostate church was that God's elect could expect piti-
less persecution before the true Gospel could finally prevail.
Here, in embryo, is the Protestantizing of English history.

It was within the framework of Tyndale's view of English
church history that men such as Robert Barnes, Nicholas Ridley,
Hugh Latimer, John Philpot, John Bradford, John Hooper, and
Thomas Cranmer preached, wrote, and even suffered martyrdom. John Foxe was intimately acquainted with the lives and
works of these men. We have already mentioned his close association with John Bale, who as a historiographer is his link with
Tyndale, and we will further observe the latter's influence on
Foxe's own views.

In the Elizabethan period, it is significant to notice that the
first archbishop, Matthew Parker, was deeply interested in English church history. He secured from the government the cus-
tody of "ancient records." The fruit of his own scholarship, *De
Antiquitate*, is a history of the church in England prior to the
arrival of the monk Augustine from Rome.[99] His objective was
to "prove" that pure, primitive Christianity had its roots in England before any representative from Rome had set foot on English soil.

In Wales, Bishop Richard Davies, with whom Archbishop
Parker was acquainted, wrote a "Protestant" history of the early

---

[98] Glanmor Williams, *Reformation Views of Church History* (London,
1970), pp. 27 ff.

[99] Matthew Parker, *Correspondence*, Parker Society (Cambridge, 1853),
passim, esp. 425–426, 327.

church in Britain (*Address to the Welsh Nation*). It was prefaced to the first Welsh version of the New Testament (1576).[100] While George Buchanan's *Rerum Scoticarum Historica* (1582) deals with secular history, it still discloses the author's Protestant sympathies in his evaluation of his country's Christian past.[101]

John Foxe towers above all the Englishmen who contributed to shaping English history into a Protestant mold; but no matter how much Foxe and the others sought to write an English Protestant history, they never isolated that history from the universal church. This point should be kept in mind when one evaluates to what extent Bale and Foxe, with other returning exiles, intended to create a doctrine of the elect nation.

First of all it should be noticed that Foxe, in his original design of the *Acts and Monuments*, had planned an ecclesiastical history covering not only England, but also the Continent. The title of the small Strassburg edition of 1554 reads that he had all of Europe in mind, with the history of England comprising the first volume of this work. Foxe did not finish the second volume.

In the Basel edition of 1559 Foxe again had in mind the kingdoms and nations of Europe as the title page states. He dedicated the work to the Duke of Norfolk and expressed the hope that his work would "not be read by him alone, but by men from the highest to the lowest, not in England merely, but in every part of the world."[102] In the preface he specifically mentions that in a second volume he will deal with the martyrs of Germany, Geneva, France, and Italy.[103] That Foxe was collecting material for this second volume is revealed by letters written to Bullinger during the summer of 1559.[104] His return to England in the autumn no doubt accounts for the fact that he did not complete the work. However, it was completed by Henry Pantaleon, a physician and friend of Foxe's, and printed in Basel in 1563.[105] In the preface Pantaleon mentions that for many years people had waited in vain for the second part of John Foxe's work; he

---

[100] See Glanmor Williams, *op. cit.*, p. 63.

[101] *Ibid.*, p. 65. [102] *Pratt*, p. 28.

[103] *AM*, (1559), p. 1.

[104] *Zurich Letters*, Parker Society (Cambridge, 1842), pp. 25–26, 35–37, 41–42.

[105] Henrico Pantaleone, *Martyrvm Historia* (Basel, 1563).

calls Foxe "my worthy friend." Being encouraged by so many, Pantaleon takes it upon himself to finish the work. Among those who encouraged him he mentions by name John Bale and states that Bale and Foxe were together in Basel. It is interesting to notice that only when Pantaleon speaks about those who influenced him to write the second volume of the "Book of Martyrs" in order to extend its scope to the whole of Europe does he mention specifically the name of John Bale.[106] This would indicate that Bale was interested in a work which dealt not only with England but with the church as a whole.

In Bale's major work on prophetic interpretation, *The Image of Both Churches*, he discusses the issue that historiographers considered to be their main task: the welfare of the church. Foxe deals with this topic also. To the Queen he writes:

> I thought also not vnprofitable to adioyne vnto this your godly procedings, and to the office of the ministery, the knowledge also of Ecclesiasticall history, which in my mind ought not to be separate from the same: that like as by the one the people may learne the rules and preceptes of doctrine: so by the other they may haue examples of Gods mighty working in his church, to the confirmation of their faith, and the edification of Christian life.[107]

Foxe adds the hope that the *Acts and Monuments* "may be to the aduancement of his [God's] glory, and profite of his Church."[108] The objectives of the *Acts and Monuments* thus described are also made obvious from the title of the various editions. The frontispiece of the 1563 and 1570 editions portrays the struggle between the apostate church and the true church of Christ.

When Foxe issued the 1563 edition, he had no plans for another one; however, the dedicatory epistle to the Queen in the 1570 edition indicates that Foxe's work had come under Papist attack. For example, Thomas Harding had criticized it in his debate with Jewel.[109] As Foxe collected new and additional material to the stories already told, he felt that he could improve his work. He was especially anxious to prove that the reformed church was

---

[106] *Ibid.*, sig. 3v.   [107] *QE* (1570), sig. iiv.
[108] *Cong.*, sig. iir.
[109] Harding, *Confvtation*, sig. 14r; *A Reionidre to M. Jewels Replie* (Antwerp, 1566), sig. 186r.

"not the beginning of any new church of our own, but the renewing of the old ancient church of Christ,"[110] while the Papists had departed from the ancient church and created a new one. Thus in the 1570 edition Foxe compares at great length the early and latter churches of Rome.[111]

In both the 1563 and 1570 editions Foxe begins his story by expressing his burden for the church. Whatever influences the *Acts and Monuments* may have had on English nationalism, Foxe clearly states that his personal intention is "to profit the Church of Christ" rather than "to delite the eares" of the nation.[112]

Still another point to keep in mind is the style of Elizabethan writers, especially on formal occasions or in writing to or about prominent persons. Haller speaks of "the elaborately conceited style in which Elizabeth's subjects and Elizabeth herself liked to wrap up their thoughts on formal occasions."[113] It is obvious that Foxe, in his description of Queen Elizabeth at the close of the *Acts and Monuments*,[114] is, as Haller writes, "instructing his royal mistress in the way she should conduct her affairs by praising her for already having done so."[115] In the 1563 edition where Foxe compares Elizabeth to Constantine, he applies the same principle, as he also does in his praise of her in the dedicatory preface of the 1570 edition. Extolling the Queen's good purpose "to furnish all quarters and countreyes of this your Realme with the voyce of Christes Gospel, and faithfull preachyng of his work," he adds, "speedely I trust,"[116] as if the Reformation had not progressed as fast as he had expected. The two dedicatory epistles clearly state that the Queen is the monarch but under Christ, the Supreme Head. They also clearly outline her duties as a godly ruler. If the Queen did not fulfill or fell short of the ideal of the godly monarch as presented by the *Acts and Monuments* (as the Puritans believed), then the question could be raised: Would not Foxe's dedicatory epistles to the Queen become a hindrance rather than a furtherance of the national myth? William M. Lamont,[117] who to some degree follows

[110] *AM*, I, 9.
[111] *AM*, I, 3–86.
[112] *AM* (1563), p. 1.
[113] Haller, *op. cit.*, pp. 124–125.
[114] *AM*, VIII, 600–625, 672–673.
[115] Haller, *op. cit.*, p. 125.
[116] *QE* (1570), sig. iiv.
[117] Lamont, *Godly Rule: Politics and Religon, 1603–60* (London, 1969).

William Haller's thesis, places Foxe among those who prefer a godly prince to a godly bishop. However, from our study of Foxe's concept of the ministry, we see that he could just as well be considered a proponent of the godly bishop; for example, he states that he could not place greater importance on Constantine, the Ruler, than on Eusebius, the Bishop.

William Haller emphasizes Foxe's "apocalyptical conception of England which he brought back from exile at the death of Mary in a valid historical perspective focussed on the place and function of kingship now devolving upon Elizabeth."[118] When Foxe, as an Englishman, wrote a work about English martyrs in the language and style of his time, it would only be natural for him to bring out points that emphasize the Christian Anglican heritage. For one who had witnessed the persecution of Mary, the new Queen was as sent from God. For one who had embraced the Reformation and hoped to see it fully established in England, the Queen and her government were looked to as God's instruments to help accomplish this. It could hardly be otherwise. However, Foxe's apocalyptic interpretations and concepts seem to be focused upon the church rather than on the nation. Prior to the Basel edition of the *Acts and Monuments*, Foxe had published *Christus Triumphans*, an apocalyptical drama, also in Basel in 1556. Since this book contains Foxe's earliest and most comprehensive view of the church in history, its content is significant; however, the historical, theological, and apocalyptic structure of *Acts and Monuments* has not previously been considered in the light of this early writing. It was translated into French in 1562, and reprinted in Latin in 1672.

Foxe's concept of the church and his philosophy of history as first expressed in *Christus Triumphans*, then put in historical perspective in the *Acts and Monuments* in its apocalyptic setting, is more fully developed in *Eicasmi seu Meditationes in Sacram Apocalypsin*. This is a Latin exposition of the first seventeen chapters of the Apocalypse and is the last writing we have from the pen of Foxe. Death prevented him from bringing the work to completion, but Samuel, his oldest son, published as much as his father had written. In this book of nearly four hundred

[118] Haller, *op. cit.*, p. 225.

43

quarto pages Foxe's philosophy of history and his own theological concept of the church are richly illustrated. Although Foxe's commentary on the Apocalypse was first printed after his death, the concepts expressed therein were those that had lived with him since his days as an exile. The *Eicasmi*, like his first apocalyptical interpretation, *Christus Triumphans*, is centered in the church, and especially in the struggle between the true church and the apostate church. In neither of these works are apocalyptic references made to England as a nation, and in the *Eicasmi* Queen Elizabeth's name is mentioned only three times in passing.[119] The apocalyptical framework of the *Acts and Monuments* cannot be fully appreciated except in the light of Foxe's other apocalyptic works.

Closely related to Foxe's apocalyptic concepts is his eschatological view. When examining his concept of the church in history we notice that the message of the *Acts and Monuments* is written in the charged atmosphere of the last days, and that Foxe, with the Reformers in general, posited a one-directed movement of history toward the Second Advent of Christ. John Sleidan writes that the believers should "not be discouraged, but shuld waite for deliuerance by the comming of Christ, who will come shortly after these afflictions."[120] Interpreting Revelation 14:14: "And I looked, and behold a white cloud, and upon the cloud one sat like unto the Son of man, having . . . in his hand a sharp sickle," Bale comments: "This sickle received he of his everlasting Father, such time as he gave over unto him his universal judgments. By the order of this vision should the preachers seem in the last age of the church much to admonish the people of the latter day, with the coming of Christ again to judge both the quick and the dead, as is in their creed or belief." Bale also writes that "the time is at hand to reap: for we are those upon whom the ends of the world are come."[121] Sleidan and Bale have been quoted because Haller mentions their influence upon Foxe.[122] Haller calls Bale one who returned from exile full "of

---

[119] *Apoc.*, pp. 61, 251, 327.

[120] Sleidan, *A Briefe Chronicle*, sig. 104 v.

[121] John Bale, *The Image of Both Churches* in *Select Works of John Bale*, Parker Society, (Cambridge, 1849), pp. 463, 464.

[122] Haller, *op. cit.*, pp. 67, 160.

apocalyptical urgings" which led "to the aspiration after nationality, not the expectation of a messiah out of the blue, but to the idea of an hereditary monarch called by the grace of God to rule the realm and defend the faith."[123]

As Magisterial Reformers, Bale and Foxe placed great importance upon the ruling monarch and expressed great hopes for their country and the Reformation; however, the Advent was always looming on the horizon. John Jewel, who, according to Haller, "had undoubtedly heard the hundred sermons which Bullinger preached on the Apocalypse,"[124] expressed the apocalyptic views of the latter in his exposition upon the two epistles of Paul to the Thessalonians.[125] Jewel advocates the apocalyptic idea that the Messiah can be expected to come "out of the blue." Believers should stand "in readiness, and watch, and pray, that we may be caught up into the clouds to meet our Redeemer." He says: "You shall be caught up into the clouds to meet the Lord," and he emphasizes: "We which shall see all these things shall also be caught up ourselves."[126]

John Bradford's attitude toward England is reminiscent of John Aylmer's, as quoted by Haller,[127] in his statement that "no people heretofore hath had or now hath such cause and so great occasion . . . to be thankful, as we have."[128] But in a meditation, "On the coming of Christ to Judgment," and a treatise, "Meditation on the kingdom of Christ," he refers to the "messiah out of the blue" idea.[129] Thomas Becon calls the Church of England "a glorious church" and compares it to "a pleasant and goodly

[123] *Ibid.,* p. 62.

[124] *Ibid.,* p. 90. The sermons of Bullinger were translated into English. See Henry Bullinger, *A Hundred Sermons vpon the Apocalips of Jesu Christe* (n.p., 1561). In his sermons Bullinger expresses himself in terms similar to that of Jewel and other expositors. See, for example, pages 24 and 699.

[125] John Jewel, *Works,* Parker Society (Cambridge, 1847), II, 813–946.

[126] *Ibid.,* pp. 873, 871, 870.

[127] Haller, "John Foxe and the Puritan Revolution," in *The Seventeenth Century: Studies in the History of English Thought and Literature from Bacon to Pope,* ed. Richard F. Jones (Stanford, 1951), p. 209.

[128] John Bradford, *Sermons,* Parker Society (Cambridge, 1848), p. 13.

[129] *Ibid.,* pp. 185–187; Bradford, *Letters,* Parker Society (Cambridge, 1853), pp. 359–362.

vineyard," planted by God "in the realm of England." Further-more, God is "dressing and trimming it after the best manner."[130] Becon also refers to such apocalyptic literature as the book of Daniel, the Revelation, and 2 Thessalonians.[131] Concerning the Advent of Christ, he writes that "we are not certain of the day and hour; yet we may plainly perceive that it is not far off."[132] Edwin Sandys, in one of his sermons, speaks about "the mercies of God toward the church of England," and mentions among the blessings, that God "hath given us Moses our sovereign, a pru-dent and gentle magistrate, who seeketh not revenge, but bear-eth with the muttering of the people."[133] He also offers a beau-tiful prayer for the Queen, comparing God's help to England with the deliverance of the people out of Egypt.[134] However, in another sermon Sandys emphasizes that "all things do shew that the end of all things is at hand."[135]

These quotations from Bradford, Becon, and Sandys illustrate how they combined a concept of a national church or a Christian commonwealth with the idea of "messiah out of the blue." John Foxe did the same. Incidentally, he complained that one of the faults of the Papists was that they did not desire "the Lord to come in the clouds."[136] Guided by the index of the publica-tions of the Parker Society, Karl Holl interprets statements from Bradford, Becon, and other Elizabethan Divines from the point of view of national self-consciousness and does not balance the quoted statements with the basic eschatological outlook of the writers.[137] In view of Foxe's doctrine regarding the nature of the church as well as his eschatological concepts, it would seem that

[130] Thomas Becon, *Prayers*, Parker Society (Cambridge, 1844), pp. 11, 206.

[131] *Ibid.*, pp. 504, 505, 511, 517, 519; Becon, *Catechism*, Parker Society (Cambridge, 1844), pp. 152, 409.

[132] Becon, *Prayers*, p. 624; see also p. 286.

[133] Edwin Sandys, *Sermons*, Parker Society (Cambridge, 1842), pp. 217, 218.

[134] *Ibid.*, pp. 415, 349.

[135] *Ibid.*, p. 364; see pp. 364–369, 387–388.

[136] *CC*, p. 93.

[137] Karl Holl, *The Cultural Significance of the Reformation* (New York, 1959), pp. 74, 176. See also the index of the publications of the Parker Society under the word: England.

he looked forward to an "apocalyptical vindication" of the church rather than of the nation.[138] Foxe's concept of the church confirms the suggestion made by A. G. Dickens that "in so many respects Foxe is a mid-Tudor individualist rather than an ancestor of seventeenth-century Puritanism,"[139] as Professor Haller would have us believe.

The Protestant reshaping of church history within apocalyptic periodizations has a direct bearing upon the whole Foxian tradition. The high regard for Foxe as an historiographer was not shared by Roman Catholics. After the publication of the first English edition of the *Acts and Monuments*, Thomas Harding, as already mentioned, referred to it as "that huge dongehill of your stinking martyrs, which ye haue intituled Actes and monumentes." Under the name of Alan Cope, Nicholas Harpsfield published his *Dialogi Sex* in 1566. The last section of this book is an attack on the Protestant martyrs in general and on John Foxe in particular.[140] At the close of Elizabeth's reign the Jesuit Robert Parsons made a direct assault against Foxe in his *A Treatise of Three Conversions of England*. Nor were the many other Protestant historiographers left unchallenged by Roman Catholics. A countermeasure is found in *Annales Ecclesiastici* by Cardinal Baronius.[141] The hermeneutical principles underlying Protestant exegesis of the apocalyptic books of the Bible were counteracted by Catholic theologians, who advocated either a futuristic or praeteristic view regarding the historical fulfillment of the prophecies.

The Counter Reformation is generally considered to have three aspects: the Jesuits, the Inquisition, and the Council of Trent. In view of the significance of the Protestant apocalyptic interpretation of history which prophetically pinpointed step by step the events covering the whole Christian era from the beginning to the end, it seems justifiable to suggest a fourth aspect, namely the praeteristic and futuristic interpretations launched by Catholic expositors as a counterattack. In modern

---

[138] Haller, *Elect Nation*, p. 244.

[139] A. G. Dickens, from *The English Historical Review*, No. CCCXVI (July 1965), pp. 589–590.

[140] Nicholas Harpsfield, *Dialogi Sex* (Antwerp, 1566), pp. 638–998.

[141] Caesare Baronius, *Annales Ecclesiastici* (Antwerp, 1593).

times the most notable attack upon Foxe was that by S. R. Maitland, the librarian of Lambeth Palace. Through a series of articles published in the *British Magazine*, beginning in June 1837, Maitland threw doubt on the historicity of Foxe's great work. Maitland's influence is reflected in the article on Foxe in the *Dictionary of National Biography*[142] and in Charles Whibley's essay in the *Cambridge History of English Literature*.[143] The fourteenth edition of the *Encyclopaedia Britannica* charges Foxe with "wilfull falsification of evidence."[144] Maitland's assault upon Foxe has up to the present been examined only in the realm of historiography; it has not previously been noticed that it had a background in their different concepts of the church, especially as those concepts were viewed within the framework of apocalyptic ideas. Before attacking the historicity of the *Acts and Monuments* and the personality of its author, Maitland had already been involved in disputes concerning a view of church history based on apocalyptic periodizations. The periodizations themselves reflect a definite concept of the church and church history. The *Acts and Monuments*, therefore, cannot be fully appreciated except in the light of Foxe's concept of the church.

Maitland's attack was made in the setting of the general discussion of the concept of the church and the view of church history during the Oxford Movement. In the intensified quest for an understanding of the doctrine of the church, Protestants restated their Protestant view of church history; Bishop Thomas Burgess, in his *Tracts on the Origin and Independence of the Ancient British Church*, published in 1815, affirmed the British church to be a "Protestant Church nine centuries before the days of Luther."[145] Likewise in *The Anglo-Saxon Church* in 1835,[146] Henry Soames confirmed the Protestant view of English

---

[142] Sidney Lee, "John Foxe," *The Dictionary of National Biography*, VII, 581–590.

[143] Charles Whibley, "Chroniclers and Antequaries," *Cambridge History of English Literature*, III, 331–334.

[144] *Encyclopaedia Britannica*, 14th ed., s.v. "Foxe, John."

[145] Bishop Thomas Burgess, *Tracts on the Origin and Independence of the Ancient Church* (London, 1815).

[146] Published in London in 1844.

church history. Some major editions of the *Acts and Monuments* also appeared at this time. S. R. Maitland attacked the 1837–1841 edition. The motivation of his attack upon this first nineteenth-century edition is the same as that of Thomas Harding in his assault on the first English edition published at the beginning of Elizabeth's reign, for both men sought to counteract a specific Protestant view of church history.

A word should also be said about the present status of Foxian studies. S. R. Maitland's attack upon the life and work of Foxe was challenged in 1940 by J. F. Mozley in *John Foxe and His Book*. Mozley met Maitland's assault by correcting suppressed historical inaccuracies and misconceived ideas. Where historical mistakes appear, plausible excuses are presented. The studies by A. G. Dickens and his students of some dioceses in England indirectly confirm Foxe's historical reliability. We have already referred to other recent writers on Foxe and their contributions. The different studies of Foxe have mostly been in the realm of historiography, and the research has been confined to the *Acts and Monuments* or a few smaller writings which appear in main editions of his major work. The *Acts and Monuments* has, most often, also been the main source of information for topical approaches to the study of Foxe. While these studies have made significant contributions, it is unfortunate that Foxe's great influence as a historiographer has overshadowed the significance of his other writings. Their contribution is nevertheless of such a nature that by themselves they would place Foxe among the eminent writers of the Elizabethan period. Addressing Queen Elizabeth in the close of the *Acts and Monuments*, Foxe writes: "I take not upon me the part here of the moral or of the divine philosopher, to judge of things done, but only keep me within the compass of an historiographer."[147] This statement by Foxe himself, an example of the conceited style so common to Elizabethan writers, is misleading unless we realize that the whole nature of Protestant historiography was to impart a Protestant theology of history. Accordingly, in the preface of the 1559 edition of the *Acts and Monuments*, Foxe expressed the hope that

[147] *AM*, VIII, 672.

the Duke of Norfolk (to whom the work was dedicated) would be established in the Protestant religion by the reading of his work.

It appears from Foxe's minor works that he is basically a theologian and a preacher, and that as such, and only as means to an end, he became an historiographer. However, that end is clearly revealed in his doctrine of the church. Foxe does not systematically write on the doctrine of the church; however, a coherent concept of the church is found throughout his writings. An attempt will be made to evaluate Foxe as a theologian from this specific viewpoint, and at the same time to obtain a greater insight into his personality and the aims of his life. When a deepened understanding of his personality and purposes is brought to the study of the *Acts and Monuments*, then this larger work may take on a deeper meaning. At least it should be of help to better understand Foxe's basic purposes, and so safeguard against drawing wrong or one-sided conclusions regarding his objectives.

Gordon Rupp, in his evaluation of Mozley's book on Foxe, made this comment: "J. F. Mozley may be said to have begun the needful 'rebunking' (to coin a needed word) of John Foxe and his book."[148] It is hoped that this study, which is indebted to the many who have previously been engaged in research on John Foxe, may be a part of this "needful 'rebunking' of John Foxe" and his major and minor works.

---

[148] Gordon E. Rupp, *Six Makers of English Religon, 1500–1700* (London, 1964), p. 54.

I. The Church in History

*T*HE CHURCH, according to John Foxe, did not come into being with the incarnation of Christ and the ministry of the apostles: It antedates New Testament times. Foxe would agree with the "Belgic Confession" of 1561 that the "Church hath been from the beginning of the world, and will be to the end thereof,"[1] and with the "Scotch Confession of Faith," 1560: "We maist constantly beleeve, that God preserved, instructed, multiplied, honoured, decored, and from death called to life, his Kirk in all ages fra Adam, till the cumming of Christ Jesus in the flesh."[2] *Bishop Overall's Convocation Book of 1606* expresses the same sentiment when it states that after the Fall of Adam and Eve, Christ "began the Erection of that one Church, selected people, and Society of Believers, which ever since hath been, and so shall continue his blessed Spouse for ever."[3] In emphasizing the existence of the church, either from the time of the Creation or the Fall, the Reformers sought to identify the church of the Reformation with God's redemptive acts in past history. Since the centrality of faith is the same at all times, and the true church is likewise the same at all times, it became supremely important

[1] "Belgic Confession," art. xxvii, in *Creeds of Christendom*, ed. Philip Schaff (New York, 1931), III, 417.

[2] "Scotch Confession," art. v, *ibid.*, III, 442.

[3] J. Overall, *Bishop Overall's Convocation Book of 1606* (London, 1690), pp. 151–152.

to be able to unfold the true tradition for the reformed church.

Foxe unites Christ with the church of the Old and New Testaments when commenting on the image of the beautiful woman and the child of Revelation 12. Calling the church the mother of Christ, he states that "the one and universal church bore Christ," and "the first church, which brought forth Christ into the world, spread his faith throughout all nations."[4] What Foxe no doubt had in mind is expressed in more detail by his mentor, John Bale. In 1550 Bale printed a verse by verse exposition of the Apocalypse, in which he comments on Revelation 12:2:

> And she was in the woman with child. She cried travailing in birth, and was pained as one ready to be delivered. With Christ is the church big, when her members are in full faith; in the heart is he evermore conceived, and delivered forth such time as he is declared unto others. For this cause Christ called them his mother which had faith, and thereupon did the will of his Father. Of faith in the first promise that Christ should destroy the serpent was he first conceived in Adam and Eve, and so grew forth in righteous Abel, in Seth, Enos, Enoch, Noe, Sem, Tarah, Melchisedech, Abraham and Lot. And as the promises waxed stronger (as in Abraham, Moses, David, and the prophets), and the people of God more in number, so waxed the woman bigger and bigger till the fulness of her time was come that she should be delivered; which was such time as Christ appeared to the world, taught, and was conversant here among men. And this course hath she kept ever since, and shall do to the latter day in them that believe. Thus hath she had Christ in her womb since the beginning.[5]

For Foxe the past was not a dead past, for to him history was salvation history (*heilsgeschichte*) proclaiming how temporal events through God's lordship led to faith in Jesus Christ. The past was filled not only with events but with characters from which the lesson and principle of election should be learned. In salvation history the individual was a microcosm of God's actions in the world at large. Thus Foxe finds in the church of the Old Testament the paradigm of all ecclesiastical history. Foxe explains in some detail how the people of the Old Testament

---

[4] *Apoc.*, p. 198.

[5] John Bale, *The Image of Both Churches* in *Select Works of John Bale*, Parker Society (Cambridge, 1849), p. 405.

"exemplifieth and beareth a prophetical image to us, declaring what is to be looked for in the universal church of God dispersed through the world, planted in Christ Jesus his Son."[6] The story of the godly Abel who was slain by his brother Cain typifies the difference in condition between God's people and those not of God.[7] "The first age of the world," or the time before the flood, had witnesses for God, such as Noah.[8] Richard Hooker, in connection with his discussion of the visible church, writes "that in the time of the first world the family of Noah did contain all that were of the visible Church of God."[9]

According to Foxe's exposition of Romans 12, the comparison of "the church of God to an Olive Tree is metaphorical and prophetical." The root typifies Abraham and the other patriarchs "because in them appeared the first buds and blossoms of God's promise." The stock of the tree "represents unto us the church scattered upon the face of the earth; a congregation gathered together out of the whole number of the faithful." Thus in the picture of the olive tree "we have an apparent view painted out as it were, both of the old synagogue of the Jews; and the new church of the Gentiles."[10] Isaac and Jacob represent the elect, but Ishmael and Esau, the reject and reprobate.[11] The afflictions of the Israelites in Egypt are compared to the persecution of the church during the first three centuries of the Christian era. As the Israelites were delivered by Moses, so was the Christian church by Constantine, who is called God's "meek Moses."[12]

After the establishment of the Israelites as a nation in the promised land, the parallelism continues.[13] During the time of the judges they were afflicted by the invasion of new enemies—the Canaanites, Sidonians, and so forth—for 299 years. Foxe compares this period to the early persecution of the church lasting 294 years.[14] The significance of this time period is discussed later in the chapter. After the judges "the Israelites were ruled by

---

[6] *AM*, IV, 94.   [7] *AM*, IV, 94.
[8] *CC*, p. 43.
[9] Richard Hooker, *Of the Laws of Ecclesiastical Polity* (Oxford, 1885), Vol. III, pt. 1, p. 9.
[10] *OT*, p. 297.   [11] *AM*, IV, 94.
[12] *AM*, I, 292.   [13] *Apoc.*, p. 384.
[14] *Apoc.*, pp. 384–385.

kings, who, however, did not all live pious and praiseworthy lives. After Constantine the Christian church was similarly ruled by kings and emperors. Not all, however, proved pious and sincere."[15] After the Babylonian captivity, kings were succeeded by priests. In a similar way with Christendom, kings and emperors gave place to Roman popes and cardinals.[16] Further to this point Foxe writes:

> Likewise, in counting the years from their deliverance out of captivity to the end of their dissolution, we find five hundred and sixty-four years, during which years, as the church of the Jews was not governed under the authority of kings, but the high priests took all the power and authority to themselves; so we Christians, for the space especially of these latter five hundred and sixty-four years, what have we seen and felt, but only the jurisdiction and domination of the pope and high priests playing the 'Rex' in all countries, and ruling the whole? whereby, by the count of these years, it is to be thought the day of the Lord's coming not to be far off.[17]

Since Foxe, as will be noted later, considers the Papacy as representing Antichrist from A.D. 1000, he counts the above time period of 564 years from that date. Foxe, we will see in several instances, makes various prophetic time periods expire in the early period of Elizabeth's reign, thus making significant the English Reformation in its relationship to church history at large.

As the Israelites were diminished by the rejection of the ten tribes, so the greatest part of the church of Christ "both in Asia, in Africa and almost in Europe," had been reduced; but as God delivered the two tribes, so God again would deliver His church. As the church of the Old Testament, during the last three centuries before Christ, had been afflicted by the Syrians, so the Christian church had been persecuted by the Turks. Foxe emphasizes the similarity by pointing out that the Syrians were the Antichrist of the Old Testament as the Turks were of the New. Antiochus Epiphanes of Syria had begun to persecute God's people 191 years before the passion of Christ; the year Foxe fixes for the Turks is A.D. 1375. Adding 191 years to that

[15] *Apoc.*, p. 385.　　　　　　[16] *Apoc.*, p. 385.
[17] *AM*, IV, 95.

date, Foxe comes to A.D. 1566; he thus calculates that the end of the afflictions by the Turks is at hand.[18] In two other comparisons Foxe minutely fixes time periods to expire in his own time.

Foxe reckons the period from the lawgiving by Moses to the destruction of the temple by Titus to be 1564 years. Applied to the New Testament, the period should begin with the incarnation of Christ.[19] The seventy years in which the Israelites were in the Babylonian captivity had a double application for Foxe, as explained in the following way: "And now by reuolution of yeares we are come from that tyme of 1501, to the yeare now present, 1570. In which the full seuenty yeares of the Babilonicall captiuitie draweth now well to an end, if we count from the first appearyng of these bloudy markes aboue mentioned." The bloody marks Foxe refers to are such tokens of Christ's passion as "the bloudy crosse, hys nayles, speare, and crowne of thornes," which are supposed to have fallen "from heauen vpon the garmentes and cappes of men, and rockes of women." Foxe also suggests that the beginning of the seventy years could be reckoned "from the beginnying of Luther, and his persecution, then lacketh yet XVI yeares."[20] In this way Foxe illustrates how "the actions and doings of that one nation, be as figures and types of greater matters, what shall happen in the latter times of the whole church universally in Christ collected."[21]

In his comparison between the church of the Old Testament and that of the New, Foxe also makes use of the Old Testament to vindicate the Messiahship of Christ and to emphasize the unity of Christ and the church. In so doing, he again states that the greater part of the prophetic scriptures "doth nothing but foreshow and report, that all those things should come to pass, which the evangelical history expressly pronounces to be already accomplished."[22] Foxe's exposition of the Old Testament, both metaphorically and prophetically, is illustrated in the following statement:

> What doth the delivery of Jonas out of the whale's belly on the third day prefigure unto us other than the resurrection of Christ? What doth the translating of Elias into heaven, in a fiery

[18] AM, IV, 97.   [19] AM, IV, 95.
[20] Cong., sig. iiiiv.   [21] AM, IV, 95.
[22] OT, p. 316; see also CC, pp. 58, 59, 65, 68.

chariot, signify, other than the ascension of Christ? What doth that brazen serpent foreshow other than Christ crucified upon the cross? What do the manifold afflictions of king David represent, but the continual persecution of Christ in this world? What doth Moses signify, but a deliverer? Joshua, but the victorious conquest of Christ over all his enemies? What doth the rule and government of Joseph, with a certain royal majesty over the Egyptians, imply, but the kingdom of Messias, at whose book all things in earth and heaven should be obedient and subject? It would require a long discourse to overrun all the mystical sayings of the prophets.[23]

The unity between the coming of the Messiah, as predicted by the prophets, and the beginning of the Christian church is especially emphasized when Foxe speaks about the kingdom of God. The perpetual kingdom of David found its fulfillment in the Christian church.[24] Referring to the imagery of Daniel 2, he speaks about "the stone, which being hewn out of a great hill without man's hands, smote the image that represented the four monarchies of the world and brake his head, his breast, his legs, and his feet, in pieces, so that no place was found for them, but the stone itself became a great mountain, and filled the whole earth." Foxe follows Augustine in making the stone that became a great mountain represent the church. He further states: "I could vouch out of the same Daniel sundry sentences, many also out of other prophets to the like effect; for what else doth the whole prophetical history of the bible, even from the beginning to the end thereof, describe unto us, than Christ Jesus and his kingdom."[25]

As Foxe's periodization of church history is minutely fixed, so also is the time for the coming of Christ and the inauguration of the church of the New Testament minutely predicted. In Daniel 9 a time period of seventy weeks is mentioned. Foxe follows other expositors when he counts each week as seven years, beginning the period of 490 years with the rebuilding of the Jewish temple after the return from the Babylonian exile, and ending it with the termination of the Jewish nation.[26] Thus Foxe could state that the "so incomprehensible majesty of this kingdom, the

23 *OT*, p. 359.　　　　24 *OT*, pp. 329–331.
25 *OT*, pp. 358–359.　　　26 *OT*, pp. 350–359, 393–394.

prophet does not in one place alone prophesy should come, nor does he promise it only, but discovers also the very minute and instant of time wherein this kingdom should flourish."[27]

Foxe not only ties the history of the church to that of the Old Testament, he also brings the coming of Messiah and the foundation of the church into close relationship with world history at large. Reference has already been made to the image in Daniel 2. This image of gold, silver, bronze, and iron was supposed to represent the four ancient monarchies: Assyria or Babylonia, Medo-Persia, Greece, and Rome. Foxe, at great length seeks to prove that this common interpretation of Daniel 2 should also be applied to the first four seals of Revelation 6.[28] In so doing, Foxe admits that he deviates from other expositors who either explain the seven seals as seven ages from the time of creation to the end of time, or as seven significant periods in the history of the Christian church. In the first four seals, four horsemen are seen following one another. The first horse is white, the second red, the third black, and the fourth pale, and "his name that sat on him was Death, and Hell followed with him." The closing scene of Daniel 2 is the establishment of a fifth kingdom, the kingdom of God. The interpretation is that this kingdom was ushered in by the coming of the Messiah and the establishment of the Christian church. The significance of Foxe's interpretation in paralleling the four ancient monarchies with the four horsemen is that the fifth seal then announces the kingdom of God. Foxe writes: "After you have heard about the political empires and their turmoils and the issue of them, revealed from the secret counsels of heaven in the preceding four seals, we now come to the fifth, sixth, and seventh. In these are opened to us wondrous mysteries, concerning the kingdom of Christ and the church, and things pertaining to the church up to the consummation of the age."[29]

The fifth kingdom of the book of Daniel depicts the church triumphant, but the fifth seal of the book of Revelation describes the church as being under the cross. Thus Foxe in his prophetic interpretation has laid down and united the two basic character-

[27] *OT*, p. 358.
[28] *Apoc.*, pp. 41–54.
[29] *Apoc.*, p. 54.

istics of the early church. When the fifth seal was opened, John "saw underneath the altar the souls of those who had been slaughtered for God's word and for the testimony they bore. They gave a great cry: 'How long, sovereign Lord, holy and true, must it be before thou wilt vindicate us and avenge our blood on the inhabitants of the earth?' "[30] Foxe asks, "At what time, and under what tyrant, was seen the affliction of this fifth seal?" He answers: "Doubtless in the first period of the church, when under profane emperors, for nearly three hundred years, the church of Christ suffered most grievously by the death of the godly." After this affliction, Foxe states, there will be a relaxation of persecution for a thousand years because Satan will be bound. After the thousand years the loosing of Satan will be pronounced. "Then will come the second persecution and this, it is to be understood, will complete the number of the holy martyrs. This will take place in the last days of the world under Antichrist and has continued already for almost three hundred years."[31]

Foxe not only brings the history of the Christian church into relationship with that of the Old Testament and world history at large, but he also places the church in the center of a great cosmic drama which began back in eternity. The last scenes were taking place in his own time or would be accomplished in the immediate future. The major events and most significant periods in ecclesiastical history are as acts and scenes in a theater. He refers to the church and Christendom as "this theater of religion."[32] Because Foxe wrote Latin plays, the setting of a play was familiar to him. Simeon Foxe, in the biography of his father, tells us that Foxe "wrote divers Latine Comedies yet to be seen, in a copious, and gracefull style, but somewhat lofty."[33] The influence of the *Acts and Monuments* upon late sixteenth- and early seventeenth-century English religious plays is revealed by the fact that "no less than twelve plays draw all or parts of their plots from the *Acts and Monuments*."[34]

[30] Rev. 6:9–10. [31] *Apoc.*, p. 55.
[32] *Exc.*, sig. A5r. [33] *AM* (1641), II, sig. A4r.
[34] Leslie Mahin Oliver, "The Acts and Monuments of John Foxe: A Study of the Growth and Influence of a Book" (Ph.D. dissertation, Harvard University, 1945), pp. 4, 221–231.

In the preface of *Christus Triumphans* Foxe informs the reader that he has transferred "from the sacred writings, to the theatre, what was most pertinent to ecclesiastical matters."[35] Accordingly Foxe adopts the form of a religious play in which he depicts historically and theologically the most significant events of the church from Adam and Eve to the End, or the Second Advent of Christ. The starting point is the Fall. Eve is lamenting over the fact that the grave holds her children "in its perpetual penitentiary."[36] Mary appears, also burdened with great sorrow because of the rage against her son.[37] The two women talk of their common sorrow. Mary raises the question, "But what if God has joined us equally, but has joined to the sorrow a greater consolation?"[38] Eve points to the promise that someday "the pain of the wound will be healed" and "the head of the serpent cast into the infernal regions"[39] (obviously a reference to Genesis 3:15). Mary then speaks of the birth of her son and also his crucifixion. The conversation, which takes place "the second day after his crucifixion,"[40] closes by Mary's making reference to a war in heaven and the casting out of the old serpent described in Revelation 12.[41] Thus is introduced the significance of this chapter which, as will be noticed later, has such a central place in Foxe's concept of the church.

Next, Satan appears on the scene,[42] saying that he is "cast out of heaven, having lost all position in the council and lawgiving."[43] However, he states: "If we are not allowed in heaven, even the stars themselves being unwilling, we shall reign on earth."[44] The resurrected Christ now approaches Satan,[45] facing him with the fact "that he scattered the works of Diabolus." Satan has to admit: "I am despoiled in heaven and earth."[46] Act One is concluded by Christ's commanding: "For 1,000 years let no one go to him, let him be imprisoned."[47]

The second act begins, as the first ended, by pointing out the

---

[35] *CT* (1556), sig. A5v.

[36] *CT*, p. 8.

[37] *CT*, pp. 9–15.

[38] *CT*, p. 10.

[39] *CT*, p. 13.

[40] *CT*, p. 14.

[41] *CT*, p. 15.

[42] *CT*, pp. 15–19.

[43] *CT*, p. 17.

[44] *CT*, p. 18.

[45] *CT*, pp. 19–21.

[46] *CT*, pp. 20, 21.

[47] *CT*, p. 21.

binding of Satan. Thus already in this early writing Foxe emphasizes the significance of the thousand year period. He writes: "Captive now of the high imperial Prince, mighty Satan is bound 1,000 years. He who bound others, himself is bound with chains."[48] Before Foxe begins his story of the early church, he brings out the other point so important to him in his view of church history, that after the thousand years Satan "will be freed from darkness, and with him the multitudes he led into error. He will seduce the wide world, and at that time the church will be troubled with painful calamities."[49]

The progress of the early Jewish Christian church disturbed the Jewish leaders. Foxe depicts a council by the chief priests, a priest, a scribe, and Saul discussing the situation. Next he mentions Saul's response to the call to persecute the Christians.[50] The chief priest's final order is, "Let Herod co-operate with what I have decreed. He will bring out Petrus, whom he holds in fetters, to us for execution. Thus we will stop their mouths."[51] The next scene describes Peter's miraculous deliverance from prison.[52] Having described persecution on the one hand and deliverance on the other, Foxe has a messenger come forward to tell that after a thousand years Satan will emerge anew.[53] No doubt Foxe wishes his audience, who experienced that persecution, to remember that, in the latter as well as in the early days of the church, God's deliverance will be manifested. The renewed reference to the thousand years should further remind them that the persecution and final deliverance are part of a great historical drama.

Beginning with Act Three, the character Ecclesia appears, calling Christ "my betrothed."[54] What mankind lost in the Fall of father Adam and mother Eve will be restored through mother Ecclesia. In Eve's conversation with Mary, the first reference is made to Nomocrates, the law personified. Theologically, Nomocrates stands for the power of death through sin. About Eve's son who was not killed, Mary asks, "Is he yet alive?" Eve an-

---

48 *CT*, pp. 21–22.
50 *CT*, pp. 23–28.
52 *CT*, pp. 28–29.
54 *CT*, p. 37.

49 *CT*, p. 22.
51 *CT*, p. 28.
53 *CT*, pp. 30–31.

swers, "I know not. Nomocrates, the tyrant, led him away captive, and delivered him into slavery to the lictor Thanatus; he was exiled from the Congregation, from home, wife, children, in Asia, Europe, Africa."[55] When Ecclesia appears she finds herself in Eve's situation. She says, "Now I, Ecclesia, am left alone with three offspring: Asia, Africa and Europe; and in my misery am despoiled of these, whom Nomocrates the implacable tyrant has cast into the most sordid prison."[56]

First Ecclesia speaks with Nomocrates,[57] and here again Foxe emphasizes the relationship between her and the first parents. Nomocrates says, "I have found again the woman whom I wished to find. I declare to thee woman, thou art Ecclesia sprung from Adam, and posthumous descendant of the sinner Eve." Ecclesia answers, "I am ashamed neither of my parents, nor of my name."[58] Nomocrates argues that he has the right over all who sin, but Ecclesia declares her innocence.[59] Next[60] Christ's victory over sin and death is brought out, emphasizing that Christ destroyed Thanatus, nailed Nomocrates to the cross, and bound "Diabolous himself with chains."[61] Ecclesia expresses great joy, saying, "In the meanwhile I delayed too long in imparting this joyful news to my children."[62] In these statements Foxe unites the appearance of the church with the proclamation of the Gospel. Asia, Africa, and Europe are rightfully the children of the church, and the proclamation of "the joyful news" will win them back to the mother. Foxe thus emphasizes the central Gospel message as the essential mark of the church.

The proclamation of the Gospel by the church and the persecution against the church, especially during the first three centuries and during the latter three hundred years, have a prominent place in Foxe's view of church history as expressed in the *Acts and Monuments*, beginning with the 1570 edition and further developed in his commentary on the book of Revelation. However, this view was already outlined in *Christus Triumphans*. After Ecclesia has said that she would tell the "joyful

---

[55] *CT*, p. 13.
[57] *CT*, pp. 38–39.
[59] *CT*, p. 39.
[61] *CT*, p. 41.

[56] *CT*, p. 37.
[58] *CT*, p. 38.
[60] *CT*, pp. 41–43.
[62] *CT*, p. 43.

news" to her children, Dioctes, the persecutor, appears on the scene,[63] stating that "the mighty Leader and God of this world, Satan, sends me here out of the vast sea, and has made me the ruler of his inheritance."[64] In Foxe's historical scheme ten persecutions of the early church play an important role.[65]

At the close of the three hundred years Dioctes appears again, saying, "We have fought with our enemies the Christians, the greater number, if not all, of whom, I think we have broken down and trampled upon by rare valour and the might of my ten Caesars."[66] Triumphantly he adds, "The day had gone happily, with the shedding of Christian blood."[67] However, his joy does not last very long. The message is brought to him that Constantius is dead and has been succeeded by his son, who "is now a friend of Christ; a most bitter adversary to us he has become."[68] The advice given to Dioctes is to "sustain the present with hope of what the future will bring: Satan himself will emerge unfettered; it will not be long, till he stretch hither his Athenian hand."[69]

The importance of Constantine for the church is pointed out when Ecclesia says, "From the day when Constantine of Britain became ruler we have enjoyed peace for a long time, except during the frightful madness of the Turk."[70] Thus Foxe praises not only Constantine but also the time following. (Notice that he points out that the first Christian emperor was "of Britain.") Foxe does not discuss the condition of the church until the time when Satan is to be loosed; according to his early view, that is about A.D. 1000.

With the loosing of Satan, Foxe introduces Pseudamnus, that is, Antichrist, and Dioctes reappears. When Satan looks at the world anew, he exclaims, "See what my absence has done!"[71] Next he summons Pseudamnus to "come forth out of the third inferno."[72] Satan points out to Pseudamnus "with how much power the name of Christendom was established by the aid of Christ. Now there is just one final plan by which we can con-

[63] *CT*, pp. 44–46.
[64] *CT*, p. 44.
[65] *CT*, p. 46.
[66] *CT*, p. 56.
[67] *CT*, p. 57.
[68] *CT*, p. 59.
[69] *CT*, p. 60.
[70] *CT*, p. 62.
[71] *CT*, p. 64.
[72] *CT*, p. 65.

quer: not by force but by subtlety."[73] Satan orders Pseudamnus, "Go to Babylon where you will besiege the abode of the Pontiff."[74] Then he gives him the following advice: "When you have gotten through to the highest, be careful to conduct yourself discreetly as Pontiff. You will appear as the unique vicar of Christ, and as such you will be applauded."[75] Satan's directions to Pseudamnus described how Antichrist will obtain full control of the church: "You will enact laws, written in the blood of martyrs. You will control the world. You will bring it to your opinion as if led by the nose. Even the concerns of the church will be in your control, and she will be your bride."[76]

Expecting the appearance of Antichrist, Ecclesia brings a warning to two of her children, Africa and Europe.[77] The common position of the Protestant Reformers, that the Antichrist is represented by both the Turks and the Pope, is presented. Europe answers, "It is well known, Mother, that Antichrist is to rise, and I think he is Mahomet of Asia, who has distracted our family for long." Ecclesia replies, "That is so, but he is not alone." Europe promises, "We will take the greatest care." And Africa says, "We shall never forget the name of Christ."[78] However, the warning is not heeded nor the promise kept. Dioctes approaches Africa and Europe and presents to them "Papa, an excellent man in life, servant of God, and piety itself."[79] "Papa," or Pseudamnus, then says to them, "Thou, Europe: be defender of the faith ... Africa shall be called most Christian."[80] Foxe further describes the continued apostasy of the universal church by letting Pornapolis, the Babylonian harlot, enter the scene.[81] She tells the audience: "When I first appeared they ran to me from all sides as if I were God. ... They said: 'It is the Ecclesia of the omnipotent God, the bride of the Lamb, the ultimate truth.' "[82] Foxe has now come to the time of a true and a false church, the former more or less invisible, the church not considered by many; the latter the great and visible ecclesiastical structure of Rome, called Antichrist or the Babylonian harlot.

[73] *CT*, p. 66.
[74] *CT*, p. 68.
[75] *CT*, pp. 68–69.
[76] *CT*, p. 69.
[77] *CT*, pp. 74–75.
[78] *CT*, pp. 74–75.
[79] *CT*, p. 78.
[80] *CT*, p. 81.
[81] *CT*, pp. 82–87.
[82] *CT*, pp. 82, 83.

Accordingly, Pornapolis in her conversation with Pseudamnus mentions that "one difficulty remains," namely, "Ecclesia, who is hidden, may betray us at last."[83] Ecclesia now appears. She cries, "I shudder, distressed at what comes. May Ecclesia be heard and helped by God of heaven. But where are the sons I long for?"[84] Pseudamnus asks her, "Tell us, if you please, O woman, who you are." At her reply, "I bear the name Ecclesia," various remarks are made: "Alas Anathema—Do you hear that?— Heretic." Pseudamnus asks, "Are you then Ecclesia?" and she answers, "Can I deny being what I am?" Scorn is expressed again: "Schismatic—What mad dog bit thee, O woman?"[85] Ecclesia is accused of being Anabaptist, to which she replies, "I am not Anabaptist, I am orthodox Ecclesia."[86] Pornapolis reaffirms: "I say you are not Ecclesia . . . I am Ecclesia, the bride of Christ." Ecclesia asks the question, "To be mother of Asia, Africa and Europe, which I am? at which Pseudamnus exclaims, "Ha! is she not schismatic?"[87] Foxe brings into focus the elect as the true church in Ecclesia's final statement, "The elect of God stand firm having this seal: He knows who are his own."[88]

In his further conquest of Europe, Satan tells his helpers: "Follow my example: now I am not Satan, but you must call me an angel of light." The form this should take is expressed to Psychephomis the lictor: "You must be a hypocrite under the Franciscan robe." To Thanatus, who represents death, Satan says, "Be in name and form a mock martyr. And whenever you find someone who is a truly pious Christian, copy him, in name and office."[89] In the next scene Satan is dressed in a pall.[90] Reference is made to Duns Scotus and Thomas Aquinas. The scene closes with Antichrist's making the following speech: "I say, you should act immediately as becomes strong accomplices, persecutors of martyrs, inquisitors, torturers, breakers of joints and bones, unjust judges, forgers of decretals, incendiaries. . . . Lead the way to Dioctes. Prepare for him what is needful."[91] Foxe has

---

83 *CT*, p. 84.
84 *CT*, p. 85.
85 *CT*, p. 85.
86 *CT*, p. 85.
87 *CT*, p. 86.
88 *CT*, p. 87.
89 *CT*, p. 89.
90 *CT*, pp. 93–96.
91 *CT*, pp. 95–96.

first described the subtle work of Satan when loosed; now he refers to a renewal of persecution, but at the same time he describes a revival of the Gospel.

Antichrist and the Babylonian harlot converse about the latest development: the revival of the Gospel. Pornapolis says, "Are we not now the common subject of talk for all? Now all read the Scriptures, sculptors, stonemasons, workmen, potters, and who else? and the dregs of the people (which to me means bad people), nowadays they are beginning to get learning. Yea indeed, what is more, they weigh our conduct in the scales of the Gospel."[92] To this Pseudamnus answers, "I see more evil in this than can be remedied." And Pornapolis continues by saying, "For neither fetters nor claws, rack, sword, nor torture, flame, nor vengeance, nor anything else can terrify them."[93]

The progress of the Reformation is further depicted by Ecclesia's welcoming back her children, Africa and Europe. The next event is the Advent and the consummation of all things. Ecclesia and her two children discuss the sad condition of the world. The children are ready to fight, but Ecclesia says, "Only by the Advent of Christ can these monsters be vanquished. . . . I have suffered for a long time, I hope it will not be long until he will bring an end to these evils." Ecclesia now hears some noise and asks, "But what is that commotion outside?" Africa gives the answer, "Why, maidens are pressing forward bearing lamps and torches."[94]

Ecclesia and her two children are joined by a chorus of five maidens.[95] They tell Ecclesia to prepare for the Bridegroom. Ecclesia asks, "Now what more remains?" and the choir answers, "Only that we now attend the wedding and join the marriage song."[96] Next the nuptial song is sung. It is a plea to the Bridegroom to come: "Bridegroom, mindful of our people, let your majesty burst through the clouds . . . the Spirit rejoices because you are coming, and to come to you, O Spouse! No longer delay but come quickly, Bridegroom. Everything on the globe lies open, the earth, and sea, and the pole are weary; your creation

---

[92] *CT*, pp. 97–98.
[94] *CT*, pp. 107–108.
[96] *CT*, p. 115.

[93] *CT*, p. 98.
[95] *CT*, pp. 109–115.

seeks your return."[97] The song closes with words that are repeated a number of times, "The Bridegroom is coming."[98]

The final scene is the chorus of virgins: "Behold, onlookers, the Bride is now robed and ready. Nothing remains but the Bridegroom, who will bring about the final scene. When this will happen certainly no one can say. . . .Meanwhile, I beseech you to be warned and to watch, with prudence; and utter acclamation."[99]

In *Christus Triumphans* Foxe clearly portrays his view of church history. A threefold background is given for the historical drama in which the church is placed: the Fall, the Incarnation of Christ, and the Second Advent. The following points are significant landmarks: Christ at the incarnation binds Satan for a thousand years, the church commences with the proclamation of "the good news," the first three hundred years see the ten main persecutions against the church, and with Constantine peace comes to the church for a long time. Satan is loosed after a thousand years, and through cunning devices he conquers the church. Next he persecutes her, but at the same time the true preaching of the Gospel is revived. What remains is the consummation of all things and the coming of the Bridegroom.

Not much historical material is brought together in *Christus Triumphans*, but Foxe's basic concept of the church in history is revealed; and at the same time the historical, apocalyptical, and theological framework of the *Acts and Monuments* is given. The further development of Foxe's periodization of church history is found in the early editions of the *Acts and Monuments*. The first two editions were printed in Latin, in Strassburg and Basel, respectively, in 1554 and 1559, during Foxe's exile on the Continent. They do not indicate a historical outline of the church, except that Foxe considers the Reformation to have begun with Wycliffe, Huss, and Jerome, thus emphasizing the concept that the renewal of true Christianity was begun within the English Church by Wycliffe to whom Huss and Jerome of Prague were indebted. The Strassburg edition describes mainly Wycliffe and the Lollard movements up to the year 1500, and is reprinted as Book One in the 1559 edition.

[97] *CT*, pp. 116–117.   [98] *CT*, p. 120.
[99] *CT*, pp. 121, 122.

In the first English edition of 1563, Foxe's view of church history reveals itself more clearly. He brings the beginning of his history back to A.D. 1000, because around this year the thousand year period of Revelation 20 expired and the loosing of Satan took place. In the opening paragraph Foxe states that he began his story here for "so many notable thynges worthy of knowledge, which haue hapned in ye time of these 500 yeres, since Sathan broke loose."[100]

About the year 1000 the apostasy of the church became especially corrupt; however, this did not mean that "the Churche and sea of Rome was not altogether voyde and clere from al corrupcion, during the whole time of the first thousand yeares after Christe our Saviour, but eftsones before the full thousand was expired, certayne enormities and absurdities began to crepe in to the heades of the cleargie."[101] Having enumerated some samples of "enormities and absurdities" among the leaders of the church from A.D. 600 to the tenth century, Foxe writes: "Although, therefore as I say, by these and suche other euidences, it may appeare, the state of the Churche not to stand so clere and vpright in all pointes, the full tyme of the 1000 yeares after Christ, but that some supersticion, and imperfection began to touche the prelasy then being: Yet in comparison of tymes that followed, all this might seme some thing sufferable and honest."[102]

Foxe repeats the same thought and then states that "the 1000 yeares after Christe, yet in respect of the other time that followed, it might seme a golden age full of much light, vertue, and true felicitie."[103] Having this in mind, Foxe states his objective as follows: "I intend by the grace of Christ to begin this history there, where the 1000 yeares do ende, declaring therein such actes and doings as haue happened most notable, in the church within the compas of these latter 500 yeares, especially in the churche of England and Scotland."[104] The title of the 1563 edition states the same objective and reason for it.

Foxe lays down a basic principle of his general view of church history when he writes, "In summe, to geue thee one generall

[100] *AM* (1563), p. 1.
[101] *Ibid.*
[102] *Ibid.*, p. 2.
[103] *Ibid.*
[104] *Ibid.*

rule for all, this thou shalt obserue, the higher thou goest up-warde to the Apostles time, the purer thou shalt finde the churche: the lower thou doest descend, euer the more drosse and dregges thou shalt perceyue in the bottome, and especiallye within the laste 500 yeares."[105]

Of the two major periods into which Foxe divides church history, the first is characterized as the "golden age," and the second as "the olde, or brasen age of the churche." Here Foxe refers to the image of Daniel 2 where the degradation of world powers is symbolized through the change of the metal in the image. Foxe continues by saying, "For as Daniell deuideth the times of the world, by the example of an Image . . . so the churche also (thoughe she shall neuer haue ende of her age, as other empiers haue) yet she hat her deuersitie of times, and ages."[106] Before Foxe begins his discussion of the church after A.D. 1000, he refers briefly to various periods of the church. The early years when the apostles worked within the borders of Palestine are called "the first age of the Church" or "this primi-tive age of ye church," as well as "the birth and infancy" of the church. Next Foxe speaks about the years when the apostles brought the Gospel to the far corners of the Roman empire as "the second age of the Churche."[107] This period is followed by "the florishing age of the churche" when the church became strong through persecution, and flourished when the persecution ceased at the time of Constantine. Foxe writes: "But to our purpose, concerning the youthfull age, of the virgin and spouse of Christe the churche, which now grew up, by litell and litell, through the mighty gift of God, to a more complet state of age, what time Constantinus the emperour relinquishing his idols submitted himself openly to the sacrament of Christ, being baptysed in the name of the father, the sonne, and the holy Ghost."[108]

The next period in the history of the church is called "the midle age of the Churche." Foxe's opening statement in describ-ing this period reads as follows: "Thus the catholike churche in her infancy, was innocent, in her child hode, she grew and multi-

105 *Ibid.*, p. 6.
107 *Ibid.*

106 *Ibid.*, p. 7.
108 *Ibid.*, p. 8.

plyed, in her youthe she increased and gat strength. And in her midle age she wrastled with sondrie sectes, schismes and shismatickes, especially such as contended for supremacie."[109] The church reached "to her midle age about VIII or IX hundreth yeres after Christ" and "began again to decay, by litel and litel. And as she decresed in spiritual strength, so increased in worldly power."[110] Finally "cometh the latter age of the church," and "then began corruption to enter and increase: then turned the gold and good metall, into drosse and filthinesse: then quenched the clear light of the gospel."[111] In his view of church history Foxe had now come to "the time, that the reuelation speaketh of, when Sathanas, the old serpent, beyng tied up for a thousand yere, was losed for a certaine space, of ye which space, here in these bokes...we entend some thing to entreat and speake of."[112] This is the historical and apocalyptic view of the church in which the great folio volume of nearly 1800 pages of the first English edition of the *Acts and Monuments* found its setting.

Foxe's fully developed periodization of church history is found in the 1570 edition of the *Acts and Monuments*. In this edition Foxe brings his story back to the beginning of the Christian era and modifies the historical outline sketched in the 1563 edition. He divides its history into five periods as follows:

> First, to declare of the suffering time of the church, which conteyneth 300 yeares after Christ.
> Secondly, the florishing and growing tyme of the same; conteyning other 300 yeares.
> Thirdly, the declining tyme of the church, and of true religion, other 300 yeares.
> Fourthly, of the time of Antichrist, reigning and raging in the church, since the loosing out of Sathan.
> Lastly, of the reforming time of Christes church in these latter 300 yeares.[113]

This same fivefold division is given by Foxe, but in greater detail, in a comparison between the state of the primitive church

---

[109] *Ibid.*
[110] *Ibid.*, p. 9.
[111] *Ibid.*, p. 10.
[112] *Ibid.*, p. 11.
[113] *AM* (1570), I, 49.

and the latter church of Rome. Here it is clearly stated that the loosing out of Satan "was about the thousand yeare after Christ."[114] In other words, the third period brings the history of the church down to the year A.D. 1000. Discussing the third period, characterized as "the declining or backeslyding time of the Churche," Foxe writes:

> During which space of time, the Churche, although in condicion of life, in ambition and pride, it was nowe muche altered from the simple puritye of the primitiue tyme, yet in a certaine outwarde professon of doctrine and religion was something tollerable, and had some face of a Church: notwithstanding some corruption of doctrine, with superstition and hypocrisy was then also crept in. And yet in comparison of that as followed after, it myght seeme (as I sayde) something sufferable.[115]

The fourth period lasts four hundred years, beginning in A.D. 1000 and synchronizing for the last hundred years with the first one hundred years of the fifth and last period. The fourth period covers "the time of Antichrist, or the desolation of the Churche." During this time "both doctrine, and sincerity of life was vtterly almost extinguished, namely in the chiefe heds and rulers of this west church, through the meanes of the Romane Bishops, especially Gregory the VII, called Hildebrand, Innocentius the III, and the Friars which with him crept in, etc. And this time I count from Pope Boniface the third, till the time of Wickliffe and John Husse, during 400 yeares."[116]

With the fifth period, from about the year A.D. 1300, begins "the reformation and purging of the Churche of God, wherein Antichrist beginneth to be reueled, and to appeare in his coulours, and his antichristian doctrine to be detected, and the number of his church decreaseth, and the number of the true Church increaseth. The durance of which time hath continued from 260 yeares hetherto, and how long it shal continue more, the Lord and gouernour of all times onely knoweth."[117]

In regard to his fivefold division of church history Foxe writes: "For in these fiue diuersities and alteracions of times, I suppose the whole course and state of the Church may well be

114 *Ibid.*, I, 1.   115 *Ibid.*
116 *Ibid.*, I, 1.   117 *Ibid.*

comprised."[118] It is of interest to notice that James Ussher, the archbishop of Armagh, to a large degree follows Foxe in his periodization of church history. Both of them also point out the significance of the Waldenses at the time of papal apostasy.[119]

Foxe follows the common medieval concept when he counts the thousand year period from the birth of Christ to A.D. 1000. However, the later and more typical view of Foxe is that the period spans the time from Constantine to Wycliffe, or, to be exact, from A.D. 324 to A.D. 1324.[120] In making this change Foxe formulates a periodization of church history which is original with him. Foxe arrived at this new view while studying the persecution of the early church in light of the book of Revelation, especially the numbers in chapters 11, 12, and 13.[121] In these chapters several time periods of the church are mentioned in connection with the persecution. The periods are listed as twelve hundred and sixty days; three and a half days; a time, times, and half a time; and forty-two months. According to Foxe, these numbers all refer to the same time period; yet the problem he faced was that "all this by computation coming but to three years and a half, came nothing near the long continuance of these persecutions, which lasted three hundred years."[122] This is the question that troubled Foxe:

> Why should God of his goodness suffer his children and servants so vehemently to be cruciated and afflicted? If mortal things were governed by heavenly providence (as must needs be granted), why did the wicked so rage and flourish, and the godly go so to wrack? If their sins deserved punishment, yet neither

[118] *Ibid.*

[119] Robert Buick Knox, "The Ecclesiastical Policy of James Ussher, Archbishop of Armagh" (Ph.D. dissertation, University of London, 1956), pp. 399–400.

[120] While Foxe changed the date for the beginning of the thousand year period, he did not correct the thousand year period in his two references to the fivefold division of church history already referred to. Neither is it corrected in the 1570 and 1576 editons. *AM* (1570), I, 49; *AM* (1576), I, 30.

[121] *AM* (1570), I, 139. How Foxe arrived at this concept is described in full detail in *AM* (1576), I, 101–102. Since *AM* gives the rendering of the 1576 editon, the former has been quoted.

[122] *AM*, I, 290.

were they sinners alone, and why was their death above all others so sharp and bitter? At least why should the Lord suffer the vehemency of these so horrible persecutions to endure so long time against his poor church, showing unto them no certain determined end of their tribulations, whereby they, knowing the appointed determination of Almighty God, with more consolation might endure out the same? The Israelites in the captivity of Babylon had seventy years limited unto them; and under Pharaoh they were promised a deliverance out; also under the Syrian tyrants threescore and two weeks were abridged unto them. Only in these persecutions I could find no end determined, nor limitation set for their deliverance.[123]

Foxe further describes how he came to a solution in regard to the interpretation of the prophetic time periods. Since this interpretation is the backbone for Foxe's whole framework of church history, it seems in this connection necessary to quote Foxe at length. He first writes: "For the better explication whereof, because the matter (being of no small importance) greatly appertaineth to the public utility of the church; and lest any should misdoubt me herein, to follow any private interpretation of mine own; I thought good to communicate to the reader that which hath been imparted unto me, in the opening of these mystical numbers in the aforesaid Book of Revelation."[124] Foxe then tells the story of how he arrived at his interpretation. He writes:

Thus, being vexed and turmoiled in spirit about the reckoning of these numbers and years; it so happened upon a Sunday in the morning, I lying in my bed, and musing about these numbers, suddenly it was answered to my mind, as with a majesty, thus inwardly saying within me; "Thou fool, count these months by sabbaths, as the weeks of Daniel are counted by sabbaths." The Lord I take to witness, thus it was. Whereupon thus being admonished, I began to reckon the forty-two months by sabbaths: first, of months; that would not serve: then by sabbaths of years; wherein I began to feel some probable understanding. Yet not satisfied herewith, to have the matter more sure, eftsoons I repaired to certain merchants of mine acquaintance; of whom the number of these aforesaid forty-two months being propounded

123 *AM*, I, 289.   124 *AM*, I, 289.

and examined by sabbaths of years, the whole sum was found to surmount unto two hundred ninety and four years, containing the full and just time of these aforesaid persecutions, neither more nor less.[125]

In Foxe's calculations the forty-two months are multiplied by seven, giving him 294 days. Then, reckoning each day for a year, he arrives at 294 years, which should comprise the length of the persecution in the early church. Foxe counts this period from A.D. 30 to A.D. 324, explaining his solution as follows:

> And so have ye the just years, days, times, and months of these aforesaid persecutions under the beast, neither shorter nor longer, reckoning from the death of John the Baptist under Herod the Roman king, to the end of Maxentius, and of Licinius, the two last great persecutors, the one in the West, the other in the East, who were both vanquished by godly Constantine. And so peace was given to the church; albeit not in such ample wise, but that divers tumults and troubles afterward ensued, yet they lasted not long: and the chief brunt, to speak of these Roman persecutions which the Holy Ghost especially considered above all other in this his Revelation, thus ended in the time of Constantine.[126]

The peace that came to the church by the rule of Constantine marks the beginning of the thousand years, or the millennium of Revelation 20. Speaking about the significance of the year A.D. 324 Foxe writes:

> After the which year, according to the pre-ordinate counsel of God, when his severity had been sufficiently declared upon his own house, it pleased him to show mercy again, and to bind up Satan, the old serpent, according to the twentieth chapter of the Revelation, for the space of a thousand years; that is, from this time of Licinius, to the time of John Wickliff and John Huss. During all which time, albeit certain conflicts and tumults were among Christian bishops themselves in the church; yet no universal murdering persecution was stirring before the preaching of John Wickliff, Huss, and such others.[127]

In Foxe's great work, the *Acts and Monuments*, the historical material is arranged in accordance with the historical time peri-

[125] *AM*, I, 290. [126] *AM*, I, 291.
[127] *AM*, I, 292.

ods already referred to. Furthermore, the various "books" of the *Acts and Monuments* are brought into relationship with the thousand year period. Thus Book One, which brings the history down to the end of the first three hundred years of persecution, closes with the words, "At which time it so pleased the Almighty, that the murdering malice of Satan should at length be restrained, and himself tied up for a thousand years, through his great mercy in Christ."[128]

In its opening, Book Two refers to "the tying up of Satan [which] giveth to the church some rest."[129] In closing Book Two, Foxe refers to Book Three in the following way:

> Comprehending therein the rest of the next three hundred years, with the acts and state of religion, as in that space was in the church: wherein may appear the declining time of the church, and of true religion; preparing the way to Antichrist, which not long after followed. For here is to be noted, that during yet this mean time, Satan (as is said) was bound up from his raging and furious violence; counting from which was foretold by the revelation of St. John abovementioned to be a thousand years.[130]

Book Four, which brings the reader down to the time of Wycliffe, reads in its conclusion: "Forasmuch as Satan, being chained up all this while for the space of a thousand years, beginneth about this time to be loosed and to come abroad, according to the forewarning of St. John's Revelation."[131] Thus it follows that Books Five to Eight, which contain the history from the time of Wycliffe, all have the heading, "Containing the Last Three Hundred Years from the Loosing Out of Satan."[132]

Because the thousand year period, with approximately three hundred years of persecution before its beginning and the same after its termination, is so basic and significant for Foxe's concept of the church, it is of value to compare his time scheme with that of three other British expositors of the book of Revelation, namely John Bale, John Napier, and Thomas Brightman.

John Bale's familiarity with expositors of the Apocalypse is obvious from his tabulations of interpreters from Justin Martyr

---

128 *AM*, I, 304.   129 *AM*, I, 305.
130 *AM*, I, 385–386.   131 *AM*, II, 722.
132 *AM*, II, 724; III, 580; IV, 165, 557.

and Irenaeus to Luther and Calvin.[133] His work may have influenced John Foxe when he wrote the 1563 edition of the *Acts and Monuments*.[134] In this edition, Foxe begins his story with the pontificate of Sylvester II, which coincides with the loosing of Satan, A.D. 1000.[135] In terminating the thousand year period with Sylvester II, Foxe is in agreement with Bale. However, it should be noticed that Bale states that this concept is held by "all the historiographers."[136] When Foxe changed his view regarding the beginning and the end of the thousand year period as found in the 1570 edition of the *Acts and Monuments*, he deviated not only from Bale, but from the apocalyptic historical expositors in general.

In connection with his concept of the thousand years, Foxe's calculation of the 1260 days, or 42 months, amounting to 294 years and covering the early ten persecutions, is of basic significance. This concept he did not borrow from Bale. Bale applied this period, as Thomas Aquinas did, to "the time of the gospel preaching from Christ's ascension to the latter end of the world,"[137] the end of which "is in the Lord's hands."[138]

John Foxe was followed by John Napier (1550–1617), a distinguished Scottish mathematician and devoted adherent of the Protestant cause, in beginning the thousand year period with the cessation of the early persecution at the time of Constantine.[139] However, there are some basic differences in their views of church history. For Foxe the thousand years meant a period of no major persecution against the church, and the condition of the visible church was considered excellent in the beginning and tolerable for several centuries following; first toward the end of the period, the antichristian forces became evident. For Napier, on the other hand, the thousand years covered from its very beginning a time of apostasy in the visible church, an interpretation that has already been noticed in the historical periodi-

---

[133] Bale, *op. cit.*, pp. 255–258.

[134] William Haller stresses the influence of Bale upon John Foxe. See Haller's *Elect Nation*, pp. 54, 64–67.

[135] *AM* (1563), p. 11.   [136] Bale, *op. cit.*, p. 560.

[137] *Ibid.*, p. 411.   [138] *Ibid.*, p. 413.

[139] John Napier, *A Plaine Discouery of the whole Reuelation of Saint Iohn* ... (Edinburgh, 1593), p. 62.

zation of Servetus and the Radical Reformers. For Napier the binding of Satan meant that he was held back from stirring up universal wars; accordingly, the loosing of Satan was fulfilled in the wars begun by Ottoman about A.D. 1300.[140]

As for Foxe, so also for Napier a very close connection is found between the 1260 days of chapter 12 of the book of Revelation and the thousand years of chapter 20,[141] but here also the application reveals the different concept of the visible church from the time of Constantine. In Napier's exposition of the book of Revelation, he lays down thirty-six basic propositions. The first states that "in propheticall dates of daies, weekes, moneths, and yeares, euerie common propheticall day is taken for a yeare."[142] Accordingly the 1260 days stand for 1260 literal years. In the calculations of Napier these 1260 years take their beginning about A.D. 300[143] and cover the reign of Antichrist. Napier writes "that betwixt the yeare of Christ 300, and 316, hath the Antichristian and Papisticall raign begun, reigning vniuersallie and without any debatable contradiction 1260. yeares; and so (as is said) about the yeare of God 1560. began their first publike decay, and the open repining against their kingdom to their confusion, ever more and more."[144] During these years "the whol outward visible church lay whollie as dead, and corrupted with Papisticall errours, and began not to bee raised vp nor quickened by the word of life, till after the yeare of God, a thousande three hundred."[145] During these years only the invisible church was the true church.[146]

Thus Napier reacted against Foxe and the Magisterial Reformers' concept of the golden era of the Constantinian church. However, he is still within a modified Augustinian view of the millennium, believing that the era in which he lived was the last. He fixed a number of dates by manipulating apocalyptic numbers. The 1260 years ended in 1576 and other apocalyptic periods expired respectively in 1541, 1590, 1639, 1688, and the last in 1786. On account of the belief that God would shorten the time

---

140 *Ibid.*, pp. 62–64, 232–235.   141 *Ibid.*, 237–238.
142 *Ibid.*, p. 1.   143 *Ibid.*, p. 64.
144 *Ibid.*, p. 68.   145 *Ibid.*, p. 234.
146 *Ibid.*, pp. 161–162.

for the sake of the elect, he expected the final judgment to take place sometime between 1688 and 1700.[147]

At the close of the Elizabethan reign the premillennial idea began to be advocated; therefore, it should be noticed that Napier believed, with the Reformers, in the imminent Second Advent of Christ, bringing the last judgment, the last resurrection, the second and everlasting death, followed by eternity.[148] The description of the new Jerusalem in Revelation 21 refers to the eternal heavenly kingdom; accordingly, he speaks against the sect of "*Chiliasts* or *Millenaries*, who thought our raign with Christ to be on earth, and temporal."[149] It should be noticed that Napier's exposition on the Revelation "occupies a prominent place in Scottish ecclesiasticall history, for it is the earliest Scottish work on the interpretation of the scriptures."[150]

Napier's concept of the church is further emphasized by Thomas Brightman (1562–1607), a Puritan scholar and one of the founders of English Presbyterianism. Like Foxe and Napier, he explains the thousand years to span the time from Constantine to Wycliffe.[151] That Satan was bound during this period meant that there was "brought in such a manner of gouernment, as left the open enemies no power to Dominere and tyrannize in and ouer the Church, as they had bene accustomed to doe in former times."[152] However, Brightman also emphasizes that Antichrist will reign during the thousand years,[153] since this period and the 1260 years begin at the same time.[154] Thus Brightman and Napier are one in their application of the 1260 years but differ from Foxe.

Thomas Brightman's influence upon the Puritans in the seventeenth century has been pointed out by William M. Lamont.[155] On the other hand, William Haller has emphasized the influence

---

[147] *Ibid.*, pp. 9, 12, 15–16, 21–22, 179.
[148] *Ibid.*, pp. 236–240.   [149] *Ibid.*, p. 240.
[150] Joseph Frederick Scott, "John Napier," *Encyclopaedia Britannica* (1964), XVI, 77.
[151] Thomas Brightman, *A Revelation of the Revelation* (Amsterdam, 1615), p. 840.
[152] *Ibid.*   [153] *Ibid.*, p. 841.
[154] *Ibid.*, p. 840.
[155] Lamont, *Marginal Prynne* (London, 1963), pp. 59–66.

of Foxe upon the same period.[156] In view of the fact that Brightman in his concept of the church not only deviates from Foxe, but counteracts some of his basic views about the church, Lamont seems correct in suggesting that what Haller "has failed to show is the extent to which Foxe's influence could retard the Puritan Revolution."[157] What Lamont does not mention is that Brightman's view was shared by Napier twenty-two years before Brightman's English edition was published. Thus a reaction against part of Foxe's view of church history seems to have begun at the close of the sixteenth century. Napier's work was published in Edinburgh in 1593, and Brightman, who died in 1607, doubtlessly worked on his exposition before the death of Queen Elizabeth.[158]

In evaluating the role played by Constantine in the history of the church as viewed by Foxe, Napier, and Brightman, two different points must be kept separated: the importance of Constantine as such at a certain given time in history, and then the status of the church as such from the time of Constantine. Foxe praises both Constantine and the visible church which followed for some centuries. Napier and Brightman do the former in no less glowing terms than Foxe, but not the latter. It seems that Lamont does not keep these two points separated when he writes: "In his devaluing of Constantine and Elizabeth, Brightman struck at the imperial myth."[159]

In his description of Constantine, Brightman goes even further than either Foxe or Napier. In chapter 12 of the book of Revelation, the woman and the child were generally interpreted to represent the church and Christ, and so by both Foxe and Napier. Deviating from that, Brightman could not be unaware of the significance he gave to Constantine when he stated that Constantine was represented by the child, thus making him the central figure in the important drama of Revelation 12. Revela-

[156] Haller, "John Foxe and the Puritan Revolution," in *The Seventeenth Century: Studies in the History of English Thought and Literature from Bacon to Pope*, ed. Richard F. Jones (Stanford, 1951).

[157] Lamont, *op. cit.*, p. 66.

[158] Prior to Brightman's English edition printed in Amsterdam in 1615, the first Latin edition was printed at Frankfurt in 1609. His collected works were issued in London in 1644. See bibliography.

[159] Lamont, *op. cit.*, p. 60.

tion 12:5 reads: "She gave birth to a male child, who is destined to rule all nations with an iron rod. But her child was snatched up to God and his throne." In his interpretation of this text Brightman writes:

> The Church doth at length bringe forth this manlike and stout Champion, when she instructed Constantine the great in the Christian faith.... For this man is that man-child, who did first of all the Romane Emperours, take vppon the open patronage of the truth....
>
> He it was that did indeed deliuer the Church like a man from the tyranny of the enemies, he did likewise defende it valiantly, he did augment it and did enlarge the bounds of it meruailously, he brought peace vnto it that was so much desired, and did establish it for euer.
>
> ... For this Emperour ruled them with an Iron rodd, that is, he did so curbe and keepe down all his enemies with his martiall power, that no man durst so much as stirre a finger against the Church.[160]

In spite of this specific role, predicted and fulfilled in Constantine, according to Brightman, Antichrist, "vvich Beast is the Pope of Rome vvho sprunge vp at once vvith Constantine, vvas made great by the Nicene Councell,"[161] and for a thousand years "from Constantine the Church abidinge in most secret lurkinge places, vvas together with Christ, but did no great matter famous & remarkeable by the vvorld. Those 1000. yeares beinge ended, Wicklefe preacheth the gospel in the world."[162] Napier and Brightman seem to say that Constantine, in granting peace to the church, fulfilled the role given to him by God; yet, the visible church became the seat of Antichrist. Therefore, although Queen Elizabeth had played a God-given part in the Reformation, her established church could still become the seat of Antichrist.

So far Brightman agrees with Napier, but he moves a great step further away from Foxe by making a double application of the thousand year period. He writes:

> And they shall raigne vvith him a thousand yeares. These thousand yeares begin, where the former ended, that is in the yeare

---

[160] Brightman, *op. cit.*, pp. 404–405.
[161] *Ibid.*, sig. B2v.   [162] *Ibid.*, sig. B3r.

1300; Whereby continuance of the truth is promised for a thousand yeares, from the restoring thereof (of which we haue spoken) in these our natiōs of Europe of which also this first resurrection belōgeth.[163]

Understood spiritually a second "first resurrection" would take place and, in comparison with the first at the time of Constantine, it would be greater, for Christ would reign "most gloriously vvpon earth, by ministery of his Seruants, so as he shall aduance his Church vnto the highest honour that can be, euen aboue all Empire that is."[164] The holy city and the new earth of Revelation (chapters 21 and 22) are symbols describing the new millennial church, which the Jews will join; thus, Jerusalem "shalbe sealed vpon earth."[165]

In the erection of this new Jerusalem in which "all men shall acknowledge the hand of God," England has a specific role to play. Brightman interprets the Seven Churches of the Apocalypse as so many periods. The church of Ephesus applies to the church during the first century, Smyrna under Constantine, and Pergamus after A.D. 800—here he mentions the beginning of Waldenses and Albigenses. Thyatira is the church represented by Occam, Marsilius, Dante, John Huss, and Jerome of Prague; and the false prophetess of this church is "Rome, that Queene, that Idolatresse, that Inchauntresse, that Harlot, that Killer of Martyrs . . ." and so on.[166]

The Reformation is prophetically portrayed in the three last churches, applying Sardis to the Lutheran Reformation, Philadelphia to the Reformed churches of Switzerland, France, Holland, and Scotland, and Laodicea to the Church of England.[167] The characteristics of Laodicea are fulfilled in the Church of England. In his comments on these characteristics we find confirmed the suggestion already made, that Brightman on the one hand praises Elizabeth and the English Church, but on the other finds the seat of Antichrist in her midst. The former should be dealt with first.

Elizabeth is that most beautiful star which arose to augment

---

[163] *Ibid.*, p. 851. [164] *Ibid.*, p. 852.
[165] *Ibid.*, p. 878.
[166] *Ibid.*, pp. 48 ff., 58 ff., 65 ff., 73 ff.
[167] *Ibid.*, pp. 91 ff., 109 ff., 126 ff.

the Christian empire with England which in turn should bring the fifth kingdom of Daniel 2 to fruition.[168] Is not the truth of this, he asks, confirmed by the fact that "so many & mighty enemies against England alone and our most gracious Queene haue vanished away like smoke, and come to nothing? He whose Scepter they striue to ouerthrowe, laugheth at their foolish and vain enterprises."[169] God has given Himself to "our English Laodicea" in a threefold way; "namely, in his constancy in promisinge, his truth and fidelitie in teachinge, and then his inuincible power in defendinge of vs."[170]

The church of Laodicea is characterized by being "neither cold nor hott." Here Brightman finds the Scriptural anchorage for a more thorough reformation. He exclaims: "I would thou wert either all Romish, or els wouldest at last admitt of a full reformation."[171]

Brightman deals at some length with the needed reformation and points out the wrongs as they were seen by the Puritans in the closing decades of Elizabeth's reign. First reference is made to the antichristian and Romish manners in "the degrees of cleargil mē, in elections & ordinations, & the whole administration of the Church-censures." His strongest condemnation is directed against the worldly clergy, especially the wealthy bishops, who "are blinded with the vain-glorie of the world." Brightman blows the trumpet of battle against these negligent, lukewarm men, who are "strangers frō him [God] altogether," and warns that "a great and shamefull iudgment doth waite" them. "We must not measure the perfection of a Church, by the multitude of professours, or by the great estate of riches and earthly honours, but by the integritie of Gods institution, and by the abundance of heauenly gifts." The Church of England can only be preserved by "skillful Pastours and Teachers." On account of his criticism of the clergy, it is not surprising that he speaks about the people's favorable reception of the *Marprelate Tracts*.[172]

After having opened "this rotten vlcer," as he says, he suggests (in the language of the message to the church in Laodicea) a

---

168 *Ibid.*, p. 389.
170 *Ibid.*, p. 129.
172 *Ibid.*, pp. 132, 141, 135–136, 140, 128, 152.
169 *Ibid.*
171 *Ibid.*, p. 133.

threefold medicine. First they should buy "gold refined in the fire, to make you truly rich." This meant that men should not seek office for the sake of wealth, neither should simony be practiced. The minister of the Gospel should be promoted "not by there money, but by there honestie, not by fauour, but by learninge, not at any one mans pleasure, but by the voices and consent of theire flocke." The second advice is that they acquire "white clothes to put on to hide the shame of your nakedness." This means "worthines," "learninge," "sanctifyed hart and carriage" as contrary to "former honours and nakednes." Finally they are told to receive "ointment for your eyes so that you may see" against the blindness of "fleshly wisedome, and ignorance of spirituall thinges." The admonition is given:

> Purge out all thy Romish leuen; hange not any longer in the midst betweene the reformed Churches and that that is Antichristian: Cast away thy honours and riches for his sake who became most contemptible and poore for thee: Lett faithful Pastours be sett ouer euery Congregation: Lett them that are sett vppe & called to places of charge ouer soules bee compelled to be diligent: Let innouaters and corrupters of doctrine be retayned: let the Pastours haue the power restored vnto them, of exercisinge the Censures vppn there owne flockes; And doe not dispute with Christ how profitably a Church-policy, that is in vse amonge the enemyes of the Gospell, may bee ioyed with the Gospell.[173]

Brightman refers to the work of the High Commission when he tells the bishops to repent of "thy iniuryes which thou hast done to thy brethren, in castinge some of them into Prison, in turninge others out of there liuinges & estates, in depriuinge many of them of the power to preach the word, in reuilinge them all." He further makes a significant reference to the use of the word "Puritan" when he says that those who claimed a thorough reformation to be urgently needed had been slandered "with the odious names of *Anabaptists* & *Puritans*." He then explains: "Thou knowest these men haue nothinge at all to doe with those Sectaryes: They who doe reprehend thy superstitions, doe teach most purely & holily concerninge the Magistrate, as whome they honour and obey with no lesse faithfullnes and

[173] *Ibid.*, p. 158.

reuerence then any other men whosoeuer." It is the lukewarm bishops who had harmed the relationship between the Queen and the progressive Reformers. "It was a notorious slaunder wherewith thou hast bleared the eyes of the Princesse & brought thy brethren into hatred with her." Finally it was said, "Christ is determined certenly to spue thee out of his mouth vnles thou will speedily repent."[174] Since God, on the one hand, had destined England to play an important apocalyptic role in establishing the fifth monarchy of Daniel 2, but the leading clergy, on the other hand, did not repent, Brightman's words "Christ is determined certenly to spue thee out of his mouth" could easily become an axiom for the men of the Civil War years.

Bale and Foxe would agree with Brightman's call for a spiritual religion, but we see an evolution in the writings of Bale, Foxe, Napier, and Brightman regarding the millennium. Bale and the early Foxe held the Augustinian concept, but Foxe modified it by placing the beginning with Constantine and giving the period the exact numerical value. Napier adhered to the Foxian interpretation including the importance of Constantine, but he saw in Bishop Sylvester the embryo of Antichrist (being a member of the Kirk of Scotland and one of the Edinburgh commissioners to the General Assembly in 1588, and in 1593 appointed one of the committee members to ensure the safety of the Kirk, he favored the Presbyterian form of church government), and therefore fixed the beginning of the 1260 years at the same time as the millennium. However, he adhered to the Augustinian idea of the last age.

Brightman, being one of the fathers of English Presbyterianism, held Napier's view of the 1000 and 1260 year periods; thus both men reacted against Foxe's view of the Constantinian church. From a reference to the Whitgift-Cartwright controversy it is evident that Brightman stands on the side of the latter.[175] When Foxe praised Constantine and Elizabeth, it was as a Magisterial Reformer; but when Brightman did the same, it was within the framework of what became seventeenth-century apocalyptic expectations of the millennium as a new age on earth. Thus there is a great gulf between Foxe and Brightman,

[174] *Ibid.,* pp. 154–155, 158–159. [175] *Ibid.,* p. 139.

and not the former but the latter is the ancestor of the apocalyptic hopes of the men of the 1640s. To make this important difference still clearer, short references should be made to a few of the expositors within the latter group.

Joseph Mead, or Mede (1568–1638), broke fully away from the Augustinian-Foxian tradition and is the link between Brightman and the premillennialism of the seventeenth century. His work, *Clavis Apocalyptica*, was first published in 1627 and reprinted in 1632. In 1642 the House of Commons authorized its publication, and it was printed the following year in English under the title, *The Key of the Revelation*. Two other works dealt with apocalyptic interpretations, namely, *Daniel's Weeks* (1643, 1648, 1677) and *The Apostasy of the Latter Times* (1641, 1644).

Mead's philosophy of the millennium, which was so very different from the Augustinian in whatever modified form the latter might have appeared, is presented in its full significance and with its characteristics, when he asserts that it is

> ... circumscribed within two resurrections, beginning at the iudgement of Antichrist, as the morning of that day, and continuing during the space of 1000 yeeres granted to new Ierusalem, (the Spouse of Christ) upon this Earth, till the universall resurrection and iudgement of all the dead, when the wicked shall be cast into Hell to be tormented for ever, and the Saints translated into Heaven, to live vvith Christ for ever.[176]

For Mead, and contrary to the Continental Reformers and the Elizabethan Divines, the literal Second Advent of Christ would precede the millennium. After the thousand years the final judgment would take place, and then the eternal heavenly kingdom would be realized. Not all the premillennialists who succeeded Brightman held to the literal resurrection; while some were specific about the conditions during the millennium, others were rather vague, but they all had this in common: they believed that a new millennial age would precede the final consummation. The appearance and growing influence of chiliasm during the last decade of Elizabeth's reign are reflected in the

---

[176] Joseph Mede, "Compendivm on Chap. 20, "*The Key of the Revelation* (London, 1643), sig. ss4*v*.

criticism of it as expressed in the writings of Napier and others. George Gyfford, in some published sermons on the Revelation (1596), speaks about the "error of the Chiliastes, or Millenaries," who say "that after the ouerthrowe of Antichrist, the Lorde Iesus would come, & with the faithful raign here a thousand yeres vpon the earth."[177] Arthur Dent, in his *Exposition vpon the whole Revelation*, 1603, writes:

> The *Chiliasts* or *Millenaries*, doe fondly gather from this scripture, that after the ouerthrow of Antichrist, the Lord *Iesus* would come & raigne vvith the faithful, heere a thousand yeeres vpon the earth, and that in this time, that *Christ* should so raigne, as a great and glorious king vpon the earth, his subiects should enioy all manner of earthly pleasures, and delights. This foolish error is confuted by the words that follovv in the text, as wee shall see afterward.[178]

Andrew Willet, in a commentary on the book of Daniel published in 1610, asserts that the kingdom of Daniel 2 "shall not be in earth" as expressed by "the Chiliastes" in their mistaken interpretation of Revelation 20.[179] John Cotton expresses himself similarly in his exposition of Revelation 16, saying:

> ... many devises there are in the mindes of some to thinke that Jesus Christ shall come from Heaven againe, and reigne here upon Earth a thousand yeares, but they are but the mistakes of some high expressions in Scripture.[180]

In one of his books, the Scottish Presbyterian divine Robert Baillie devotes a whole chapter to criticism of the premillennialist. The proposal is that "The thousand yeares of Christ his visible Raigne upon Earth, is against Scripture."[181]

---

[177] George Gyfford, *Sermons Vpon the Whole Booke of the Revelation* (London, 1596), p. 389.

[178] Arthur Dent, *Exposition vpon the whole Reuelation* (London, 1603), p. 274.

[179] Andrew Willet, *Hexapla in Danielem* ... (Cambridge, 1610), pp. 228–229.

[180] John Cotton, *The Powring ovt of the Seven Vials* ... (London, 1642), p. 26.

[181] Robert Baillie, *A Dissvasive from the Errours of the Time* ... (London, 1645).

In spite of criticism of the premillennial view, the fact remains that the Augustinian-Foxian tradition largely came to an end with the Elizabethan age. A few examples of the apocalypticism of the men of the 1640s will substantiate how different they are from Foxe.

Having as his text 2 Peter 3:13, "But we have his promise, and look forward to new heavens and a new earth," Nathaniel Homes preached a sermon before the Parliament in May 1641. The title page of the printed sermon reads, *The Nevv VVorld, or the Nevv Reformed Chvrch*, pointing out the author's chiliastic belief. The members of the Parliament were addressed as "you worthies in this our Israel."[182] The title page of John Archer's book (1642) speaks for itself: *The Personall Reign of Christ vpon Earth. In a Treatise, Wherein is fully and largely laid open and proved, That Jesus Christ, together with the Saints, shall visibly possesse a Monarchicall State and Kingdome in this World.*[183] Johann Heinrich Alsted of the Netherlands wrote several works on biblical prophecy. His *Diatribe de mille annis apocalypticis* ... (1627) was translated into both German (1630) and English (1643). The English title follows the German, when it reads: *The Beloved City or, the Saints Reign on Earth a Thovsand Yeares; Asserted, and Illustrated from LXV. places of Holy Scripture; Besides the Judgement of Holy Learned men, both at home and abroad; and also Reason it selfe.*[184]

From the pen of Thomas Goodwin we have not only some expositions on the Revelation,[185] but also a few printed sermons dealing with the same subject as that already referred to. One

---

[182] Nathaniel Homes, *The Nevv VVorld, or the Nevv Reformed Chvrch* (London, 1641).

[183] John Archer, *The Personall Reign of Christ vpon Earth* ... (London, 1642).

[184] Johann Heinrich Alsted, *Diatribe de mille annis Apocalypticis. Christliches ... Bericht von der künfftigen Tausand-Jährigen Glückseligkeit der Kirchen Gottes auff dieser Erden, nach der Weissagung des ... Propheten Daniels; vnd ... Apostel Johannis ... Verdeutschet durch Sebastianum Francum*, with a table (1630). English translation, *The Beloved City* ... (London, 1643).

[185] Thomas Goodwin, *The expositione of ... T. G. ... on the Book of the Revelation* (London, 1843); *The French Revolution foreseen in 1639* (London, 1843).

of these is entitled *A Sermon of the Fifth Monarchy*....[186] In October 1543, Henry Wilkinson preached a sermon before the House of Commons. It was printed the same year with the apocalyptic time periodizations of Brightman and Mead. In this tract, *Babylons Ruine, Jerusalems Rising*, he tells how it had become common talk "that Christ their King is comming to take possession of his Throne."[187] It should be noticed that Thomas Hayne, in his exposition *Christs kingdome on earth ... the thousand years of the saints reign with Christ* (1645), largely restates the views of Brightman, Alstede, Mead, and Archer as expressed on the title page.[188]

The fact that the men who formulated the apocalyptic concepts that became an intricate part of the total historical involvement of the mid-seventeenth century do not refer to Foxe confirms my thesis that they were not indebted to him for their apocalypticism. This is an evidence from silence, but nevertheless noteworthy. Foxe's relationship to the millennialism of the seventeenth-century Puritans has now been considered, and a comparison between his and the Roman Catholic view of biblical prophecy calls for a brief examination.

The Catholic reaction shows the impact of the influence of apocalyptic expositions, as found in the writings of Foxe and others during the whole Reformation period, upon the doctrine of the church. To counteract the concept of the church and the view of church history which were explained and illustrated through historical interpretation of the books of Daniel and Revelation, Roman Catholic theologians advanced the view that these two books could not be interpreted historically, since all their pictures and images portray events that would take place

---

[186] Thomas Goodwin, *A Sermon of the Fifth Monarchy, proving by invicible arguments that the saints shall have a kingdom here on earth ...* (London, 1654).

[187] Henry Wilkinson, *Babylons Ruine, Jerusalems Rising* (London, 1643), p. 21.

[188] Thomas Hayne, *Christs Kingdome on Earth, Opened according to the Scriptures. Herein is examined, What Mr. Th. Brightman, Dr. J. Alstede, Mr. I. Mede, Mr. H. Archer, The Glympse of Sions Glory, and such as concurre in opinion with them, hold concerning the thousand years of the Saints Reign with Christ, etc.* (London, 1645).

during a short period at the end of time. This "futuristic" view was advocated by two Catholic theologians, Fransisco Ribera (1537–1591) and Robert Bellarmine (1542–1621). In contrast, a Spanish Jesuit of Seville, Luis de Alcazor (1554–1613), founded the Praeterist School, which maintained that the message of the Revelation was fulfilled in the early church and the pagan Roman Empire.[189] Thus, historically the Revelation concerned itself only with a short period either at the beginning or at the close of the Christian era. The Revelation had nothing to do historically with the centuries in between.

The clash between the Roman Catholic view and that of Protestant expositors is seen in the work of Thomas Brightman. To a large degree he wrote his work to counteract the influence of Ribera and Bellarmine and to substantiate the unified view of church history as expressed in such works as the *Magdeburg Centuries* and the *Acts and Monuments*, even though he deviated from Foxe. About Ribera, Brightman wrote: "Indeed Francis of Ribera the Iesuite, thrusts this whole Prophecy almost into theis straits, wisely indeed, to saue his Popes skonce, but as touchinge the truth, exceedinge perversely. For why, were men that lived by the space of theis 1500 yeares, which are nowe past, since the writinge of the Apocalypse, altogether devoyd on this felicity?"[190] Brightman at great length seeks to counteract Bellarmine's views.[191] This conflict between the two different concepts of apocalyptic exposition has a definite bearing upon the whole Foxian tradition.

The attack on Foxe by S. R. Maitland in the nineteenth century had its background in their differing concepts of the church, especially as viewed within the framework of apocalyptic ideas. During the years prior to his attack on Foxe, Maitland had studied the question regarding the time period of the 1260 years and its relationship to Antichrist. The pamphlets he printed as

[189] For a summary of the principle of interpretation of these men, see E. B. Elliott, *Horae Apocalypticae* (5th ed.; London, 1862), IV, 480–484; Henry Alford, *The New Testament for English Readers* (Cambridge, 1863), Vol. II, pp. 348–351; Joseph Tanner, *Daniel and the Revelation* (London, 1898), pp. 16–17.

[190] Brightman, *op. cit.*, p. 5.

[191] *Ibid.*, see chap. "Against Bellarmine," pp. 622–770.

a result of this study expressed the same basic view as that of Bellarmine and Ribera, thus revealing a close connection with the conflict concerning the two opposite concepts of the church as found in the writings of Foxe and other expositors at the time of the Reformation.

In 1826 Maitland made an enquiry into the question of the 1260 years or days, and came to the conclusion that they denoted "a period of 1260 natural days."[192] While he makes reference to a number of expositors of the historical school,[193] he makes especial reference to G. S. Faber because his work "on the 1260 years ... is generally known and respected."[194] Faber believed, as stated in the *Magdeburg Centuries*, that the 1260 years began in A.D. 606.[195] A member of the Church of England made a reply to Maitland two years later in which he wrote, "I apprehend that Mr. Faber and other commentators, have written all the truth of their dissertations under the influence of the Holy Spirit of Truth, and not from their own wisdom and power."[196] The following year Maitland made a second inquiry into the question "whether the 1260 days are literal days, or years."[197] In 1830 two more writings came from his pen on the same subject.[198] William Digby wrote a book occasioned by Maitland's attack on the year-day principle in which he challenged Maitland.[199] The latter made a reply the same year, 1831.[200]

[192] S. R. Maitland, *An Enquiry ... of 1260 Years* (London, 1826), p. 2.
[193] *Ibid.*, pp 55–56.
[194] *Ibid.*, p. 2.
[195] G. S. Faber, *A Dissertation on the Prophecies* (London, 1807), II, 456–461.
[196] A Member of the Church of England, *Reply to an Enquiry by S. R. Maitland ... of 1260 Years* (London, 1828), p. 8.
[197] S. R. Maitland, *A Second Enquiry ... the Prophetic Period ... Supposd to Consist of 1260 Years* (London, 1829), p. iv.
[198] S. R. Maitland, *The Twelve Hundred and Sixty Days in Reply to a Review* (London, 1830); *An Attempt to Elucidate the Prophecies Concerning Antichrist* (London, 1830).
[199] William Digby, *A Treatise on the 1260 Days of Daniel and St. John: Being an Attempt to Establish the Conclusion that they are years* (Dublin, 1831).
[200] S. R. Maitland, *A Letter to the Rev. William Digby, A.M., Occasioned by His Treatise on the 1260 Days* (London, 1831).

In the view of Foxe and other Protestant expositors up to the nineteenth century, the true visible church had been preserved by the Waldenses, Albigenses, and other sectarian groups throughout the time when Rome represented Antichrist. This view was closely related to the theory of the 1260 years. Consequently Maitland wrote a book about the Albigenses and Waldenses. In his preface he clearly states the relationship between the question of the 1260 years and the two religious groups just mentioned. Maitland writes:

> Many writers have supposed the Albigenses and Waldenses to be the Witnesses predicted in the Apocalypse, and one of the most recent and popular advocates of this Prophecy, has endeavoured to maintain the high antiquity and orthodoxy of these sects. That part of his work being comparatively new, and only published by him since I had ceased to think that any of the systems, founded on the mystical interpretation of the 1260 days, required minute examination, remained almost unknown to me until my attention was recently called to it.[201]

In 1834 William Cuninghame attacked Maitland,[202] and Maitland replied.[203] The historian Joseph Milner had spoken about the Albigenses and Waldenses as representing the true church prior to the Reformation.[204] Speaking about their catechisms, he said, "The ancient catechism for the instruction of their youth, contains the same vital truth in substance, which form the catechisms of Protestant churches."[205] Consequently Milner was attacked by Maitland. A letter was written to Hugh James Rose discussing Milner's treatment of the two groups.[206] Milner was

---

[201] S. R. Maitland, *Facts and Documents Illustrative of the History, Doctrine, and Rites of the Ancient Albigenses and Waldenses* (London, 1832), p. iii.

[202] William Cuninghame, *On the Jubilean Chronology ... And 1260 Years* (Glasgow, 1834).

[203] S. R. Maitland, *The Twelve Hundred and Sixty Days: in Reply to ... William Cuninghame* (London, 1834).

[204] Joseph Milner, *The History of the Church of Christ* (London, 1834), III, 92–155.

[205] *Ibid.*, p. 114.

[206] S. R. Maitland, *A Letter ... with Strictures on Milner's Church History* (London, 1834).

defended by John Goulter Dowling[207] and by John King.[208]
S. R. Maitland replied again.[209]

For ten years Maitland had studied and had been engaged in polemics regarding a concept of the church and a view of its history, framed within apocalyptic periodizations. It is with this background that Maitland makes his attack on the historicity of the *Acts and Monuments*, as well as on Foxe's personal history.

Maitland's assault upon Foxe began with a series of thirteen consecutive articles printed monthly in the *British Magazine* beginning in June 1837.[210] In these attacks Maitland seeks to discredit the historicity of the *Acts and Monuments*, especially Foxe's history of the Waldenses. The same is the subject of a book by Maitland,[211] as well as a pamphlet to Rev. W. H. Mill (1839).[212] Foxe's personal story is attacked by Maitland in three booklets,[213] as well as in the *British Magazine* in connection with George Townsend's new edition of the *Acts and Monuments*.[214]

[207] John Goulter Dowling, *A Letter to the Rev. S. R. Maitland* (London, 1835); S. R. Maitland, *A Second Letter to the Rev. Hugh James Rose, Containing Notes on Milner's History of the Church in the Fourth Century* (London, 1835).

[208] John King, *Examination of Milner's History of the Fourth Century* (London, 1836).

[209] S. R. Maitland, *Remarks on that Part of the Rev. J. King's Pamphlet* (London, 1836); S. R. Maitland, *The Dark Ages A Series of Essays, Intended to illustrate the State of Religion and Literature in the Ninth, Tenth, Eleventh and Twelfth Centuries* (London, 1844). In these essays Maitland seeks to prove that the darkness of these centuries has been a good deal exaggerated.

[210] S. R. Maitland, "Remarks on the New Edition of Foxe's work, and on the work itself," *The British Magazine*, XI, 620–625; XII, 6–13, 137–144, 253–259, 376–381, 496–502, 620–627; XIII, 12–20, 122–129, 254–263, 385–389, 613–619 (1837–1838). The first six articles were reprinted in a book. See *Six letters on Foxe's Acts and Monuments* (1837).

[211] S. R. Maitland, *A Review of Foxe the Martyrologist's History of the Waldenses* (London, 1837).

[212] S. R. Maitland, *A Letter to Rev. W. H. Mill, Containing some Strictures on Mr. Faber's Recent Work entitled "The Ancient Vallenses and Albigenses"* (London, 1839).

[213] S. R. Maitland, *Notes on the Contribution of the Rev. George Townsend* (London, 1841–1842).

[214] S. R. Maitland, "On the Personal History of Fox the Martyrologist," *The British Magazine* (1843), XXIII, 493–500; XXIV, 477–489.

The fact that Maitland's principles of prophetic interpretation, rather than those of the historical school, were taken up not only by the Catholics but also by Protestants during the nineteenth century would of course discredit the historical periodization of the church as expounded by Foxe. This development is presented in a study of the history of prophetic interpretation by Charles Maitland.[215] Charles Maitland, no relation to S. R. Maitland, followed the latter in his "futuristic" interpretation. Charles Maitland says that to S. R. Maitland "belongs the honour of having effected a partial reformation in the manner of conducting prophetic investigations." He also calls him "this second Valla."[216]

S. R. Maitland's attack upon Foxe took place during a decade when the doctrine of the church was reevaluated by men of the Oxford Movement. They, too, broke with the historical prophetic periodization of church history, and thus with John Foxe. This indicates the close connection between the concept of the church and apocalyptic ideas and periodizations as found among the broad stream of Protestants up to the nineteenth century.

James H. Todd (1805–1869) of Trinity College, Dublin, in his Donnellan lectures of 1838 and 1839, discussed the prophecies relating to Antichrist. These lectures were published and dedicated to S. R. Maitland.[217] James H. Todd's colleague, William Burgh (or De Burgh), expressed his appreciation of S. R. Maitland's writings.[218] It should be noticed that Todd refers to the fact that the principles of prophetic interpretation held by most Protestants can be traced back to the Waldenses, Albigenses, and Cathari, as well as to the Spiritual Franciscans.[219] John Henry Newman in the *Protestant Idea of Antichrist* makes

[215] Charles Maitland, *The Apostles' School of Prophetic Interpretation* (London, 1849), pp. 373–401, 445–450. For a comprehensive study of the praeterist and futuristic view see H. Grattan Guinness, *History Unveiling Prophecy* (New York, 1905), pp. 284–295; Elliott, *op. cit.*, IV, 566–679.

[216] Charles Maitland, *op. cit.*, p. 394.

[217] James H. Todd, *Discourses on the Prophecies Relating to Antichrist* (Dublin, 1840).

[218] William Burgh, *Lectures on the Second Advent* (Dublin, 1932), p. vi.

[219] Todd, *op. cit.*, pp. 27–33.

reference to Todd's lectures. Newman writes, "The Discourses which Dr. Todd has recently given to the world, are, perhaps, the first attempt for a long course of years in this part of Christendom to fix a dispassionate attention and a scientific interpretation upon the momentous 'Prophesies relating to Antichrist in the writings of Daniel and St. Paul.' "[220] Newman further states that "we entirely agree with Dr. Todd" and "we take up Dr. Todd's position."[221] Newman also affirms that the idea that Antichrist is fulfilled in the Papacy sprang from three heretical bodies, the Albigenses, Waldenses, and Spiritual Franciscans.[222] Newman, with Todd, acknowledges the work of S. R. Maitland.[223] Newman's "Advent Sermons on Antichrist"[224] are in accord with the ideas expressed by these men.

In view of the close relationship between apocalypticism and the different views of church history and the bearing this in turn has upon the attack on Foxe, his commentary upon the book of Revelation becomes significant for an understanding of his philosophy of history and his concept of the church.

Foxe states that the subject matters of the Apocalypse are "of greatest usefulness and necessity for the church, and disclose the mystery and the universal history of the church, as if on a public stage one should produce dramas."[225] The entire book is "prophetical and historical."[226] He therefore writes: "What seems to be unique and outstanding, is that it depicts for us the state of the church and presents it before our eyes. The state of the church as a whole, not merely in one age but throughout all ages of all men, from the first beginnings of the proclamation of the Gospel until the very end of the world."[227]

The two great contestants are Lucifer and Christ, the former deceiving people through the apostate church or the synagogue

---

[220]John Henry Newman, "The Protestant Idea of Antichrist," *Essays Critical and Historical* (1872), I, 112.

[221] *Ibid.*, pp. 113, 114.   [222] *Ibid.*, pp. 117–123.

[223] *Ibid.*, p. 118.

[224] John Henry Newman, "Advent Sermons on Antichrist," in *Tracts for the Times* (1840), V, 83.

[225] *Apoc.* sig. 3r.   [226] *Apoc.*, p. 4.

[227] *Apoc.*, p. 4.

of Satan, the latter working through the true church of God or the church of the elect.

The threefold background for Foxe's discussion of the church in this commentary is the same as that noticed in *Christus Triumphans*. There is first the original apostasy of Lucifer with the subsequent Fall of the first parents; second, the incarnation, crucifixion, resurrection, and ascension of Christ; and third, the Second Advent of Christ and the consummation of all things. Turning to the actual history of the Christian church, Foxe brings out further details relative to its periodization.

The history of the early church during the first three centuries is described in *Christus Triumphans* and the *Acts and Monuments* in connection with the ten persecutions. Foxe shows how specific he is in his parallelism of the two most severe times of persecution by the fact that in the commentary on the book of Revelation he also enumerates ten persecutions for the latter three hundred years.[228]

The comparison between the first three hundred years and the latter three hundred years of church history is further illustrated in Foxe's interpretation of Revelation 12 and 13. The time period of "a thousand two hundred and threescore days" (Rev. 12:6) or "a time, and times, and half a time" (Rev. 12:14)

---

[228] *Apoc.*, p. 55. Quod & ipsum in persecutiones similiter decem, aut plures fortassis diffundere liceat, si singulas recensere libeat mactationes piorum martyrum, quas a tempore Ioan. Wicleui ab anno 138. hucusque per diuersas Europae plagas cuenisse compertum est, veluti sub Henrico quarto & quinto in Anglia.

Secunda sub concilio generali in Constantia & Bohemia.

Tertia sub Romanis pontificibus in Italia, vicinisque Romae prouincijs.

Quarta, sub Carolo quinto Imperatore in Germania.

Quinta sub Henrico octauo in Anglia.

Sexta sub Henrico secundo in Gallia.

Septima sub Iacobo secundo in Scotia.

Octaua sub Carolo nono in Gallia, sub cuius imperio occubuerunt vnius mensis spacio, supra viginti martyrum milia inaudita crudelitate sublata.

Nona, sub Maria regina in Anglia, in qua persecutione flammis crudelissime supra quadrigenta viua martyrum electissimorum corpora in vno fere quinquennio absumpta sunt.

Decima sub Philippo in Hispania, atq; Flandria, vbi in Hispanica inquisitione leguntur innumeri flammis & ferro contrucidati martyres, atq., etiamnum contrucidantur quotide.

is the period of 294 years through which the church, symbolized as a woman, should on the one hand be the object of severe persecution and on the other survive through God's providence.[229] Furthermore, this time period has a double application in that it refers not only to the persecution of the early church but also to the one "due partly to the Turks, partly to Antichrist,"[230] from the time of the loosing of Satan about the year 1300.

Turning to chapter 13, Foxe states that there is a close connection between this chapter and the one preceding.[231] The time periods of these two chapters and the interpretation of the two beasts depicted in chapter 13 are essential to Foxe's chronological framework of the *Acts and Monuments*, as well as to his theory of Antichrist's being fulfilled in the Turks and the Papacy.[232]

The first beast is interpreted to represent pagan Rome, which is also mentioned as the fourth beast in the book of Daniel.[233] In Daniel 7 the four ancient empires are depicted under the symbols of four beasts, a parallel description to Daniel 2. This reference is another example of how, in the opinion of Foxe, the history of the church is linked with ancient history, thus illustrating that God's hand in world history is manifested in behalf of His church, for which He has an eternal purpose and plan.

Foxe seems to agree with those commentators who are of the opinion that the seven heads of the beast represent "the city of Rome" with its "seven hills." The ten horns "may relate to the ten tyrants who instigated the first ten persecutions against the church of Christ."[234] The time allotted to the beast to make war with the saints and to overcome them is given as 42 months, but interpreted by Foxe to mean 294 literal years.[235]

The second beast of Revelation 13 "it is not difficult to see refers to Antichrist, in the name of a church, in these last days, persecuting Christ in His members. This is so graphically portrayed that it should be easy for all to understand what is intended by this beast."[236] At great length Foxe discusses why

[229] *Apoc.*, pp. 199–211.
[230] *Apoc.*, p. 206.
[231] *Apoc.*, p. 213.
[232] *AM*, IV, 103–108.
[233] *Apoc.*, p. 213.
[234] *Apoc.*, p. 214.
[235] *Apoc.*, pp. 215–216.
[236] *Apoc.*, p. 223.

the second beast is Antichrist and is fulfilled in the Papacy.[237] His interpretation of the two beasts brings again into focus the two great persecuting periods in the history of the church.[238] Furthermore, the first persecution was less insidious, did less harm and was more readily shunned because the persecutors were outside the church, while the second persecution caused more injury by the fact that the persecutors were "within the confines of the church, seated in the temple of God under the title of the name of Christians."[239]

The continuity of history should be noticed. In connection with the second beast who "wielded all the authority of the first beast,"[240] Foxe asks, "Who shall restore the renown of the fallen Roman republic? Is it not this two-horned Roman beast [the Papacy]?"[241] Rome was in turn a continuation of the ancient monarchies.

The two pictures, the one of a temple and its court, and the other of two witnesses, drawn by the Revelator in chapter 11,[242] illustrate the persecution and restoration of the evangelical church during the latter 300 years. The time periods expressed in this chapter are those of 42 months and 1260 days, obviously two ways of expressing the same length of time.[243] In computing these figures Foxe makes use of the principle previously mentioned, that of multiplying the number by seven and then making each day represent a year; thus the 42 months, or 1260 days, would amount to 294 years. This time period is of the same length as the one covering the first persecution, from the death of John the Baptist until the emperor Constantine, and gives Foxe another example by which to compare the early and the latter persecution. When, therefore, it is said that "the court . . . shall they tread under foot forty and two months," it refers to the persecution during the latter 300 years by the Turks and Antichrist, which is said to be 294 years; that is, from the first emperor of the Turks, Ottoman (A.D. 1300), until 1586. The reason given for that date is that "the Lord knows whether the period will be shortened for the elect's sake."[244] In another

[237] *Apoc.*, pp. 223–273.
[239] *Apoc.*, p. 243.
[241] *Apoc.*, p. 268.
[243] See *Apoc.*, pp. 123, 147.

[238] *Apoc.*, pp. 233, 239, 244.
[240] Rev. 13:12.
[242] Rev. 11:1–4.
[244] *Apoc.*, p. 147.

connection he writes that this period "appears to leave only eight years."[245] The picture of the two witnesses illustrates the resurgence of the Gospel during the same period, signifying to Foxe the imminent approach of the end.[246]

The principle of divine judgment and vengeance is basic to Foxe's philosophy of history, and its story in the Christian era is, according to Foxe, expressed in the pictures of the Seven Trumpets and the Seven Vials of the book of Revelation.[247] Introducing the Seven Trumpets Foxe writes: "In my judgment there is little doubt but that those seven trumpets . . . are given as signs of the divine vengeance, against the nefarious enemies of the church, because of the pouring out of the blood [of the saints]. . . . Seven seem to stand out in history."[248]

The first persecutors of the early church were the Jews, and the divine vengeance is seen "in the universal dispersal of the seed of the Jewish people under Nero and Vespasian, after the crucifixion of the Lord, and the martyrdom of the apostles."[249] These historical events are described in the First Trumpet.[250] In the *Acts and Monuments* Foxe discusses ten persecutions in the early church,[251] but in his commentary on the Revelation the Second and Third Trumpets depict the afflictions that came over the Roman Empire, as God's righteous judgment, during the same period.[252] This retribution came in the form of pestilence, earthquakes, inundations from rivers, frequent plagues, locusts, famine, and the like. In the Fourth Trumpet are portrayed these calamities which came through the Huns, the Goths, the Lombards, and so on.[253] The Fifth Trumpet brings forth an army of locusts and scorpions.[254] The particulars of this trumpet are fulfilled in the Mohammedan conquests from about A.D. 612 to A.D. 1300.[255] The Sixth Trumpet[256] begins "when we come to the restoration of the Turkish power, and to the Ottoman

[245] *Apoc.*, p. 123.
[247] See Rev. 8, 9, 16.
[249] *Apoc.*, p. 79.
[251] *AM*, I, 99–304.
[252] Rev. 8:8–11; *Apoc.*, pp. 74–79.
[253] Rev. 8:12–13; *Apoc.*, pp. 79–81.
[254] Rev. 9:1–12.
[256] Rev. 9:13–21; *Apoc.*, pp. 92–99.

[246] *Apoc.*, pp. 149–177.
[248] *Apoc.*, p. 73.
[250] Rev. 8:7; *Apoc.*, pp. 73–74.

[255] *Apoc.*, pp. 82–92.

leader, 1300."[257] The dangers of the Turks were well known to Western Europe and to the church during the lifetime of Foxe. The Sixth Trumpet covers the significant period after "the loosing out of Satan" and brings the story of God's judgment down to Foxe's own time.

In his comments on the outpouring of the Seven Vials, Foxe covers again the history of the Christian era for the purpose of illustrating the principles of divine vengeance. He writes: "Crime against the name of Christ never escapes divine vengeance; not only against individuals, but also in the form of widespread public calamities, punishing former outrages. The histories show these things have occurred in all nations and ages."[258] Regarding the first three Vials Foxe writes: "To me the simple solution is that by these first three vials a triple punishment is meant, on those who execrated and persecuted the early church."[259] Included in this period is also the Fourth Vial, for Foxe asserts that "the first four vials all have to do with the early persecution . . . the last three, being the scourge of the latter days, pertain to the conclusion of the war against the tyrant Antichrist."[260] The Sixth Vial is to be compared with the Sixth Trumpet in chapter 9, and describes the punishment through the wars of the Turks.[261] The Fifth Vial leads up to the events of the Sixth, and thus belongs to the latter days, even though it is fulfilled in the migration of the Goths, Huns, Lombards, and the like. These events weakened Rome and "prepared the coming of the kings of the East, as seems to be properly fulfilled in the Saracens and the Turks."[262]

The significance of Foxe's interpretation of the Trumpets and the Vials is not only that it historically illustrates the principle of God's retribution, but that it points to "the end of time and to the Telos of all things. The kingdoms of the world are abolished, the kings and rulers of the earth cease. There is only one King to whose empire they are subjugated universally, and who alone will rule eternally. And now this desired day of the

---

257 *Apoc.*, p. 95.
259 *Apoc.*, p. 343.
261 *Apoc.*, p. 373.

258 *Apoc.*, p. 343.
260 *Apoc.*, p. 362.
262 *Apoc.*, p. 368.

Lord may not be far from the doors."[263] The various countries
and rulers "are permitted to continue, by the One overruling
God, till the appointed time of the end of the world, when all
will return under the control of one Prince from heaven and
will abide forever under His authority. No more blessed time or
kingdom or Prince can be hoped for: we should hope for nothing more sure."[264] At the same time the church of Christ has
"a joyful peace with never-ending serenity. The so-long-desired
resurrection of the righteous will take place with rewards for
the holy martyrs; there shall be inflicted on those who destroyed
the earth the just punishment of perdition."[265]

In his closing remarks about the Seventh Trumpet, Foxe
brings its nearness into renewed focus when he writes: "This
seventh trumpet certainly is not far off, when by a marvellous
inversion of things and times the past shall grow old and all
things new, a new heaven and a new earth shall be constituted."[266] Like the Seventh Trumpet, the Seventh Vial[267] describes the events and points out the time of "the supreme day of
judgment, which will bring an end to all things and all times."[268]

Whatever message Foxe may convey in his interpretations of
the various images of the Revelation, they are always written in
the charged atmosphere of the last days. The same is the case
in the *Acts and Monuments*. Foxe makes a comparison between
worldly soldiers and the soldiers of Christ. Referring to the latter
he states: "To be shorte, they declare to the worlde what true
fortitude is, and a waye to conquer, which standeth not in the
power of man, but in the hope of the resurrection, to come, and
is now, I trust, at hand."[269] In the opening paragraph of his letter
"To the True and Faithfull Congregation of Christes Vniuersall
Church" Foxe wishes "aboundance of all peace and tranquilitie,
with the spedy commyng of Christ the Spouse, to make an ende
of all mortall miserie."[270] In his eschatological view Foxe was not
sectarian, but represented the same basic beliefs as the Continen-

---

[263] *Apoc.*, pp. 194, 195.
[265] *Apoc.*, p. 195.
[267] Rev. 16:17–21.
[269] *UPH*, Bvir.

[264] *Apoc.*, p. 195.
[266] *Apoc.*, p. 195.
[268] *Apoc.*, p. 387.
[270] *Cong.*, sig. iir.

tal Reformers[271] and the Anglican Fathers.[272] They all preached the one-directional movement of history toward the Second Advent of Christ. Foxe did not expect the apocalyptic hopes for Christ's kingdom to be fulfilled through social revolts as did many before and during the Reformation period.[273] The Puritan millennium of the seventeenth century was equally foreign to him, whether the idea of the kingdom of God was spiritualized or realized through material or political advantages.[274]

The "Telos" was for Foxe the consummation of the church. As Christ was taken to heaven at the beginning of the Christian era, so the church at its end, which was imminent, would be received into heaven.[275] Then God's church is avenged and at peace, "with never ending serenity."

[271] Regarding Luther, see John M. Headley, *Luther's View of Church History* (New Haven and London, 1963), especially the chapter on "Luther and the End," pp. 257–265.

[272] Statements illustrating this point are quoted from Sleidan, Bale, Jewel, Bradford, Becon, and Sandys in the Prolegomena.

[273] Norman Cohn, *The Pursuit of the Millennium* (London, 1962).

[274] Alfred Cohen, "Two Roads to the Puritan Millennium: William Erbury and Vavasor Powell," *Church History* (1963), XXXII, 322–338.

[275] *Apoc.*, p. 199.

II. The Nature of the Church

*T*HE CHURCH is a divine society built upon Christ and preserved by Him. Commenting upon the apostle Peter's confession, "Thou art the Christ, the Son of the living God," and Christ's words, "... upon this rock I will build my church,"[1] Foxe stresses three points: "First, that Christ will have a church in this world. Secondly, that the same church should mightily be impugned, not only by the world, but also by the uttermost strength and powers of all hell. And, thirdly, that the same church, notwithstanding the uttermost of the devil and all his malice, should continue."[2]

Concerning the concept of the church there are, according to Foxe, two particulars which are "most requisite and necessary for every christian man to observe and to note, for his own experience and profit." The first is "the disposition and nature of this world" and the second, "the nature and condition of the kingdom of Christ." Foxe compares the two by referring to "the unprosperous and unquiet state of the one, ruled by man's violence and wisdom, and the happy success of the other, ever ruled by God's blessing and providence; the wrath and revenging hand of God on the one, and his mercy on the other." The people in "the world" are defined as those who are "without or against Christ, either by ignorance not knowing him, or by

[1] Matt. 16:16–18.

heathenish life not following him, or by violence resisting him." On the other hand the kingdom of Christ is composed of "all them which belong to the faith of Christ, and here take his part in this world against the world; the number of whom although it be much smaller than the other, and always, lightly, is hated and molested of the world, yet it is the number which the Lord peculiarly doth bless and prosper, and ever will." It should be observed that "this number of Christ's subjects is it, which we call the visible church here in earth."[3]

It is also significant to notice that in defining the nature of the church Foxe laid down another basic principle. As mankind belongs either to the kingdom of the world or the kingdom of Christ, so the visible church is divided into two parts, or composed of two kinds of people, where "the one standeth of such as be of outward profession only, the other of such as by election inwardly are joined to Christ: the first in words and lips seem to honour Christ, and are in the visible church only, but not in the church invisible, and partake the outward sacraments of Christ, but not the inward blessings of Christ."[4]

When Foxe describes the relationship between the two parts of the visible church he points out another axiom, so fundamental to his concept of the church. Between the two sections there is often "great variance and mortal persecution, insomuch that sometimes the true church of Christ hath no greater enemies than those of their own profession and company." This has been true since the time of Christ, "but especially in these latter days of the church under the persecution of Antichrist and his retinue."[5] Apparently one of the major objectives of the *Acts and Monuments* is to illustrate this point. Having noticed Foxe's basic definitions regarding the nature of the church, it will be profitable to turn to his idea of predestination before a further inquiry is made into his view of the visible and invisible church.

Theologically, the question of election and predestination has a central place in Foxe's concept of the church, true also of other Elizabethan Divines.[6] In some notes upon the matter of

---

[3] *AM*, I, 88.   [4] *AM*, I, 88.
[5] *AM*, I, 88.
[6] H. F. Woodhouse, *The Doctrine of the Church in Anglican Theology, 1547–1603* (London, 1954), pp. 43–58.

election and faith, Foxe explains "what God's election is, and what is the cause thereof." He first defines the difference between predestination and election: "predestination is as well to the reprobate, as to the elect; election pertaineth only to them that be saved." For the rejected, predestination is called reprobation, while for the saved it is called election. Furthermore, "predestination is the eternal decreement of God, proposed before in himself, what shall befall on all men, either to salvation or damnation."[7] Election, on the other hand, "is the free mercy and grace of God in his own will, through faith in Christ his Son, choosing and preferring to life such as pleaseth him."

Foxe himself points out four important factors in this definition. First, "the mercy and grace of God . . . excluded all the works of the law, and merits of deserving, whether they go before faith, or come after." Second, this mercy is "free," and "thereby is to be noted the proceeding and working of God not to be bounded to any ordinary place, or to any succession of chair, nor to state and dignity of person, nor to worthiness of blood, etc.; but all goeth by the mere will of his own purpose." Third, this mercy is "in his own will." Foxe comments, "by this falleth down the free will and purpose of man, with all his actions, counsels, and strength of nature. . . . Furthermore, as all then goeth by the will of God only, and not by the will of man: so again here is to be noted, that this will of God never goeth without faith in Christ Jesus his Son." This leads to the last point in defining election. Foxe writes: "Whosoever will be certain of election in God, let him first begin with his faith in Christ; which if he find in him to stand firm, he may be sure, and nothing doubt, but that he is one of the number of God's elect."[8]

The concept of election theologically gives the assurance that

---

[7] *AM*, VII, 268.

[8] *AM*, VII, 268–269. For the significance of predestination and election, see *OT*, pp. 305–308, 374–375; *CC*, p. 82; *FJ*, pp. 60, 158, 217–219, 296, 400, 485–486; John Foxe, *Against Ierome Osorivs* (London, 1581), pp. 131–255. Foxe's discussion of election, *AM*, VII, 268–272, was printed together with a book by Beza translated into English in 1576, the subject of which was predestination. See Theodore Beza, *The Treasvre of Trueth* (n.p., 1576).

all God's eschatological promises to the church will be fulfilled. It is therefore also interesting to notice that when Foxe speaks about the church in relationship to some distressing events, he is referring to the church of the elect, which valiantly will survive and in which God's eternal plans will be realized. Those belonging to "the church of the elect are clearly immune from the plagues, which are destined to be inflicted on the reprobates."[9] When in 1586 Foxe refers to the time period of 294 years, which in his opinion began in A.D. 1300, he writes: "The Lord knows whether [the period] will be shortened for the sake of the elect."[10]

"Christ is the one Head of His church, and in a more specific sense, He is the sole Head of the elect from the beginning."[11] When Christ at the time of His resurrection founded the church "he shewed not him selfe to the world, but onely to his elect which were but few. The same Church after that encreased and multiplyed mightely among the Jewes, yet had not the Jewes eyes to see Gods Church, but did persecute it, till at length all their whole nation was destroyed."[12]

Faith in Christ and true Christian doctrines are attributes of the elect. The true worshipers are those who are united to Christ "by the grace of election" and thus "adore Him in spirit and truth," while "through the true faith and preaching they observe the proper worship of God."[13] Foxe mentions a third characteristic, godly living. The church of the elect, as opposed to the apostate church, is known by Christian living worthy of the true spiritual church or kingdom of Christ. The "elect of Christ . . . possess integrity of life."[14] Foxe explains how godly living is a visible fruitage of election and as such a sign of the true church. As a good tree bears good fruits, "so with the elect who are true members of the church; they are indeed known from their fruit, not made elect by their fruit."[15] Foxe thus defines the church with the Reformers and the Anglican Fathers "in relation to grace and faith, not to institutional continuity."

---

[9] *Apoc.*, p. 334.
[11] *Apoc.*, p. 231.
[13] *Apoc.*, p. 120.
[15] *Apoc.*, p. 277.

[10] *Apoc.*, p. 147.
[12] *Cong.*, sig. iiir.
[14] *Apoc.*, p. 281.

For them as for Foxe "the Church, in the deepest sense, was the community of the elect or those who have saving faith in Christ."[16] Hooper, Whitaker, and Hooker make use of the word invisible, thinking of "the Church as composed of sanctified individuals."[17] Foxe speaks about "the blameless church of Christ."[18]

If the elect should turn away from God and profane His worship with idolatry, neither attending His word nor following His counsels, then they would be punished in order to bring them to their senses and to their repentance. Foxe writes: "As the Israelites, being brought out of Egypt, when they sinned against God, were punished in the desert, and yet the promise of the plentiful land nevertheless still went forward—even so the elect members of Christ's church, after their deliverance, when they sin against God by fragility of weak flesh, their sins are punished with temporal scourges in this world, but yet the truth of God's everlasting favour standeth for ever, to all them that repent by faith."[19] Foxe expected that the Reformation would bring the elect back to God and thus restore the church of the elect or the true church of Christ.

The church at the time of the eschatological fulfillment is characterized by Foxe as the church of the elect. Thus when the church is glorified the song of victory is sung by the elect: "In brief, this mystic song of praise none but the elect understands." In the same connection the elect are described as "the true church, which is a congregation of men redeemed from the earth by the precious blood of the immaculate Lamb."[20]

When Foxe defines the church in its absolute and purest sense, then he has in mind only the elect. Thus he speaks about "the true Church of Christ" to be composed of "Gods elect."[21] The members of the invisible church consist of those who "by election inwardly are joined to Christ,"[22] and the church is thought to be spiritual as "respecting the elect alone."[23] Like Foxe, such English Divines as Cranmer, Hooper, Philpot, Jewel, Whitaker,

---

[16] Woodhouse, *op. cit.*, p. 57.

[17] *Ibid.*, p. 54.

[18] *Apoc.*, p. 373.

[19] *CC*, p. 28.

[20] *Apoc.*, p. 276.

[21] *FQP*, sig. iiiiv.

[22] *AM*, I, 88.

[23] *Apoc.*, p. 273.

and Field, when speaking about the invisible church, meant the elect.[24]

H. F. Woodhouse, in his analysis of the usage of the words "visible" and "invisible" by the Anglican Fathers, concludes that what "appears to be the greatest weakness perhaps of this period in regard to the doctrine of the Church is the idea of invisibility."[25] The reason for this is that there "are differences of opinion on this subject and sometimes the same author seems to say now one thing, now another."[26] Foxe does not write a systematic treatise on the subject of the visible and invisible church; yet his references to it, historically and theologically, are probably more extensive than those of most of his contemporaries. While some writers may emphasize one aspect and others another, Foxe covers both. Foxe may place different meanings on the two words; however, when the circumstances and his objectives are considered, there are no contradictions in his usage of them. No doubt, Foxe does not write anything not expressed by others, but his comprehensiveness may help to clarify the concept of the visible and invisible church among Elizabethan clergymen.

Reference has been made to Foxe's division of the church into two groups of people, the one having "outward profession only," the other "by election inwardly joined to Christ." The first are in only the visible church, but "the other are both in the visible, and also in the invisible church of Christ, which not in words only and outward profession, but also in heart do truly serve and honour Christ, partaking not only the sacraments, but also the heavenly blessings and grace of Christ." Here Foxe defines the visible and invisible church not as two churches but as one; the one church composed of "two sorts of people, so is it to be divided into two parts."[27] This means that the visible church is composed of a mixed group of people, mixed in regard to sincerity of worship and godly living. This point is further illustrated in Foxe's letter "To the True and Faithfull Congregation of Christes Vniuersall Church, with all and singular the members thereof, wheresoeuer congregated or dispersed through the

[24] Woodhouse, *op. cit.*, p. 54.
[25] *Ibid.*, p. 190.
[26] *Ibid.*, p. 45.
[27] *AM*, I, 88.

Realme of England."[28] The title of this letter is most interesting in that it speaks of the true and faithful congregation as a part of the universal church of Christ. Furthermore, Foxe writes to those members who are congregated and dispersed through the realm of England. In his introduction Foxe expresses the desire that God would bless the *Acts and Monuments* to the advancement of His glory and profit of the church just as He had answered Solomon's prayer for the blessing of the Lord's temple. Foxe writes that "as it hapned in that Temple of Solomon, that all which came thether, came not to pray but many to prate, some to gaze and see newes, other to talke and walke, some to buye and sell, some to carpe and find fault, and finally some also at the last to destroy and plucke downe, as they did in deede,"[29] so it also happened in his own time. Here Foxe is in line with Hooker whose viewpoint is summarized: "But all within the visible Church do not reveal holiness of life, for the visible Church is always mixed and imperfect and also there are some outside and some cut themselves off, even if not completely."[30]

In his discussion with the Catholics, Foxe insists that to acknowledge a visible church is not to prove the Catholic Church the church of Christ. He writes: "I know that there is never a church which is not visible in the earth. But it does not follow because a church is visible that on that account it is the church of Christ; what it does should be the criterion."[31] Foxe addresses four questions "To All the Professed Frendes And Folowers Of The Popes Proceedinges." In the close of this letter he takes up the problem: "That forsomuch as Christ must nedes haue a catholique Church euer continuyng here in earth, which all men may see and whereunto all men ought to resort: and seyng no other Church hath endured continually from the Apostles, visible here in earth, but onely the Church of Rome: they conclude therefore the Church onely of Rome to be the right catholicke Church of Christ."[32] Foxe meets their argument in the following way:

In aunsweryng whereunto this is to be sayd: that forsomuch as

[28] *Cong.*, sig. ii*r*.
[30] Woodhouse, *op. cit.*, p. 51.
[32] *FQP*, sig. iiii*v*.

[29] *Cong.*, sig. ii*r*.
[31] *Apoc.*, p. 24.

the medius terminus of this argument, both in the Major and Minor, consisteth onely in the word (visible and vnknowne:) if they meane by this worde (visible) in the Major that Christes Church must be sene here to all the world, that all men may resort to it, it is false: Likewise if they meane by the same word (visible) in the Minor: that no other Church hath ben saene and knowne to any, but onely the Church of Rome, they are likewise deceiued. For the true Church of Christ neyther is so visible, that all the world can see it, but onely they which haue spirituall eyes: and be members therof: nor yet so inuisible agayne, but such as be Gods elect, and members thereof, do see it and haue saen it though the worldly eyes of the most multitude canne not so do.[33]

In the opinion of Foxe the visible hierarchical organization of Rome does not represent the church of Christ. Therefore, when addressing the followers of the pope he emphasizes that the religion of Christ is spiritual, not corporal; his statement about the visible and invisible church was made with this in mind. Foxe further writes:

> . . . if our God, whom we serue, be spirituall, how can his Religion and seruice be corporall as we are taught by the mouth of our Saviour, saying: God is a spirite and therefore they that worship hym, must worship in spirite and veritie, etc. Nowe if ye graunt (as ye must nedes) this our Christian Religion to be spirituall, and not a corporall Religion, then shew, if ye can, any one poynt, of all these thinges which ye striue for so much with vs, to be spirituall, but altogether corporall, and externe matters and ceremoniall obseruations, nothyng conducyng to any spirituall purpose.[34]

In another place Foxe speaks about the apostasy of Rome in using the temporal sword, and then refers to the true church as the "spiritual church." Foxe writes that the armour of God "is all spiritual, so ought they which have the dealing thereof to be likewise spiritual, well furnished with all such gifts and graces of the Holy Ghost, as are meet for the governance of his spiritual church."[35] The church is "a spiritual Kingdom, I say, although it exists among men and in a visible church, which is Mt. Syon, it must be regarded as spiritual with respect to its general glory,

---

[33] *FQP*, sig. iiiiv.   [34] *GQP*, sig. iiiiv.
[35] *AM*, I, 57.

benefits, felicity and triumphal ovation, respecting the elect alone."[36] Thus in one sense the church, as "the bride of Christ," is deserted and hidden in this world."[37] On the other hand Rome is visible and yet "the synagogue of Satan."[38]

The church is maintained by the gifts of the Holy Spirit, the active force within it. Christ has no need of the pope as vicar, for the Holy Spirit is Christ's vicar. Foxe states that Christ's rule is distinguished from that of the world by the fact that he "sustains, fosters and governs the affairs of His church through the Holy Spirit, through whom He sanctifies the minds of his people, giving peace and instilling patience."[39] Elsewhere Foxe writes that "the spiritual church of God" has "the real worship," characterized by "the genuine knowledge and faith of Christ, the true invocation, the gracious favour of the Godhead, the preaching of sacred doctrine, the charismata of the divine spirit."[40] The gift of the Holy Spirit to the church is also described as follows: "I know that there are both many and eminent vertues, wherewith the Spirit of Christ always adorns his Church."[41] He adds that "the church of God must be measured, not by external splendour or amplitude, but by genuine gifts of the spiritual good."[42] Speaking about the work of the Reformation, Foxe writes: "The temple which must be repaired, I mean, is the spiritual church of Christ."[43] Foxe places great emphasis upon the spiritual aspect of the church, noticeable also in his dealing with the Christian ministry.

In defining the church, Foxe makes rich use of the expression "the kingdom of Christ," which he takes "to be all them which belong to the faith of Christ."[44] This "kingdom of Christ first began upon the cross,"[45] and whatever may happen Christ "cannot, and will not totally and finally forsake his church, which is his kingdom."[46] When Foxe refers to the church as the kingdom, he is usually speaking of either the present spiritual values of the Gospel or the eternal or eschatological aspects of the

[36] *Apoc.*, p. 273.
[37] *Apoc.*, p. 197.
[38] *Apoc.*, p. 23.
[39] *Apoc.*, p. 373.
[40] *Apoc.*, p. 125.
[41] *FJ*, p. 256.
[42] *Apoc.*, p. 118.
[43] *Apoc.*, p. 120.
[44] *AM*, I, 88.
[45] *AM*, I, 78.
[46] *CC*, p. 11.

church.[47] Foxe clearly states: "The church is the spiritual king-dom;"[48] and he speaks about "the kingdom of the gospel."[49] He comments about the remission of sins by faith: "So that to them that be repenting sinners, and be in Christ Jesus, there is no law to condemn them, though they have deserved condemnation: but they are under a perpetual kingdom, and a heaven, full of grace and remission to cover their sins, and not to impute their iniquities, through the promise of God in Christ Jesus our Lord."[50]

In another connection Foxe quotes Paul: "For ye see your calling, brethren, how that not many wise men after the flesh, nor many mighty, nor many noble, are called,"[51] then comments: "In this way, I perceive the wonderful way in which God chooses those who are to be saints, by His peculiar favour, in the kingdom of His Son."[52] In the great drama between the church and the world, the church is also described as the kingdom. Having referred to the kingdom of Satan with its great power and external magnificence, Foxe emphasizes that "none the less Christ has His kingdom, His church and the sons of His Church in the midst of these forces."[53] The eschatological aspect of the churchly kingdom is mentioned: "Christ has His kingdom and eternal riches and good things stored in heaven, which He promised to His own."[54] The church is depicted in the book of Revelation under the symbol of a beautiful woman, greatly adorned.[55] The details of her ornaments "typify the exceeding glory of the church of God, if not in this world, yet certainly it has and will always have, in the kingdom of Christ."[56]

In considering the application Foxe makes of the expression "the universal church," or "the church universally," it would be profitable to examine his interpretation of the "temple, court and city" of Revelation 11. Here he elaborates further upon the question of the church, visible and invisible. The Revelator's

[47] See *FJ*, sig. A6v, pp. 18–20, 22, 32–34, 36, 53, 69, passim; *OT*, pp. 291–292, 317–318, 320, 330, 332, 358–359; *CC*, pp. 3, 4, 11, 33, 34, 40, 67.
[48] *Apoc.*, p. 138.
[49] *Apoc.*, p. 386.
[50] *AM*, I, 80.
[51] 1 Cor. 1:26–27.
[52] *Apoc.*, p. 333.
[53] *Apoc.*, p. 204.
[54] *Apoc.*, p. 320.
[55] Rev. 12.
[56] *Apoc.*, p. 197.

picture of the measuring of the temple refers, according to Foxe, to the restoration or spiritual reformation of the church after A.D. 1300. It is not generally understood, says Foxe, that the restoration of the church applies only to those parts of the church that God has chosen to show forth His glory. Those nations that God had permitted to be overrun by the Turks He had rejected.[57] Foxe would no doubt agree with Hooker "that Saracens, Jews and Infidels are excluded out of the bounds of the Church."[58]

In his interpretation of "the city" Foxe states that it "signifies the universal church of Christians" which although suppressed by the Gentiles "will emerge victorious from this inundation, in no part extinct." This will be accomplished because "God always has his remnants, in the midst of the lost. The church therefore is never totally overthrown."[59] The true church of Christ is here characterized as the city. When Foxe calls the church a city, which in spite of difficulties within and persecution without will emerge triumphant, he has no doubt been influenced by Saint Augustine's concept of the church as the city of God. Discussing the persecution of the church he writes: "Antichrist with his church of the wicked has throughout the centuries persecuted the beloved city of God," but they do not know that their final and fatal judgment is near.[60]

In the temple building, symbolizing the Reformation, Foxe describes two groups of worshipers. He first states that "God will not build into his temple all those who are contained within the ambit of the church as part of the congregation."[61] Foxe describes one group of worshipers as "those who are united to Him by election of divine grace, whether they are pastors or people, who adore Him in spirit and truth, who by sincere faith and preaching observe and promote the true worship of God."[62] Connected with the temple are the inner and outer courts. According to Foxe true followers of Christ worship in the inner court, while the others worship in the outer one. The two groups

---

[57] *Apoc.*, p. 121.
[58] Richard Hooker, *Of the Laws of Ecclesiastical Polity* (Oxford, 1885), Vol. III, pt. i, p. 7.
[59] *Apoc.*, p. 124.   [60] *Apoc.*, p. 374.
[61] *Apoc.*, p. 120.   [62] *Apoc.*, p. 120.

here described are not merely a mixed group of worshipers within the one visible church, even though there is some over-lapping, but represent a true and a false church. Foxe clearly states that those in the inner court "signify the true church of God" but the others in the outer court "are ordered to be cut off."[63]

The "true church" is clearly related to the "invisible church," as she is the true church in its absolute and full sense. Thus Cranmer and Hooper apply the expression only to the invisible church. On the other hand, Foxe, like Hooker, Covell, Field, and Philpot,[64] would "refuse to make a rigid division between visible and invisible and to admit that the visible Church is not the true Church."[65] Foxe uses the expression "the true church" to distinguish, theologically and historically, between the true visible church and the apostate church. Regarding this point he writes: "There has been up to the present much controversy among the theologians about the true and false church. No one denies that there is one certain church of Christ on earth. But there is no agreement as to which is the true church, where it is to be sought, by what marks and signs it is to be measured."[66] The false church is composed of "those who profess themselves Catholics, who hold that incontestably the true Christian church is at Rome and so has ever been." The members of the true church are those "whose profession is nearer to the gospel, who all the more reject this Roman church. . . . Having left Rome, they cling to Christ rather than to the Pontiff."[67]

In the opinion of Foxe "the true Church of God" is not alone "but is accompanied with some other Church or Chappell of the deuill to deface and maligne the same."[68] The same was true in the time of Christ, for "who would haue thought, but the congregation and councels of the Pharisies had bene the right Church: and yet had Christ an other Church in earth besides that, which albeit, it was not so manifest in the sight of the world, yet was it the onely true Church in the sight of God."[69] In the opinion of Foxe the Pharisees represent Rome, whose church is desig-

---

[63] *Apoc.*, p. 124.
[65] *Ibid.*, p. 50.
[67] *Apoc.*, p. 389.
[69] *Cong.*, sig. iiir.

[64] Woodhouse, *op. cit.*, p. 49.
[66] *Apoc.*, p. 389.
[68] *Cong.*, sig. iiir.

nated as the synagogue of Satan.[70] This is illustrated by the following statement:

> Who beholding the Church of Rome to be so visible and glorious in the eyes of the world, so shinyng in outward beauty, to beare such a porte, to cary such a trayne and multitude, and to stand in such hye authorite, supposed the same to be onely the right Catholicke mother. The other because it was not so visibly knowne in the worlde, they thought therefore it could not be the true Church of Christe. Wherein they were farre deceaued. For although the right Church of God be not so inuisible in the world, that none can see it: yet neither is it so visible agayne that euery worldly eye may perceaue it. For as like as is the nature of truth: so is the proper condition of the true Church, that commonly none seeth it, but such onely as be the members and partakers therof. And therfore they which require that Gods holy Church should be euident and visible to the whole world seeme to define the great Synagoge of the world, rather than the true spirituall Church of God.[71]

Foxe illuminates the question of the true and false church with historical references.[72] With Constantine liberty came to the church, but as the years went by there was much deterioration in evangelical doctrine. However, up to the time of Gregory VII and Innocent III, the church remained, "albeit not without some repugnance and difficultie, yet in some meane state of truth and veritie," and it was called "the true Church of Christ." After Innocent III things were altogether "turned vpside downe." Furthermore, "the clere sunne shine of Gods word was ouershadowed with mistes and darknes," and "the true visible Church began now to shrinke."[73] From Foxe's comparison between the ancient church of Rome and the Roman church of his own time, the following words are taken: ". . . this latter pretended church of Rome hath utterly sequestered itself from the image and nature of the ancient and true church of Rome, and they have erected to themselves a new church of their own making."[74]

---

[70] See *Apoc.*, pp. 23, 198, 204; *AM*, I, 70; II, 521; *OT*, p. 310.
[71] *Cong.*, sig. iiir.
[72] *Cong.*, sig. iiir–iiiiv; *Apoc.*, 124–141.
[73] *Cong.*, sig. iiiv.   [74] *AM*, I, 12–13.

If Rome ceased to be the true church from the time of Gregory VIII, yet God always has His true church on earth, then where was the true church of Christ from that time until the Reformation? Foxe answers: "Duryng which space, the true Church of Christ, although it durst not openly appeare in the face of the world, oppressed by tyranny; yet neither was it so inuisible or unknowen, but by the prouidence of the Lord, some remnaunt always remayned, from tyme to tyme, which not onely shewed secret good affection to sincere doctrine, but also stode in open defence of truth agaynst the disordered Church of Rome."[75]

Beginning with Joachim and the Waldenses and enumerating a great number of preachers down to Wycliffe, Huss, Luther, and Zwingli, Foxe describes how the true church continued in the midst of her enemies by "faithfull witnesses of the truth, not teachyng any new doctrines contrary to the determination of holy Church: but rather shall finde that Church to be vnholy, which they preached agaynst, teachyng rather it selfe hereticall opinions contrary both to antiquitie, and verity of Christes true Catholicke Church." In this connection the following words should be noticed: "What shal nede then any more witnes to proue this matter, when you see so many yeares ago, whole armies and multitudes, thus standyng agaynst the Pope? who though they be termed here for heretickes and schismatickes: yet in that, which they call heresy, serued they the liuyng Lord, within the Arke of his true spirituall, and visible Church."[76] The reformed church of the sixteenth century is thus shown by Foxe to be the true spiritual and visible church, and as such is not a new church. Arguing against the opinion of Rome, "that neuer was any other Church demonstrable here in earth for men to follow" than Rome, Foxe writes: ". . . when as we haue sufficiently proued before by the continual descent of the Church till this present time, that the sayd Church, after the doctrine which is now reformed, is no newbegun matter, but euen the old continued Church, by the prouidence and promise of Christ still standyng."[77] Resistance against the Pope should

<hr/>

[75] *Cong.*, sig. iiiv.
[77] *Cong.*, sig. iiiiv.

[76] *Cong.*, sig. iiiir.

not therefore be considered a "new thing in these days in the church of Christ."[78]

The apostasy described by the apostle Paul as "a falling away"[79] Foxe finds fulfilled in the papacy.[80] It was "not a defection, but rather a plain destruction, and a ruin of faith; neither that this were any true church of Christ, but a new-found religion."[81] When the pope's church is compared with Christ's church, it is "like black and white."[82] Foxe makes another contrast between the true and false church. The first is represented by a beautiful woman,[83] "who was pure and beloved of God," the other by a "shameless harlot."[84] Both churches "were mothers, but their offspring were entirely different." The true church "bore His Son and daily bears sons of God," while the false church "gives birth to adulterous off-spring of Satan—popes, cardinals, boasting archpriests, executioners, inquisitors, shaven orders of priests, friars and monks."[85] Rome, though she considers herself the mother church, is "not the mother [of the church] but of fornicators and abominations of the earth."[86]

In Foxe's discussion of the pope's church and the true church of Christ, the question of apostolicity and catholicity has a prominent place. With the Protestant Reformers at large Foxe asserts that the church had been apostolic and catholic before Rome developed into the papacy; accordingly the church could be catholic without the papacy. The Reformers contended that they adhered to catholicity while Rome had forgotten its catholicity. Thus Luther, in his invective against the Catholic Duke Henry of Brunswick, said: "I shall prove that we have remained with the true, ancient church, yea, that we are the true, ancient church. But you have fallen from us, that is, from the ancient church, and set up a new church in opposition to the old."[87]

---

[78] *AM*, II, 510.   [79] 2 Thess. 2.

[80] *FQP*, sig. iiiiv; *Apoc.*, pp. 110, 148, 228, 239, 258, 286; Foxe also finds Paul's statement fulfilled in the "great defection from faith in so many churches" caused by the Turks. See *AM*, IV, 101.

[81] *AM*, I, 69.   [82] *AM*, II, 506.

[83] Rev. 12.   [84] *Apoc.*, pp. 390–391.

[85] *Apoc.*, p. 391.   [86] *Apoc.*, p. 390.

[87] Martin Luther, "Wider Hans Worst," *W. A.*, LI (Mar. 1541), 478–479.

Foxe's lengthy comparison between the primitive and latter churches of Rome purposes to disprove the apostolicity and catholicity of Rome but to prove the same regarding the church reformed.[88] Foxe says that the early doctors, "speaking of the church of Rome which then was, said not untruly, calling it catholic and apostolical; for that the same church took not only their ordinary succession of bishops but also their ordinary doctrine and institution from the apostles. But speaking of the church of Rome which now is, we say the said places of the doctors are not true, neither do appertain to the same; all which doctors neither knew the church of Rome that now is, nor, if they had, would ever have judged any thing therein worthy such commendation."[89] He expresses the same thought in this way: "... the church of Rome, as it is now governed with this manner of title, jurisdiction, life and institution of doctrine, never descended from the primitive age of the apostles, or from their succession."[90] When therefore Rome boasts of the name Catholic, it is a "false Name."[91] Referring to the reformed church Foxe states: "... our church was, when this church of theirs was not yet hatched out of the shell, nor did yet ever see any light: that is, in the time of the apostles, in the primitive age, in the time of Gregory I, and the old Roman church." Thus "we have sufficient matter for us to show that the same form, usage and institution of this our present reformed church, are not the beginning of any new church of our own, but the renewing of the old ancient church of Christ."[92]

In the opinion of Foxe Rome has broken away from and disrupted the unity of the universal church; accordingly, he accuses Rome of having her own sect of religion. Referring to her life, practices, and doctrines he exclaims: "... into what diuision of sectes they cut the vnitie of Christian Religion,"[93] elsewhere explaining, "This is the reason of that unhappy division among Christians, which has for so long disturbed the church, and is still disturbing it so lamentably."[94] Foxe was most

[88] *AM*, I, 3–86.
[90] *AM*, I, 7.
[92] *AM*, I, 9.
[94] *Apoc.*, p. 389.

[89] *AM*, I, 8–9.
[91] *FJ*, p. 225.
[93] *Cong.*, sig. iiv.

anxious to restore the unity of the church. Discussing the "great defection from faith in so many churches" by the conquests of the Turks, Foxe comments that their horrible persecutions are "the scourge of God" for "sins, and corrupt doctrine." He further states: "The consideration of this horrible persecution of the Turks rising chiefly by our discord and dissension among ourselves, may reduce us again from our domestical wars, in killing and burning one another, to join together in christian patience and concord."[95] Foxe expresses sorrow at these divisions which penetrated even into the ranks of the Protestants in his well-known sermon at Saint Paul's Cross: "Such dissension and hostility Satan hath set amongst us, that Turks are not more enemies to christians, than christians to christians, papists to protestants; yea, protestants with protestants do not agree, but fall out for trifles. So that the poor little flock of thy church, distressed on every side, hath neither rest without, nor peace within."[96]

Foxe sincerely hoped that the Reformation would restore the unity of the church: "This hope I have, and do believe, that when the church of Christ, with the sacraments thereof, shall be so reformed, that Christ alone shall be received to be our justifier, all other religions, merits, traditions, images, patrons, and advocates set apart, the sword of the Christians, with the strength of Christ, shall soon vanquish the Turks' pride and fury."[97] In his sermon at the baptism of a converted Jew, he expresses the hope that the Jews and Gentiles might someday embrace Christ in whom the unity of the church and mankind has its center. He writes: "So that at the length, all nations, as well Jews and Gentiles, embracing the faith and sacraments of Christ Jesus, acknowledging one Shepherd, uniting together in one sheepfold, may, with one voice, one soul, and one general agreement, glorify the only begotten Son, our Saviour Jesus Christ."[98] Surprisingly Foxe, who through the *Acts and Monuments* created and nourished anti-Roman feelings,[99] sought in a most kind and

---

[95] *AM*, IV, 101, 18.   [96] *CC*, p. 92.
[97] *AM*, IV, 20.   [98] *CT*, pp. 294–295.
[99] That Foxe's attack upon the church of Rome was felt by the Roman Catholics is reflected in Thomas Harding's debate with Jewell. Harding

hearty way to appeal to the Roman Catholics. He pleads with them for reform and unity in the following words:

> ... forsake your cause, and your false hopes, and saue your selues. And take me not your enemy in telling you truth, but rather your friende in geuing you good counsel, if you wil follow good counsel geuen. Returne therefore and reforme your selues, repent your murders, cease your persecutions, striue not against the Lord, but rather bewaile your iniquities, which thoughe they be great, and greater than you are aware: yet they are not so great, but Christ is greater, if ye repent betime. Ye see here I trust good counsel geuen. God graunt it may as wel fructifie in you, as on may part it hath proceded of an open and tender hart, wishing you wel to doo, as I pray God ye may, so that you and we may agree and consent together in one religion and truth in Christ Jesus our Lorde, to whom be praise for euer. Amen.[100]

In his sermon preached on Good Friday, A.D. 1570, Foxe closes his message with an appeal to Roman Catholics.[101] The same is true in the last pages of his commentary on the book of Revelation, where Foxe says that he writes especially to "the honest men of the catholic persuasion." He calls them "beloved friends and brothers in Christ." The latter he repeats when he says, "I address you: Friends and brothers." He then continues with these words: "I am not being indulgent about men's errors, I am seeking their salvation in Christ."[102] These sentiments are confirmed in his son's memoir of the father, where Foxe's plea for moderation is expressed in this way:

> That notwithstanding the case was so plain, yet neither part ought to lend too much belief to Arguments, nor be too earnest in hindering it, if by any moderation of men the matter might be brought to soundnesse and agreement. That it was not (perchance) in our power, to take from Rome her ancient honour, and the opinion of her religion so fixed already in the mindes of men.[103]

---

speaks about "that huge dongehill of your stinking martyrs, which ye haue intituled Actes and monumentes." See Thomas Harding, *A Confutation*, sig. 14r.

[100] *PGT*, sig. Bvv.
[101] *CC*, pp. 95–97.
[102] *Apoc.*, p. 389.
[103] *LJF*, sig. B5v.

Simeon Foxe describes, at some length, his father's attitude toward the Papists. He tells us that his father hoped the Papists would repent but demanded that "the conditions of agreement would be, first, that the Pope should forsake all those tenets by which he gained so great sums of money. . . . Next that he should renounce all secular jurisdiction, and not suppose himself to have title, or any thing to do with the right of Princes." The opponents of the Papacy "should not refuse that some one man may have the principall place of counsell, and government in the Church-affairs, as being a thing, which would have many conveniences in it, when it might be done with security." The choice of such a leader should "be left to the discretion of a Generall Councell of the Christians, which might be so equitable, as that neither the power, or favour of any one should be able, either from the place of meeting, or the difference in number of voices to promise it self any advantage to the injury of the rest." Until this was accomplished "it would be of great moment to hope, and speedinesse of setling all controversies, if hereafter on both sides they would give such instructions, as might cause in each party a better hope and opinion of the other, especially that they ought to leave off that stubborn conceit, whereby each of them, presuming it self to be the onely true Church, supposeth the other excluded." He hoped also that "there might one day among their own men be found some, by whose authority they should not be ashamed to amend their faults, and with more willingnesse part with their own power, to procure the peace of the whole world."[104] There is no reason to doubt that Simeon rightly expressed John Foxe's sentiments on these matters, for when he speaks about his father's attitude toward Roman Catholicism, he states that his sources were his father's "speeches, when being of ripe years, he had strengthned his judgement with much experience."[105]

While Foxe labels Rome as Antichrist and a false church, he would admit with many Anglican Divines of the sixteenth century that she retained some parts of truth and was still to some degree a part of the visible church. She was an apostate church, yet her baptism was still valid.[106] Foxe makes the point clear

[104] *LJF*, sig. B5v. [105] *LJF*, sig. B5r.
[106] Woodhouse, *op. cit.*, p. 145.

when he states: "Nor indeed do we deny to Rome any share in the communion of the Church, neither that it has any part when joined to the body of Christ. We know of so many who have been born and baptised as infants in Rome, whom we do not necessarily judge to be damned because they are Romans."[107] The word "almost" in the following statement makes it a comprehensive expression of Foxe's modified view of Rome. He writes: ". . . ye haue lost the favor both of God and men, the safety of your soules, and almost the kingdome of the Lorde, except you take the better heede."[108] The Rome of the Middle Ages was not denied the name "church," but was called "the disordered Church."[109]

In the name of the universal church Foxe asserts that the reformed church has not departed from the visible church: "We therefore do reproue certen assertions and opinions in some false teachers, from whom we sequester our selues of very necessitie; yet in such wise as we depart not at al from the visible church, in the which we have our being and reliancie as well as they."[110] He further states that the Protestants were "enforced to depart from them rather by violence, and plaine thrusting out, then of any our volunary willingnesse: so that to set down the matter in plaine termes, it may be saide more properly that we do disagree and dissent from them rather than depart from them."[111]

The following statement shows to what degree Foxe considered Rome to have the essentials that constitute the nature of the church:

> In which disagreement notwithstanding, we do not so altogether rende in pieces all the articles of their popes and deuines, nor so altogether condemne them, as though nothing were found amongst them: neither do we contend with al that church so, as though there remained no shape of a visible church in all that cities of Rome; for they haue baptisme there, wherein they make a profession of the name of the Father, the Sonne and the holy Ghost: They haue also the law of God and the Gospel: yea they retaine the worshipping of Christ, and professe the same articles of the

---

[107] *Apoc.*, p. 235.
[108] *PGT*, sig. Bvv.
[109] *Cong.*, sig. iiiv.
[110] [John Foxe], *The Pope Confvted* (London, 1580), sig. 54v.
[111] *Ibid.*, sig. 55r.

Crede that we doe. They retaine also after a certen sort the sacraments, though they abuse them after a filthy maner. All which
do carry some prety shewe of Christianitie amongst men: not
much vnlike, as the olde Jewes in times past whilest Christ liued.[112]

In defining and illustrating the nature of the church, Foxe
uses expressions other than those already mentioned. The relationship between the church and Christ is compared to that between bride and bridegroom, or husband and wife.[113] This relationship is further illustrated by other titles given to Christ. He
is identified as "Our Shepherd . . . our Head, our Husband, our
Bishop, our Pastor, our Prince and King."[114] Reference is made
to "the Arke of his true spirituall, and visible Church,"[115] and to
the church as "the ship," which "by the hidden guidance of God,
after a stormy voyage, will be safely guided into the harbour."[116]
Christ is "the Prince and Author of the Church,"[117] and He is
asked to manifest grace to "his whole beloued church."[118] The
true churches are called "devout churches, a chaste virgin in
Christ,"[119] and "thy poor church militant."[120] The church is
referred to as a commonwealth, the republic of Christ, or a
Christian society, especially where the state is under Christian
kings. Within the universal church are particular churches and
within them, congregations.[121] Foxe does not make use of the
phrase "the mystical body of Christ" as some writers do;[122] and
when he uses the word "body" as a metaphor for the church, it
is generally with reference to Christ as the head of the universal
church: "Truly, Christ is the one Head of the universal church,
fitting, principal, and vital, from whom as Chief, derive the
vital energies for the rest of the body."[123] In the headship of
Christ rests the organic unity of the universal church; and

---

[112] *Ibid.*, sig. 55r.
[113] *FJ*, pp. 144, 335, 410; *CC*, 75–76; *Apoc.*, 27, 197, 278.
[114] *CC*, p. 69.   [115] *Cong.*, sig. iiiir.
[116] *Apoc.*, p. 118.   [117] *FJ*, pp. 33, 83.
[118] *QE* (1570), sig. iiv.   [119] *Apoc.*, pp. 28, 281.
[120] *CC*, p. 91.
[121] See chapter entitled "Church and State"; *FJ*, sig. A4r, pp. 32, 69,
225, 296.
[122] Woodhouse, *op. cit.*, pp. 43–58.
[123] *Apoc.*, pp. 8, 230–231.

through the Holy Spirit the living Christ Himself infuses grace into all the members of the body, thus creating a true spiritual and visible church.

Summarizing Foxe's concept of the nature of the church, we stress the following main features: Christ will always have a church in this world, and its unity and preservation are found in Him. The visible church is the universal church. During certain historical periods it is less easily discerned than in others. The visible church is composed of two groups of people, those by outward profession only and those by election. The latter group make up the invisible church called the church of the elect. In the latter days are found a false and a true church. The former is Antichrist, the Synagogue of Satan; and the latter is Christ's true spiritual church, His bride. However, Foxe does not go so far as to say that there is no element of the true church in Rome. Christ is the head of the universal church, but in a more specific sense He is the Head of the church of the elect. When the church is referred to as "the kingdom," it is generally in connection with present spiritual values of the Gospel or the eternal or eschatological aspects of the church. Foxe's favorite designation for the church is "the church of Christ." It is used for the church universal, but especially for the true church as opposed to the false. The true church of Christ is apostolic and catholic and in Foxe's own time visible in the church reformed. Foxe emphasizes the continuity and unity of the church, and believes the church to be one, holy, apostolic, and catholic.

III. The Marks of the Church

*T*HE SIXTEENTH-CENTURY Continental Reformers generally agreed that there are two *notae ecclesiae*. In accordance with the Augsburg Confession and other Protestant confessions of the Reformation period,[1] the Thirty-nine Articles read: "The visible Church of Christ is a congregation of faithful men, in the which the pure Word of God is preached, and the sacraments be duly ministered according to Christ's ordinance, in all those things that of necessity are requisite to the same." Foxe also points out these two marks of the church: "Christ so instituted His church that wherever the sound teaching of the Apostolic faith flourished, and the true administration of the Sacraments, there would be nothing else which anyone would need either for proper salvation or for the perfect doctrine of the Church."[2]

[1] "Augsburg Confession," art. vii, *Creed of Christendom*, III, 11–12: "But the Church is the congregation of saints [the assembly of all believers], in which the Gospel is rightly taught [purely preached] and the Sacraments rightly administered [according to the Gospel]."

John Calvin, *Institutes of the Christian Religion* (Grand Rapids, Mich., 1957), chap. IV, sec. i, para. 9, p. 289: "Wherever we see the word of God sincerely preached and heard, wherever we see the sacraments administered according to the institution of Christ, there we cannot have any doubt that the Church of God has some existence, since the promise cannot fail, 'Where two or three are gathered together in my name, there am I in the midst of them' (Matth. xviii. 20)."

[2] *Apoc.*, p. 302.

For Foxe the very constitution of the Christian society as a church is found in the preaching of the pure Word, "the Doctrine of Faith rightly taught."[3] The church is not preserved by outward succession, he states, since it "was not bound to any certain place or person, but only to faith: so that wheresoever (that is to say, in whatsoever congregation) true faith was, there was the church of Christ. And because the true faith of Christ must needs ever remain on earth, therefore the church also must needs remain on earth."[4] In another connection he writes: "The divine promise does not limit the kingdom of Christ to Rome or England or France. Wherever the spirit of truth is active, wherever there is genuine piety, wherever the instruction in evangelical doctrine is established without fermentation of error, wherever the worship of the supreme Godhead is retained undiminished—there is the church."[5] Where these things are lacking, "there the title of the church may reside but not the church itself."[6]

In his book *Of Free Justification by Christ* Foxe pinpoints what he meant by "the Doctrine of Faith rightly taught." He defines it in the following words:

> ...we should search for a righteousness, which is no moral humane vertue, but which is a Spiritual Grace and gift of God, which is not ours, but which is proper to Christ; whence he only is called holy and just, and we are called justified in him, not upon the account of works, but faith, which God imputes for righteousness unto them that believe in his name. And hence it is rightly called the righteousness of faith, and therefore faith it self is righteousness; whereby we are accounted righteous before God.[7]

Foxe calls the doctrine of free justification "that most glorious Light...purchased by the great bounty of Christ, and confirmed by the Eternal Covenant of God."[8] He also defines it as the "Doctrine of Evangelical Justification" or the "Evangelical Doctrine."[9] The one who disannuls God's promises of free grace in Christ Jesus destroys "the whole Doctrine of the

[3] *FJ*, sig. A5r.
[5] *Apoc.*, p. 12.
[7] *FJ*, p. 112.
[9] *FJ*, sig. A2v, pp. 41, 343.

[4] *AM*, I, 8.
[6] *Apoc.*, p. 12.
[8] *FJ*, pp. 1–2.

Gospel, yea and the foundations of all Religion."[10] The doctrine of justification by faith is the sign of the true spiritual church.[11]

Because Christ is the center of the Gospel, its message is called "the sound doctrine of Christ"[12] or the rule of Christ's doctrine."[13] Accordingly, Foxe asks rhetorically: "What more, I ask, could be added to the true constitution of the church than that Christ should dwell in the midst of His elect?"[14] Therefore Foxe complains that "the name of Christ and faith in Him has today scarcely any trace in our doctrine and profession."[15] He attacks Rome for the same reason.

On the other hand, "wicked and impious is the doctrine of them, first, which seek any other cause of remission, than only the blood of our Saviour; secondly, which assign any other means to apply the bloodshedding of Christ unto us, besides only faith."[16] Stating that Rome does not accept justification by faith, Foxe writes:

> This error and heresy of the church of Rome, though it seem at first sight to the natural reason of man to be but of small importance, yet, if it be earnestly considered, it is in very deed the most pernicious heresy that ever almost crept into the church; upon the which, as the only foundation, all, or the most part of all the errors, absurdities, and inconveniences of the pope's church are grounded. For, this being once admitted, that a man is not justified by his faith in Christ alone, but that other means must be sought by our own working and merits to apply the merits of Christ's passion unto us; then is there neither any certainty left of our salvation, nor end in setting up a new means and merits of our own devising for remission of sins. Neither hath there been any heresy that either hath rebelled more presumptuously against the high majesty of God the Father, nor more perniciously hath injured the souls of the simple, than this doctrine.[17]

However, Foxe is confident that the Reformation will change the error of Rome, "if only the pious representatives and preachers of the Evangelical doctrine, by Luther's example, are not remiss in their office, and disseminate, through the soul-

[10] *FJ*, p. 297.
[11] *FQP*, sig. iiiiv.
[12] *PGT*, sig. Bvv.
[13] *AM*, I, 9.
[14] *Apoc.*, p. 303.
[15] *Apoc.*, p. 39.
[16] *AM*, I, 80–81.
[17] *AM*, I, p. 72.

saving proclamation of the Evangel, the faith of Christ the Son of God, far and wide in the church."[18] Having referred to Wycliffe, Huss, Jerome, Luther, Melanchthon, Zwingli, Oecolampadius, and others, Foxe writes: "They restore the ruins of the temple of old, and the collapse of sincere doctrine, and repair by faith and piety its structure, and restore the genuine vigour of the church."[19]

In his dedication of the 1570 edition of the *Acts and Monuments*, Foxe expresses to Queen Elizabeth the hope that she will "furnish all quarters and countries of this your realm with the voice of Christ's gospel and faithful preaching of his word." He implies, of course, that only thus can the true church be established and preserved. He indicates that his own work, the *Acts and Monuments*, should add to the edification of the church:

> I thought also not vnprofitable to adioyne vnto this your godly procedings, and to the office of the ministery, the knowledge also of Ecclesiastical history, which in my mind ought not to be separate from the same: that like as by the one the people may learne the rules and preceptes of doctrine: so by the other they may haue examples of Gods mighty working in his church, to the confirmation of their faith, and the edification of Christian life.[20]

From the earliest period of Foxe's literary activities, his basic theological thinking was rooted in that proclamation of the Gospel which characterized the early creative and dynamic period of the Reformation, as illustrated in the translation of a catechism by Urbanus Regius. The latter summarizes the theme: "In so moche al the effecte and summe of our salvacion consysteth only vpon fayth and knowlage of the sonne of God Jesu Christ, all the scriptures and prophets berynge wytnes."[21] In

---

[18] *Apoc.*, pp. 291–292.   [19] *Apoc.*, p. 149.

[20] *QE* (1570), sig. iiv.

[21] Urbanus Regius, *An Instruccyon of Christen fayth howe to be bolde vp on the promyse of God and not to doubte Our Saluacyon*, translated and prefaced by John Foxe (London, 1548?), sig. Aiir.

The little catechism, *A most brief manner of Instruction* by I. F., ascribed to Foxe in the *Short Title Catalogue* (no. 11238), appears to be by John Field, ca. 1585. The only copy is now in the Folger-Shakespeare Library, Washington, D.C. See J. F. Mozley, *John Foxe and His Book* (London, 1940), p. 245.

the preface Foxe writes: "Suerly the faith in Christe is only that maketh a trew christen man: doubtyng and incredulite makyth a man no christiane."[22] Foxe also wrote a preface to one of Luther's translated sermons in which Luther clearly sets forth the distinction between Law and Grace.[23] In his treatise against Osorius, the cardinal doctrine for Foxe is justification by faith.[24] The same is true in his sermon, *Of Christ Crucified*, later republished, 1759, with a recommendatory preface by the great preacher, George Whitefield.[25] Whitefield writes that this sermon "is a specimen of that foolishness of preaching, which, in the days of our forefathers, was so mighty through God.... And would to God, that not only all the ministers of our established church, but of all the protestant reformed churches, were not only almost, but altogether, such preachers."[26]

H. F. Woodhouse reflects the teaching of the Anglican Fathers regarding the nature and marks of the church when he writes: "The foundation of the Church must be Christ and his holy Word, and he consequently is always over and above, the Lord of the Church, the Lord over the Church, to such an extent that the distinguishing fact of the Christian religion is Jesus Christ himself."[27] It has been noticed that Foxe points out this significant role of Christ when dealing both with the nature of the Church and with the Gospel rightly preached. He is also in line with the Anglican writers of the sixteenth century when they state: "The Church was known by the Word of God, and ... the Church must correspond to that Church found in the holy and canonical Scriptures."[28]

In his lengthy comparison between the primitive and later churches of Rome, Foxe uses the Scriptures as the measuring rod, for "to the word of God neither must we add, nor take from it."[29]

---

[22] *Ibid.*, sig. Avv.

[23] Martin Luther, *A Commentarie vpon the Fiftene Psalmes* (London, 1577).

[24] John Foxe, *Against Osorivs*, esp. sig. 87r–131r, 479r–481r, 502v–507r.

[25] John Foxe, *A Sermon of Christ Crucified* (1838).

[26] *CC*, p. 3.

[27] H. F. Woodhouse, *The Doctrine of the Church in Anglican Theology, 1547–1603* (London, 1954), p. 30.

[28] *Ibid.*, p. 34; see also pp. 34–37.   [29] *AM*, I, 71.

Measured by the Scriptures Rome is found no longer to be a true church. The Papists "adjoin other conditions, which the Lord in his word never appointed, nor knew." They have "done wickedly in adding (as they do) to God's word" or "in making the authority of the Scripture insufficient." Rome is teaching a doctrine which "far differeth from the true teaching of holy scripture" and is contrary to the "ordinances of the Scripture."[30]

Foxe lays great emphasis upon faithful adherence to the apostolic faith; in other words, he stresses the importance of apostolicity. Therefore he writes that the church should be judged "according to the rule of truth taught in God's word, and public examples of the ancient church of Christ in the primitive time."[31] Rome had brought in "uncatholic and almost unchristian absurdities and defections from the apostolic faith;"[32] consequently the church of Rome no longer had the mark of apostolicity and neither preached the Gospel rightly. Foxe states that "they teach not rightly, nor after the institution of the apostles and the ancient church of Rome."[33] In view of the situation created by Rome, Foxe asks: "And where now is the Grace of Imputation, and the Imputation of Faith unto Righteousness, so oft repeated in Scriptures, taught by the Apostles, testified by the most Ancient Fathers, received and delivered by the Church?"[34] He answers that the preaching of the pious ministers of the Reformation has not revived heretical doctrines, but has renewed after long intermission the doctrines of the ancient fountains of the prophets and the apostles.[35] Foxe is in harmony with the Anglican writers who as a whole would say: "If any Church seeks to be reckoned apostolic, such a Church should follow the steps and doctrine of Christ and his apostles. . . ."[36]

Throughout his writings Foxe makes reference to the early church councils and the fathers.[37] Because of the Reformation, he writes, "men were now able, by the reading of the Scriptures and the most learned Fathers, which had been for so long hidden

---

[30] *AM*, I, 72, 73, 85, 77, 83.

[32] *AM*, I, 81.

[34] *FJ*, p. 134.

[36] Woodhouse, *op. cit.*, p. 71.

[31] *AM*, I, 60.

[33] *AM*, I, 76.

[35] *Apoc.*, p. 108.

[37] See index to *AM* and *Apoc.*

in darkness and dust, and besides by the study of languages and disciplines, to judge more accurately and certainly."[38]

In some detail Foxe discusses the use of the fathers, quoting two of these to express his own opinion: "I reply with Jerome: Whatever has not the authority of Scripture is readily to be disparaged; whatever has it, is to be approved. As in Augustine's ruling: whatever in the writings of all the fathers conforms to Scripture, that only is to be accepted and held as Catholic."[39] While, as the above statements indicate, Foxe considered important the catholicity of the Christian message, this catholicity could not be separated from fidelity to the Scriptures. Analyzing the usage of the word "Catholic" among Foxe's contemporaries, Woodhouse writes: "The apostolic Church was catholic because the doctrine was perfect and was to be received and preached everywhere. Universality was equivalent to catholicity only when it was linked to verity, for catholicity meant fidelity all down the ages to . . . the retention and proclamation of a true faith."[40] This was also the way in which Foxe interpreted catholicity. When Foxe agrees to give "credit to the things contained in the Articles of the Creed, and that are expressly mentioned in the Scriptures,"[41] he follows other Elizabethan writers who "speak of the Creed as a summary of evangelical and apostolic faith and doctrine."[42]

In a time when it was not uncommon to write catechisms for Christian instruction and to formulate articles and statements of faith, Foxe, as already noticed, translated and prefaced a catechism by Urbanus Regius,[43] and he himself outlines what to him are the basic doctrines of the Scriptures. He summarizes the doctrines of Paul in nineteen points, later reducing them to five points, as follows:

First, in setting forth the grace, great love, and good will, and free promises of God the Father in Christ Jesus his Son, to mankind.

The second point consisteth in preaching and expressing the

---

[38] *Apoc.*, p. 144.
[40] Woodhouse, *op. cit.*, p. 69.
[42] Woodhouse, *op. cit.*, p. 41.

[39] *Apoc.*, p. 224.
[41] *FJ*, p. 280.
[43] Urbanus Regius, *op. cit.*

glorious and triumphant majesty of Christ Jesus the Son of God, and the excellency of his glory.

Thirdly, he declareth the virtue of his cross and passion, and what exceeding benefits proceeds to us by the same.

The fourth branch is, to teach us and inform us, to whom these benefits of Christ's passion and victory do appertain, by what means the same is applied and redoundeth unto us; which means is only one, that is, only faith in Christ Jesus, and no other thing; which faith it pleaseth almighty God to accept for righteousness. And this righteousness it is, which only standeth before God, and none other, as we are plainly taught by scriptures, and especially by the doctrine of Paul.

The fifth branch, which I note in St. Paul's doctrine, is this: that after he hath thus established us in certainty of our salvation through faith in Christ, then after that, he exhorteth us vehemently, and with all instance, to good works, showing the true use and end of good works; which is, First, to show our obedience and dutiful service (as we may) unto God, who hath done so great things for us: secondly, to relieve our neighbours with our charity and kindness, as God hath been kind to us his enemies: thirdly, to stir up others, by our example, to praise God, to embrace the same religion, and do the like. For requisite it is, that as God hath been so merciful to us and gracious in eternal gifts, we should be merciful likewize to others, in temporal commodities.[44]

He lists twenty main truths of the Scriptures:

The first principle.—As sin and death came originally by the disobedience of one to all men of his generation by nature: so righteousness and life come originally by the obedience of one to all men regenerated of him by faith and baptism (Rom. 5:17).
The second.—The promise of God was freely given to our first parents, without their deserving, that "the seed of the woman should break the serpent's head" (Gen. 3:15).
The third.—Promise was given freely to Abraham before he deserved any thing, that in "his seed all nations should be blessed" (Gen. 12:3).
The fourth.—To the word of God neither must we add, nor take from it (Deut. 4:2).
The fifth.—"He that doeth the works of the law shall live therein" (Gal. 3:12; Lev. 18:5).

[44] *AM*, I, 62–69.

The sixth.—"Accursed is he which abideth not in every thing that is written in the book of the law" (Deut. 27:26; Gal. 3:10).

The seventh.—God only is to be worshipped (Deut. 6:5; Luke 4:8).

The eighth.—"All our righteousness is like a defiled cloth of a woman" (Isa. 64:6).

The ninth.—"In all my holy hill they shall not kill nor slay, saith the Lord" (Isa. 11:9; 65:25).

The tenth.—God loveth mercy and obedience more than sacrifice (Hosea 6:6; 1 Sam. 15:22).

The eleventh.—The law worketh anger, condemneth and openeth sin (Rom. 3:19).

The twelfth.—The end of the law is Christ, to righteousness, to every one that believeth (Rom. 10:11).

The thirteenth.—Whosoever believeth and is baptized, shall be saved (Mark 16:16).

The fourteenth.—A man is justified by faith without works, freely by grace, not of ourselves (Gal. 2:16; Eph. 2:8).

The fifteenth.—There is no remission of sins without blood (Heb. 9:22).

The sixteenth.—Whatsoever is not of faith is sin (Rom. 14:23). Without faith it is impossible to please God (Heb. 11:6).

The seventeenth.—One mediator between God and man, Christ Jesus (1 Tim. 2:5). And he is the propitiation for our sins (1 John 2:2).

The eighteenth.—Whosoever seeketh by the law to be justified, is fallen from grace (Gal. 5:4).

The nineteenth.—In Christ be all the promises of God, Est and Amen (2 Cor. 1:20).

The twentieth.—Let every soul be subject to superior powers, giving to Caesar that which is Caesar's and to God that which is God's (Rom. 13:1).[45]

These "Principles, or general Verities, grounded upon the truth of God's Word" Foxe no doubt expected to be included in that preaching of the pure Word of God which should be a mark of the church. Regarding these twenty principles he comments:

> And to the end to open unto the simple reader some way whereby he may the better judge in such matters of doctrine, and not

[45] *AM*, I, 71.

be deceived in discerning truth from error; first we will propound certain principles or general positions, as infallible rules or truths of the scripture, whereby all other doctrines and opinions of men being tried and examined, as with the touchstone, may the more easily be judged whether they be true or the contrary, and whether they make against the scripture or no.[46]

The influence of Foxe's evangelical and apostolic faith is reflected in a booklet printed in 1645. It quotes Foxe's teaching on justification by faith and reprints his twenty main doctrines. The author writes: "... the first comfort I received, for the assurance of the pardon of my sinne, and justification in the sight of God, was from reading this excellent Treatise of Mr. Fox, in his Difference betwixt the Law and the Gospel."[47] This personal testimony could no doubt be multiplied. It reveals the great influence Foxe must have had in conveying to generations the central message of the Gospel.

Turning to the sacraments as the second mark of the church, Foxe states that "Christ commended only two sacraments for His church."[48] The Papists err in teaching more than two sacraments and in saying that they are "effectual without faith" and "that they give grace, and not only do signify, but also contain and exhibit that which they signify."[49] Both in attacking the sacramental system of Rome and in teaching what to him is the correct theological concept of the sacraments, Foxe emphasizes the spirituality of the Christian religion: "... the doctrine of Christ is altogether spiritual, consisting wholly in spirit and verity, and requireth no outward thing to make a true christian man, but only baptism (which is the outward profession of faith), and receiving of the Lord's supper."[50]

Writing against the doctrine of transubstantiation, Foxe asks: "If the Spirit only in the sacrament is to be partaken of, why is it not admitted that the meal is only spiritual? Why do we not, with Paul, compare spiritual things with spiritual?"[51] He answers his question in the following statement:

---

[46] *AM*, I, 70–71.

[47] Francis Cornwell, *King Jesvs is the Beleevers Prince, Priest, and Lawgiver* (London, 1645), sig. A3r–A3v.

[48] *Apoc.*, p. 245. [49] *AM*, I, 82.

[50] *AM*, I, 85. [51] *Apoc.*, p. 24.

If ye affirme it to be corporall, as was the old Religion of the Jewes consistyng in outward rites, sacrifices, ceremonies of the law: then shewe if ye can, what any one outward action or obseruation is required in Christian Religion by the scripture, as necessary in a Christian man, for remission of sinnes and saluation, saue onely the two Sacramentall ceremonies of outward Baptisme, and of the Lordes Supper? Howbeit neyther these also as they are corporall, that is to say neyther the outward action of the one, nor of the other conferreth remission of sinnes, nor saluation, but onely are visible shewes of inuisible and spirituall benefites. And furthermore if our God, whom we serue, be spirituall, how can his Religion and seruice be corporall as we are taught by the mouth of our Saviour, saying: God is a Spirite and therefore they that worship hym, must worship in spirite and veritie, etc.[52]

In his discussion of the sacraments, Foxe never omits the doctrine of faith in Christ Jesus as the only means of salvation. Having explained what faith in Christ means, he mentions that "many other things are incident also to the doctrine of our salvation"; among these are the sacraments,

Albeit as no causes therof, but eyther as Sacramentes and seales of fayth, or as declarations therof, or els as fruites and effectes following the same. So Baptisme and the Supper of the Lord be as testimonies and profes: that by our fayth onely in Christ we are iuistified, that as our bodies are washed by water, and our life nourished by bread and wine: so by the bloud of Christ, our sinnes be purged, and the hunger of our soules releued, by the death of his body.[53]

Speaking of the mystical significance of both the sacrament of baptism and the Lord's Supper, Foxe states that it "is nothing else but Faith in Christ Jesus: for as Baptism is called a Sacrament of Faith, . . . so those that are well instructed in the knowledge of Christ, understand, that to eat the flesh of Christ, is the same with believing in him."[54]

As the Jews have circumcision and the Turks the Koran as a special mark of their religion, so the Christian religion has baptism. The distinguishing characteristic of baptism is twofold: external and internal. Externally it distinguishes the believer

[53] *FQP*, sig. iiiiv.   [54] *FJ*, p. 419.
[52] *FQP*, sig. iiiiv.

from the unbeliever and thus becomes "in many ways the necessary initiation into the church."[55] and its fellowship. Rebaptism
is denied by Foxe even though the baptizer be a heretic or he
and the godfathers have taught things not in harmony with true
Christian doctrines.[56]

Baptism, which Foxe also calls "the Sacrament of Faith"[57]
and an "ordinance,"[58] consists in faith and the hidden inspiration
of the divine Spirit."[59] Thus external baptism and internal faith
given by the Spirit become a mark of the church. Furthermore
baptism distinguishes Christian from non-Christian nations,[60]
and should be administered to children.[61] Baptism is the door
into the church and brings the person into fellowship with
Christ in whom the unity of the church is found. Since baptism
confirms faith in Christ, and the baptized through the Holy
Spirit is united with Christ, baptism becomes a means to holiness.
"The baptism of water signifies the public washing of sins
through the death of Christ."[62] In another connection Foxe calls
baptism "the Sacrament of Faith in Regeneration."[63]

In Foxe's discussion of the Lord's Supper, "sola fide" is the
essential doctrine:

> If we rightly consider the nature of this Sacrament, there cannot
> be a more evident demonstration that we are justified by no other
> thing, but Faith only. For by what Argument could it more mani-
> festly set before our Eyes, how great benefit redounds to us from
> the shedding of the blood of Christ, than by the Institution of the
> Sacramental Bread and Wine, for a memorial of his Body and
> Blood?[64]

Throughout his writings Foxe refers to the Eucharist as a
figure, sign, seal, symbol, or memorial of Christ's body and
blood. Discussing the Catholic doctrine of transubstantiation he
states: "It cannot be at one and the same time both the body
and the figure, the sign of the thing and the thing signified."[65]

[55] *Apoc.*, p. 294.
[56] *AM*, I, 9.
[57] *FJ*, pp. 134, 145, 358, 419.
[58] *Apoc.*, p. 294.
[59] *Apoc.*, pp. 294–295.
[60] *Apoc.*, p. 295.
[61] *FJ*, pp. 170, 435.
[62] *Syl.*, sig. G4v.
[63] *FJ*, p. 134.
[64] *FJ*, p. 419. See also Foxe, *The Pope Confvted*, sig. 95v.
[65] *Apoc.*, p. 25.

Foxe finds his own concept of the Eucharist to be that held by the Protestants in general. He writes:

> ... but al ingeneral with one voyce do proclaime that bread and wine is a signe of Christs body and blood: some call it a figure, others an exemplar, others a type, some a likenesse and token, many a memorial, and al with one voice confesse too bee a sacrament of the body: of some the body is sayde to bee represented by the bread, of many too bee shewed, of others too be signified, and many also too bee figured.[66]

Foxe's claim of a common Protestant theology of the Eucharist must be modified. His definition seems applicable only to the Reformed theologians; he disapproves of Lutheran concepts, even though he expresses great regard for Luther. In the preface to one of Luther's translated sermons, Foxe writes: "I wyll not say this author in all poynts to stand vp ryght and absolutely, as in the sacramentes, but what humane wryter hathe there ever bene but some defaute he hathe left behynd hym. Also Peter was not without his reprehension. In euery thyng the best is to be taken."[67]

The Papists are wrong in administering this sacrament under the form of bread only. Accordingly Foxe commends King Edward VI for reestablishing the practice, instituted by Christ and used by the apostles and the early church, "that the said holy sacrament should be ministered unto all christian people under both the kinds of bread and wine."[68]

In the *Acts and Monuments* the denial of the doctrine of transubstantiation is often the main issue and the chief reason for martyrdom. In some instances Foxe makes comments revealing his personal views of the Eucharist, as for example in the case of Bishop Peacock of Chichester,[69] who was afflicted and tormented in 1457, as well as in the case of the Oxford dispute of 1554.[70] In both instances Foxe emphasizes his concept of the bread and wine as figures and symbols, and participation in the Lord's Supper as an act of remembrance of Christ's sacrifice on

---

[66] Foxe, *The Pope Confvted*, sig. 101r.
[67] Martin Luther, *A Frutfull Sermon* (1547?), sig. Aiiv.
[68] *AM*, V, 715.   [69] *AM*, III, 724–734.
[70] *AM*, VI, 439–520.

the cross. He also stresses faith as the only means of salvation.

Early in Queen Elizabeth's reign, circa 1560–1564, Foxe wrote a single Latin work of 152 pages on the Eucharist.[71] It was dedicated to John Harding, principal of Brasenose College, Oxford, in gratitude for the help he gave Foxe as a young man in pursuing his university studies. Now he hopes with Harding's help to draw the attention of students and theologians to his study on the Eucharist. There follows a letter and appeal to the popes and the people of the Roman Church; we will refer to this later. The first part of the treatise proper presents, in the form of syllogisms, arguments and proofs on either side of the controversy about transubstantiation. Next is furnished a theological explanation of Christ's statement: "This is My body." A very short exposition of chapter 6 of the Gospel of John concludes Foxe's treatise. What already has been noticed regarding Foxe's view of the Eucharist is confirmed in the *Syllogisticon*.

Foxe's arguments against transubstantiation echo those of the Reformed theologians. Christ's words, "This is My body," should be understood as parable or metaphor, such as when the disciples are called the salt of the earth or the light of the world and when Christ calls Himself the vine, the shepherd, or the bread of heaven.[72] Further, the doctrine of transubstantiation denies the spirituality of the Christian religion and makes it corporal.

Foxe's basic idea in this exposition is that the true food and spiritual nourishment is "the eating of His flesh," but he adds: "you understand that [salvation is] not by the bread of the Eucharist, nor by the drinking of the blood, but by the power of His passion and faith in Him, who offered Himself to save us sinners by His blood."[73] The important point, which Foxe wishes to stress, is "that only faith in Jesus Christ can give salvation and justification to men."[74] Therefore, no matter how deeply a person wishes to scrutinize the meaning of the bread and the wine, he will have to begin by contemplating the passion of Christ and its effect.[75] Accordingly Foxe writes: "This sacra-

---

[71] John Foxe, *Syllogisticon* (London, 1560–1564?).
[72] *Syl.*, sig. 1v, G1r.   [73] *Syl.*, sig. I6r–I6v.
[74] *Syl.*, sig. I6v.   [75] *Syl.*, sig. G3v–G4r.

ment of the Lord's table indicates nothing other than the ordinary earthly food by means of which the passion of Christ is provided for us all."[76] Christ was not intending that the bread should be transubstantiated into His body, and the wine into His blood, "but, through these external and material symbols of bread and drink [was] striving to place thereupon before our eyes the very power and operation of His passion."[77] This is for Foxe the *mysterium sacramenti*, the "underlying wisdom," and "the most hidden mystery of his body."[78]

The doctrine of ubiquity, that Christ's body can be both in heaven and in the Eucharist at one and the same time, is contrary to observed truth. The absurdity of the "ubiquity" is especially demonstrated through the doctrine of the resurrection of Christ and His promise of the Paraclete.

> Unless Christ had departed in the body, completely from us, in no way could the Spirit have come on our behalf, as Christ so plainly promised to Philip. Wherefore the Holy Spirit comes to fill the place vacated by the Lord, as we read in the Gospel: Unless I depart, the Paraclete cannot come unto you. Now in what way can you say that he who is absent is present with you? But these things are so clear that almost all the doctors agree, for with one voice they say that the Presence in the sacrament cannot be held to be other than a mystery.[79]

The resurrection and ascension of Christ teach a "local" presence of the body of Christ in heaven, and consequently the resurrected Lord is above the earthly elements in the Eucharist. The Holy Spirit came to fill the place vacated by the ascension of the Lord,[80] and Christ comes now not in order to be eaten, but that "He might minister in the Spirit." It is true that for man "Christ is food, but that of the spirit, not of the body."[81]

In the closing paragraph of his exposition Foxe expresses his soteriological concept of the Eucharist: "Just as bread, taken into the stomach, is employed for the nourishment and increment of the body, so Christ, received through faith, quickens and strengthens all and renews the spirit; and that is the sole

---

[76] *Syl.*, sig. G4v–G5r.
[78] *Syl.*, sig. F5v, G1r, G15r.
[80] *Syl.*, sig. G1v.

[77] *Syl.*, sig. G5r.
[79] *Syl.*, sig. G2r.
[81] *Syl.*, sig. G5v.

meaning."[82] This means that for Foxe there is a positive and dynamic side to the sacrament, which is expressed also in his comments on the Oxford dispute.

In the month of March 1554, Archbishop Cranmer, Bishop Ridley, and Master Latimer were summoned to the University of Oxford to dispute with some of the professors of both Oxford and Cambridge. The question for discussion was the Eucharist. Foxe quotes the disputation in detail[83] and points out three basic errors of the Papists. First, "they consider not the nature of a sacrament; which is, not to exhibit the thing in deed which it doth represent, but to represent effectually one thing by another." The second error is "that they consider not the operation of faith, which, penetrating up to heaven, there apprehendeth the real body of Christ, no less, yea, and more effectually, than if he were here bodily present to the eye." The Papists seemed not to regard "the operation of Christ's passion enough, or else, not to feel the heavy torment of sin and miserable hunger of man's soul; which, if they did not feel, they would easily perceive what a necessary and opportune nourishment to man's conscience, were the body of Christ on the cross broken, and his blood shed."[84] Another point the Papists overlook is the spiritual eating of Christ without the sacrament. Foxe writes:

> ... they see not, neither do consider, how Christ is eaten, not only with the symbols of sacrament, but also without the sacrament: which eating standeth inwardly by faith, and pertaineth to the spirit of man, in apprehending or digesting with the stomach of faith those things which by the outward sacrament are represented.[85]

Foxe clarifies the points under discussion in the Oxford dispute: "The body of Christ, either to be present with us, or to be eaten of us, or to be united to us; which presence, eating, and uniting of him to us, standeth three manner of ways, Really, Spiritually, and Sacramentally."[86] In a table Foxe defines the "manner of ways" in which the body of Christ should be understood, and it presents the most comprehensive statement regard-

[82] *Syl.*, sig. G6r.
[84] *AM*, VI, 521–522.
[86] *AM*, VI, 521.

[83] *AM*, VI, 439–520.
[85] *AM*, VI, 522.

ing his view of the Eucharist.[87] It should be noticed that in his description of the operation of the sacraments Foxe suggests a concept which C. W. Dugmore, in his discussion of the Oxford dispute, calls "the Reformed Catholic, or Augustinian realist-symbolist tradition of eucharistic doctrine handed down from the days of the early Church."[88] Foxe writes that the sacraments themselves do not "give life and salvation, but that they are certain means and instruments of that life and salvation, which cometh to us from God."[89] By the words "certain means and instruments," Foxe expresses the same concept of the sacraments as that held by the Reformed theologians when they signed "Consensus Tigurinus" in order to define a view more positive than Zwingli's. The "Consensus Tigurinus" calls the sacraments "marks and badges of Christian profession," and adds "that God by means of them attests, represents, and seals His Grace in us."[90] While this statement falls short of Dugmore's definition referred to above, there is in Foxe's comment, as in "Consensus Tigurinus," "at least an echo of Augustine's belief that while the res sacramenti is distinct from the sacramentum, or signum, the two cannot be wholly disjoined, because a sign is only a sign in that it causes us to think of that which it signifies."[91] Accordingly, Foxe touches the periphery of the "realist-symbolist tradition."

Both in the introduction of the *Syllogisticon*, and in the evaluation of the Oxford dispute in the Latin edition of the *Acts and Monuments*, Foxe expresses great sorrow over the discord among Christians because of different concepts of the Eucharist. He has in mind not only the conflict between the Catholics and the Protestants on account of the doctrine of transubstantiation but is no doubt also thinking of the eucharistic controversies between Luther and Zwingli, as well as Joachim Westphal's

[87] See Appendix.

[88] C. W. Dugmore, *The Mass and the English Reformers* (London, 1958), p. 200.

[89] *AM*, VI, 524. See appendix.

[90] "Consensus Tigurinus," art. vii, *Documents Illustrative of the Continental Reformation*, ed. B. J. Kidd (Oxford, 1911), p. 653.

[91] Dugmore, *op. cit.*, p. 162.

attack upon Calvin, the followers of "Consensus Tigurinus," and the Melanchthonians.

> Now while each holds to his own opinion and faction fights with faction, hardly paying attention to the arguments of others, almost all freedom of letters perishes. Leaders of different schools and opinions almost lose sight of justice and amenity as they contest in tribunals with bitterness, hatred, favouritism, and clamouring, and so there are multiple disputations and nothing seems to come out of it all.[92]

In words demonstrating his desire for peace and concord Foxe writes: "I know that these important matters are everywhere strenuously contested, not only in England, but abroad, even among brethren of the same Gospel and congregation." This is so much more regrettable since the Eucharist should be "the symbol of peace and harmony."[93] In *Syllogisticon* he writes a letter of appeal to the pope, saying: "Since we see that so many and so great storms of contention about the nature and material of one sacrament have been fermented among Christians, the unbroken communion of that internal charity can scarcely ever be restored while we quarrel so persistently ourselves about the sacred communion."[94]

While Foxe recognizes that it may be difficult to be optimistic, nevertheless he states: "I trust we shall not cast away all good hope of healing these wounds, so that from the theological schools some help may come to subdue gradually this tyranny."[95] He then expresses his desire to be a peacemaker: "O that indeed, like the ancient fabled lute of Orpheus, I might at last be able by your decision or by this speech of mine, to call back your minds from this inveterate and pertinacious dissension to unity or at least some condition of concord."[96] There is no doubt that Foxe hoped that his record of the eucharistic disputes, as well as his personal writings on this subject, would be an aid to convince the Papists of their faults and heal the eucharistic conflict as a whole.

C. W. Dugmore, in his analysis of John Bale's concept of

---

[92] *Syl.*, sig. A4r.
[94] *Syl.*, sig. A5r.
[96] *Syl.*, sig. A4v.

[93] *AM* (1559), p. 639.
[95] *Syl.*, sig. A4r.

the Eucharist, notices Bale's violent attack upon the Papacy and the doctrine of transubstantiation. Having quoted Bale, he states:

> This violent passage is typical both of Bale and of the language of many of the popular attacks on the Mass published at the beginning of the reign of Edward VI. It was occasioned by the crude realism of the later fourteenth and fifteenth century popular teaching which we have noted above, but that does not excuse the well-nigh blasphemous language of Bale and some of his contemporaries.[97]

Foxe, both before and during the Marian exile, was a close associate of Bale. He too made strong attacks upon the Papacy, yet his approach to the Papists, not only in the discussion of the doctrine of transubstantiation but on other subjects as noticed elsewhere, reveals a somewhat different spirit from that of Bale.

Comparing the different concepts of the Eucharist, it has been proposed that the three reformers, "Bucer, Calvin and Martyr, represent a unified theology of ecumenical dimensions and purpose, reflecting their historical position as united in a task of reformation which was essentially catholic."[98] The sacramental unity is found in the "Consensus Tigurinus." It appears that Foxe has a good right to occupy a position in this triumvirate.

While it was common to designate two marks of the church, a third, discipline, was implied in the teaching and practices of the Reformed church and was directly stated in the "Scotch Confession of Faith" (1560; art. xviii), the "Belgic Confession" (1561; art. xix), and the "Hiedelberg Catecism" (1563; quest. 83).[99] Practical applications of the doctrine of discipline can be traced back to the establishment of a domestic relations court in Zürich. In 1525 certain regulations were formulated regarding matrimonial matters. Zwingli was the main author of this document[100] as well as the inspiration behind the matrimonial tribune,

---

[97] Dugmore, *op. cit.*, p. 235.

[98] Joseph C. McLelland, *The Visible Word of God: An Exposition of the Sacramental Theology of Peter Martyr Vermigli* (London, 1957), p. 280.

[99] Schaff, *Creeds of Christendom*, III, 337, 419, 462.

[100] Zwingli, *Opera*, Vol. II, Sec. ii, 356–359. "Ordnung und ausehen, wie hinfür zu Zürich in der statt über eelich sachen gericht soll werden" (May

the so-called Zürcher Ehegericht.[101] Laws and regulations, including discipline and punishments, to guide the magistrate in cases of divorce and other marriage problems were laid down. These injunctions were supposed to be in harmony with the teaching of Christ, thus making it possible for the magistrate to act from a "thus saith the Lord."[102] In other words, Zwingli sought to realize the principle that nothing is more conducive to the exercise of secular authority than the teaching of Christ. Seen in historical perspective this is significant, for it has correctly been pointed out that the Zürcher Ehegericht was the real ancestor of the Genevan Consistory.[103] In turn Calvin's Geneva became the cradle of Presbyterianism and Puritanism with their theory of social ethics, which was based upon the Bible and brought into relationship with the universal kingdom of God.

Discipline as a third *nota ecclesiae* is mentioned earlier in England than on the Continent. In "The Form and Manner of Making and Consecrating Bishops, Priests, and Deacons," this third mark is pointed out in the editions of both 1549–50 and 1552. At the time of his ordination the priest is asked:

> Will you then give your faithful diligence always, so to minister the doctrine and Sacraments, and the discipline of Christ, as the Lord hath commanded, and as this realm hath received the same, according to the commandments of God, so that you may teach the people committed to your cure and charge, with all diligence to keep and observe the same?[104]

10, 1525). See also "Züricher Chorgerichtsordnung," in Aemilius Ludwig Richter, *Die evangelischen Kirchenordnungen des sechzehnten Jahrhunderts* (Weimar, 1846), I, 21–22.

101 "Ordnung und satzung von ei(ne)m ersamen R. der stadt Zürich von wegen der straf des ebruchs und unelicher biwonung" (Dec. 15, 1526), printed in Emil Egli, *Achtensammlung zur Geschichte der Zürcher Reformation in den Jahren* 1519–1533 (Zürich, 1879), Nr. 1087, pp. 521–523.

102 For a further discussion see V. Norskov Olsen, *The New Testament Logia on Divorce* (Tübingen, 1971), pp. 67–70.

103 Walther Köhler, *Zürcher Ehegericht und Genfer Konsistorium* (Leipzig, 1932–1942).

104 *The Two Liturgies . . . in the Reign of King Edward VI*, Parker Society (Cambridge, 1844), pp. 177, 346.

It is generally recognized that Martin Bucer wrote *De Ordinatione Legitima Ministrorum Ecclesiae Revocanda* in order to influence Cranmer in the composition of his ordination rites, and that he to a very large degree succeeded in doing so.[105] During Bucer's sojourn in England from April 1549 to his death two years later, he wrote *De Regno Christi* (1550) and dedicated it to the young King Edward as a token of appreciation;[106] however, it was first printed in Basel in 1557.[107] This work aimed to reveal the nature of the kingdom of Christ and to point out the ways and means whereby it could be established.[108] The book was esteemed by theologians in England and elsewhere, being translated into French[109] and German.[110] Nearly a century after its dedication to Edward VI, John Milton translated into English large sections dealing with marriage and divorce.[111] The original Latin edition is composed of two hundred and forty-nine folio pages, and nearly one third deals with marriage matters, especially divorce. The work reflects the philosophy behind the Zürcher Ehegericht and the Genevan Consistory in seeking to make real the concept that nothing is more vital to successful exercise of secular authority than the teaching of Christ.

Bucer concludes his discussion of "what the Kingdom of Christ is, and what is necessary for its restoration" by stating: "The duties of this sacred ministry include the teaching of

[105] E. C. Ratcliff, "The Liturgical Work of archbishop Cranmer," *Journal of Ecclesiastical History*, Vol. VII, no. 2, p. 201; Jasper Ridley, *Thomas Cranmer* (Oxford, 1962), pp. 307–308.

[106] Burnet, *The History of the Reformation of the Church of England*, Vol. II, pt. i, p.156.

[107] Martin Bucer, *De Regno Christi Iesu seruatoris nostri* (Basel, 1557).

[108] An analysis of *De Regno Christi* has been made by W. Pauck, *Das Reich Gottes auf Erden* (Berlin, 1928).

[109] Martin Bucer, *Deux Livres dv Royavme de Iesvs Christ Nostre Savvevr* (n.p., 1558).

[110] Martin Bucer, *The Ivdgement of Martin Bucer, concerning Divorce das selbige von allen Christlichen Oberkeiten anzustellen, vnd ins werck zubringen seye* (Strassburg, 1563). A rare copy of this edition is found in Bibliothèque du Consistoire, Colmar, France.

[111] Martin Bucer, *The Ivdgement of Martin Bucer, concerning Divorce* (London, 1644), printed in *The Works of John Milton* (New York, 1931), IV, 1–61.

Christ, the dispensation of his sacraments, and the administration of his discipline."[112] Thus we find that the Ordinal of 1549–50 and 1552 and Bucer's *De Regno Christi* (1550) express the identical view; further, they seem to contain the earliest direct statements regarding a threefold sign of the true church.

Peter Martyr, or Pietro Martiri Vermigli, was a close associate of Bucer during his professorship at the University of Strassburg from 1542 to 1547. He accepted Cranmer's invitation and came to England in 1547, two years before Bucer, and remained there until 1553. His first lectures as Regius Professor of Divinity at Oxford were on the First Epistle to the Corinthians. Although his commentary on this epistle was printed posthumously in 1567, as were most of his other commentaries, there is good reason to believe that it represents his teaching at Oxford. In his comments on I Corinthians 1:2, he characterizes the true church:

> And to define it, we say that it is a company of believers (coetum credentium), and of the regenerate, whom God gathers together in Christ, through the Word, and Holy Spirit, and governs through the ministers by purity of doctrine, by the lawful use of the sacraments, and by discipline.[113]

In his treatise "De Schismate," the same three notes are emphasized: "the three marks of the Church which are wont to be shown by men of our side, namely doctrine, the right administration of the Sacraments, and the care of discipline."[114]

The political theorist John Ponet, who became chaplain to Cranmer in 1547 and successively bishop of Rochester and Winchester, had much influence with Cranmer. A short catechism issued by the King's authority is attributed to Ponet. This catechism was published together with the Edwardian Articles of 1553. In defining the true church Ponet confirms discipline as a significant mark:

> The marks therefore of this church are: first, pure preaching of the gospel: then brotherly love, out of which, as members of

---

[112] Martin Bucer, *De Regno Christi*, as translated by Wilhelm Pauck, *Melanchthon and Bucer*, the Library of Christian Classics, vol. xix (Philadelphia, 1969), p. 232. See also *Martini Bvceri Opera Latina*, ed. F. Wendel (Paris and Gutersloh, 1955), XV, 62.

[113] Quoted by Joseph C. McLelland, *op. cit.*, p. 123.

[114] *Ibid.*, p. 125.

all one body, springeth good will of each to other: thirdly, upright and uncorrupted use of the Lord's sacraments, according to the ordinance of the gospel: last of all, brotherly correction, and excommunication, or banishing those out of the church, that will not amend their lives. This mark the holy fathers termed discipline.[115]

Nicholas Ridley, who during the reign of Edward VI worked closely with Cranmer in carrying through the English Reformation, also left his testimony regarding the marks of the church. In the record of some conversations between him and Hugh Latimer while they were in prison prior to their execution in 1555, we read:

> The holy catholic or universal church, which is the communion of saints, the house of God, the city of God, the spouse of Christ, the body of Christ, the pillar and stay of the truth; this church I believe, according to the Creed: this church I do reverence and honour in the Lord. But the rule of this church is the word of God, according to which rule we go forward unto life. 'And as many as walk according to this rule,' I say with the St. Paul, 'peace be upon them and upon Israel, which pertaineth unto God.' (Gal. vi.) The guide of this church is the Holy Ghost. The marks whereby this church is known unto me in this dark world, and in the midst of this crooked and froward generation, are these— the sincere preaching of God's word; the due administration of the sacraments; charity; and faithful observing of ecclesiastical discipline according to the word of God.[116]

In the interval between the accession of Queen Elizabeth and the acceptance of the Thirty-nine Articles, Archbishop Parker, the northern metropolitan, and other English prelates formulated, in 1559 or early 1560, the Eleven Articles as a provisional

---

[115] "A Short Catechism, or Plain Instruction, containing the Sum of Christian Learning, set forth by the King's Majesty's Authority, for all Schoolmasters to teach." See *The Two Liturgies ... in the Reign of King Edward VI*, p. 513.

[116] "Certain Godly, Learned, and Comfortable Conference between the two Reverend Fathers and Holy Martyrs, Dr. Nicholas Ridley, Late Bishop of London and Master Hugh Latimer, Sometime bishop of Worcester, during the time of their imprisonment." *The Works of Nicholas Ridley*, Parker Society (Cambridge, 1841), pp. 122–123.

test of orthodoxy.[117] Article Three supports the third mark of the church: "I do acknowledge also that Church to be the spouse of Christ, wherein the word of God is truly taught, the sacraments orderly ministered according to Christ's institution, and the authority of the keys duly used."[118]

Although the Thirty-nine Articles, along with the Forty-two Articles, state only two *notae ecclesiae*, the third seems to be indirectly confirmed. Article XXVI deals with the question "of consecration of Bishops and ministers," and instructs that the clergy be ordained in accordance with the injunction of the Edwardian Ordinal, which, we have already noticed, instructs the priest to subscribe to a threefold mark of the church.

The significant place given by the English Reformers to the doctrine of discipline, reflected in the official statements of faith, was a product of the English Reformation as such and not merely a result of influences from across the English Channel. This is illustrated in the formulation of new ecclesiastical laws of which the *Reformatio Legvm Ecclesiasticarvm* was a result.

During 1534, when Henry VIII made his break with Rome complete, a commission was appointed to frame a new set of ecclesiastical laws to reverse and replace the old existing canon laws. The work seems to have been completed in 1545 or 1546, but it never received the official sanction of the King, no doubt because of the opposition of Gardiner and other Roman Catholic bishops who considered this enterprise an innovation.[119] No copy of these revised laws is in existence, but they are generally considered to be different from those formulated during the next reign, when Edward VI appointed a commission for the establishment of a new code of ecclesiastical laws. The commission was composed of thirty-two members: eight bishops, eight divines, eight laymen, and eight lawyers.[120] In letters to Bullinger written during the year 1552, Peter Martyr and Martin

[117] Charles Hardwick, *A History of the Articles of Religion* (London, 1888), pp. 117–118; Schaff, *Creeds of Christendom*, III, 615.

[118] Hardwick, *op. cit.*, p. 357.

[119] Strype, *Memorials of Cranmer*, Vol. I, pt. xxx, pp. 132–133.

[120] Strype, *Memorials of Cranmer*, Vol. II, pt. xxvi, p. 271; Vol. II, pt. xxxv, p. 299.

Micronius tell him about the work of the commission, hoping that the new laws will obtain the sanction of the Parliament and that the present opposition will be ineffectual.[121] While the report of the commission was a result of the work of the whole committee, it seems that Archbishop Cranmer and Peter Martyr carried the main responsibility.[122]

The work was completed before the end of Edward's reign, and Cranmer was eager to have the reformed canon law adopted, but the record reads: "[Cranmer] with indefatigable Pains had been, both in this and the last King's Reign, labouring to bring this Matter about, and he did his part, for he brought the Work to perfection. But it wanted the King's Ratification, which was delayed, partly by Business, and partly by Enemies."[123] During the reign of Mary the religious situation was reversed, but when Elizabeth came to the throne the report of the commission was read in Parliament, although no action was taken. In the Convocation in 1563, the matter was brought up anew by Bishop Sandys, again with no result. The next and final step in the history of the new ecclesiastical laws was taken in 1571. With the permission of Archbishop Parker a new edition was presented to Parliament, which discussed its acceptance. "But it made no progress. The Queen, averse to all interference of the Commons in ecclesiastical matters had conceived an especial displeasure against the individuals by whom the measure was recommended."[124] The *Reformatio Legvm Ecclesiasticarvm* was composed during the years when the Edwardian Reformers "creedalized" the doctrine of discipline as the third mark of the church. There is no doubt that the new ecclesiastical laws were intended to be a basis for a needed restoration of discipline, for they stipulated a local church board which would administer discipline and bring before the congregation names of members liable for excommunication. When the bishops came for visitation they

---

[121] *Original Letters, Letter* CCXXXVI, Vol. II, p. 503; Letter CCLXVII, Vol. II, p. 580.

[122] John Foxe, ed., *Reformatio Legvm Ecclesiasticarvm* (London, 1571; repr. Oxford, 1850). See preface by Edward Cardwell, p. vi.

[123] Strype, *Memorials of Cranmer*, Vol. II, pt. xxvi, p. 271.

[124] Foxe, *Reformatio Legvm Ecclesiasticarvm*, p. xi.

were obliged to find out not only if the first two marks of the church were evident in the life and worship of the congregation but also if church discipline was exercised.[125]

The English Reformers apparently envisaged discipline within an episcopalian framework as the right form of government for the Church of England. Elizabeth's rejection of the *Reformatio Legvm Ecclesiasticarvm* illustrates their failure to bring this to pass. The doctrine of discipline is commonly associated with Presbyterian Puritanism. May it be suggested that if this doctrine, as an outgrowth of pietistic motives, has any part in formulating the concept of Puritanism, then the English Reformers might be classified as Anglican Puritans. What was the position of John Foxe on the doctrine of discipline, and did he play any part in stating it in definite terms? We do not find him defining it directly as a third mark; however, he employs the doctrine to that effect.

In 1550 Foxe was ordained Deacon by Bishop Ridley of St. Paul's. At this occasion the Edwardian Ordinal was used for the first time. Although Foxe was not ordained priest until 1560, he was no doubt acquainted with the clause of discipline to which the priest had to subscribe. Foxe had no active part in formulating the *Reformatio Legvm Ecclesiasticarvm* during the reign of Edward VI, but he definitely was in harmony with the endeavors. In 1551 he himself wrote a smaller treatise, one of his earliest works, on the subject of excommunication, which was also thoroughly discussed in the new ecclesiastical laws. Further, it was Foxe who was commissioned with the permission of Archbishop Parker to edit the 1571 edition. Thus Foxe in his own life and writings links the endeavors for discipline during the reign of Edward VI with those progressive Reformers during the early years of Elizabeth's reign who worked and hoped for a more thorough reformation in line with the new ecclesiastical injunctions. Having analyzed the question of discipline among the Anglican writers during the Elizabethan period, H. F. Woodhouse writes that discipline would "include the power to excommunicate and to receive the repentant back again; to maintain and keep order; and to exercise correction

---

[125] *Ibid.*, pp. 93–94, p. 133.

where needed. Such discipline is very necessary."[126] In his discussion of excommunication Foxe deals with these aspects. We
should further notice, as a general observation regarding this
treatise, that discipline and its correlative, excommunication,
have not only a theological significance, but are also of practical
importance for society as a whole. The formula of success or
failure for the state is religious: obey God and be blessed; dis-
obey and be cursed.

This treatise of 74 pages is directed to the archbishop of Canterbury, the other bishops, and the clergy as a whole. In the
opening paragraph Foxe addresses them: "I venture to press on
you this treatise of what is so important to me. I dare to solicit
your interest—I who am but a rustic. Not I alone, but Christ
Himself, and the universal church beg with tears your concern.
I believe you will accept this responsibility." There is reason
to believe that Foxe's appeal and the work itself encouraged
the discussion of discipline during the formative and formulative
period of the English Reformation.

Following the dedicatory preface and a lengthy appeal on
the significance of ecclesiastical censure and excommunication,
Foxe treats excommunication in nine chapters: One, what excommunication means; two, its necessity and practicability;
three, the form of excommunication which should be used and
why; four, against what sins should it be chiefly employed; five,
about extravagance and certain other follies; six, regarding not
associating with the excommunicated, and the purpose and ends
of excommunication; seven, concerning the distinction between
the two governments, and the need of repentance; eight, the
chief obstacles that impede excommuncation; nine, who should
administer excommunication.

Foxe begins his discussion by stating that "the Christian
church . . . has lapsed from discipline."[127] To the Christian ministry has been entrusted the spiritual sword, which should lead
to that purity prescribed in God's Word. Preaching and teaching will have little effect except there "be added correction and
sedulous castigation."[128] Foxe points out that the Scriptural basis

---

[126] Woodhouse, *op. cit.*, p. 107. [127] *Exc.*, sig. A4v.
[128] *Exc.*, sig. A7r.

for excommunication is found in Acts 13, I Corinthians 5, and
1 Timothy 1 and 5.[129] Excommunication was also mentioned by
the Fathers,[130] and the authority to exercise excommunication
remains with the church as "it shares in the gifts of Christ and
the keys of Peter";[131] accordingly, Foxe admonishes "that the
old and apostolic discipline be restored in the Church of
Christ."[132]

Foxe defines excommunication, as would be expected, as
nothing else than removal from the general Congregation of
Christ";[133] excommunicants are thus separated from the church's
belief "in one faith, one God, and one baptism, as is contained
in the same sacraments, and offers the same hope of salvation to
all. Without this there is no participation in grace."[134] The latter
statement clearly indicates Foxe's belief that there is no salvation
outside the church. He further writes: "Excommunication is
exile from the church, and can be termed death of the spirit,
until the person is received back into grace by the Church."[135]

Foxe distinguishes between two forms of excommunication.
The lowest form, private or pastoral excommunication,[136] is a
censure of anyone who by word or act associates with those
who appear alienated from the institution and purity of Christians. The pastor or any member of the church should privately
warn such a person by a severe glance and sharply rebuke him.[137]
Foxe has in mind the duty, right, and power of the church to
control its members and exercise necessary discipline by warning and rebuke. Actual excommunication Foxe calls "the second
grade of excommunication"; that is, when the church of one
spirit assembles "together openly, in public congregation, and
proscribes some one from the records of Christians."[138] However, Foxe emphasizes that this form should be used only in
most extreme cases "when either private admonition produced
no effect, or when something outstanding has been committed

---

[129] *Exc.*, sig. A7v–A8r.
[131] *Exc.*, sig. B3r.
[133] *Exc.*, sig. C2v.
[135] *Exc.*, sig. C3r.
[137] *Exc.*, sig. C4r.

[130] *Exc.*, sig. A8v.
[132] *Exc.*, sig. B7v–B8r.
[134] *Ibid.*
[136] *Exc.*, sig. C4r–v.
[138] *Exc.*, sig. C6r.

which involves public disgrace to the Church, and his own fall."[139]

Foxe considers excommunication to be not only useful but "even more necessary."[140] He sees deplorable results which could have been avoided had this censure not been neglected.[141] He therefore appeals to the Christian ministry to improve the spiritual and moral condition of the church "by sharply refuting, warning, rebuking and by excommunicating."[142] Foxe also stresses the great influence of the pastor's right example as well as his sincerity and dignity when dealing with those who must be censured.[143]

Against what sins should excommunication be used? Foxe enumerates them as adultery, incest, blasphemy, idolatry, perjury, violation of parents and magistrates, rebellion, heresy, murder, and robbery.[144] In the case of lesser faults, the pastor should make it clear that correction is necessary and "should be ready to admonish where advice and warning is called for."[145] The purpose of excommunication is that the guilty party be made to see his sin and be ashamed, and thus be led to better spiritual health.[146] In view of Foxe's statements on excommunication, it would be correct to say that in this small treatise he implies that discipline is a mark of the church.

While most theologians affirm two *notae ecclesiae* and the Edwardian Reformers list three, we should notice that a fourth is listed both by Ridley and in the catechism ascribed to Ponet. Ridley adds "charity," and Ponet, "brotherly love, out of which, as members of all one body, springeth good will of each to other."[147] Foxe does not mention this fourth mark directly; yet, few, if any, emphasize its reality so strongly. Its significance is taken for granted throughout his writing. It is rooted in his own charismatic nature and humanistic upbringing, but it is also considered by him to be the essence of true Gospel teaching and the ground for religious toleration.

139 *Ibid*.
140 *Exc.*, sig. C6v.
141 *Exc.*, sig. C7.
142 *Exc.*, sig. C7v.
143 *Exc.*, sig. C8v–D2r, D8v–E1r.
144 *Exc.*, sig. D5.
145 *Exc.*, sig. D6r.
146 *Exc.*, sig. Ev.
147 See p. 145 above.

IV. The Church and Its Ministry

*I*N THE DEBATE between John Whitgift and Thomas Cartwright after the publication of *An Admonition to the Parliament* in 1572, both men quote Foxe in order to substantiate their
views. Both also express great personal regard for him. Their
references to Foxe, in the midst of critical conflict concerning
the ministry within the Elizabethan Church, make a suitable
beginning for an examination of Foxe's concept of the ministry
of the church.

Whitgift closes the part of *The Defence of the Answer to
the Admonition* dealing with episcopal authority and clerical
superiority "with the very words of that worthy man (who hath
so well deserved of this church of England), Master Fox." Whitgift quotes Foxe saying:

> "In the eccesiastical state we take not away the distinction of
> ordinary degrees, such as by the scripture be appointed, or by the
> primitive church allowed, as patriarchs or archbishops, bishops,
> ministers, and deacons; for of these four we especially read as
> chief: in which four degrees as we grant diversity of office, so we
> admit in the same also diversity of dignity; neither denying that
> which is due to each degree, neither yet maintaining the ambition
> of any singular person. For, as we give to the minister place above
> the deacon, to the bishop above the minister, to the archbishop
> above the bishop, so we see no cause of inequality why one minis-
> ter should be above another minister, one bishop in his degree
> above another bishop to deal in his diocese, or one archbishop

above another archbishop; and this is to keep an order duly and truly in the church, according to the true nature and definition of order by the authority of Augustine, . . . (Order is a disposition of things equal and unequal, attributing to each their proper places)." Hitherto M. Fox.[1]

Thomas Cartwright, in his *Reply to the Answer*, seeks at some length to undo the strength of this quotation. He first refers to the fact that Whitgift mentions neither the name nor the page of the book from which he quotes. Cartwright suggests the reason to be "either for fear that the place should be found, that there might be answer, or for fear that M. Fox should give me the solution, which hath given you the objection."[2] He expresses himself willing to subscribe to all the good which Whitgift says about Foxe but challenges Whitgift's knowledge of the *Acts and Monuments*: "I think I have read more of him than you. For I have read over his Book of Martyrs, and so I think did never you."[3] He further states that Whitgift's quotation does not say what it appears to say, if it is read in its context. In this connection Cartwright's opinion of Foxe as a historiographer should be noticed. He writes:

> Moreover, I say that M. Fox, writing a story, doth take greater pain, and looketh more diligently to declare what is done, and in what time, and by whom, than how justly or unjustly, how conveniently or inconveniently it is done. Last of all, if anything be spoken there to the hinderance of the sincerity of the gospel, I am well assured that M. Fox, which hath travailed so much and so profitably to that end, will not have his authority or name therein to bring any prejudice.[4]

Whitgift meets Cartwright's arguments by giving the page in the *Acts and Monuments* from which his quotation is taken. Cartwright's ignorance of this passage does not commend his knowledge of Foxe. On the other hand Whitgift says: "I can bring forth good testimonies of my reading of these books, though I make no brag thereof or vain comparisons."[5] Strype

---

[1] John Whitgift, *Works*, Parker Society (Cambridge, 1851–1853), II, 333–334. For the statement of Foxe, see *AM*, I, 50.
[2] Whitgift, *op. cit.*, p. 334.   [3] *Ibid.*, p. 334.
[4] *Ibid.*, p. 335.   [5] *Ibid.*, p. 336.

writes: "Our Archbishop openly in print (in his answer to Cartwright) confessed, that he had read over Mr. Fox's *Acts and Monuments* from one end to the other."[6]

Whitgift asserts that Foxe in the statement under discussion shows himself to be " 'no enemy' either to 'archbishop, primate,' or bishop; for I am sure he speaketh as he thinketh."[7] When the quotation is read in its context[8] there is no doubt that Whitgift is correct; the words are Foxe's own "and express his own judgment of these degrees and offices in this church of England."[9]

In his *Second Replie* Cartwright can say only, "I stand to that before made, and refer to it to the readers judgement."[10] Cartwright was not ready to admit that he had misinterpreted Foxe. It would mean much to him if Foxe spoke his case, and it would be a great disadvantage to him if he should oppose Foxe. This indicates the high esteem Foxe had in the English nation and church.

In his first reply to Whitgift, Cartwright had made this insinuation: "I perceive you fear M. Fox is an enemy unto your archbishop and primate, and therefore it seemeth you went about to corrupt him with his praise, and to seek to draw him, if it were possible, unto the archbishop; and, if not, yet at the least that he would be no enemy, if he would not nor could not be his friend. You make me suspect that your praise is not hearty, but pretended."[11]

Whitgift replied that Foxe "is not a man like to be 'corrupted with praise;' and therefore in so saying you do us both great injury. You may not judge my heart: I think of M. Fox as of one that I love and reverence; I will not utter all that I could, lest I should seem to flatter."[12] However, in his *Second Replie* Cartwright writes: "In saying he went about to corrupt him

<hr />

6 John Strype, *The Life and Acts of John Whitgift* (Oxford, 1822), I, 486. For Strype's whole discussion, see: *ibid.*, pp. 485–487; John Strype, *Annals of the Reformation* (Oxford, 1824), Vol. III, pt. i, pp. 738–739.

7 Whitgift, *op. cit.*, 336.   8 *AM*, I, 49–51.

9 Whitgift, *op. cit.*, 335.

10 Thomas Cartwright, *The Second Replie of Thomas Cartwright: agaynst Maister Doctor Whitgiftes Second Answer touching the Churche Discipline* (1575), p. dcxxxiii.

11 Whitgift, *op. cit.*, p. 335.   12 *Ibid.*, p. 336.

with his praise, I doo M. Fox injurie: yt being no fault to be assaulted, but to be ouercome; Whether I doo (the) Fox any let the reader iudge."[13] Cartwright seems to be saying that he was in harmony with Foxe's statements in the *Acts and Monuments*; he however realized that he was losing ground in his personal relationship to Foxe, not through any fault of his own but because Foxe had been corrupted by Whitgift's praise. In his discussion about Foxe it seems that Cartwright tries to do all that he can to make it appear that while Foxe is not his friend, neither is he his enemy. Whitgift, in his *Defence of the Answer*, makes six other references to Foxe on the questions of the name and offices of metropolitans and archbishops and of superiority among the clergy,[14] but Cartwright deals with only two of these.[15]

Foxe's writings in general support Whitgift's assertion that Foxe believed in degrees of superiority within the Christian ministry. When Foxe discusses whether excommunication and absolution should be pronounced by the bishops alone or by all the pastors, he suggests that whenever the bishop is unable to be present he may request that the "lower ministers" or "lesser clergy" absolve penitents.[16]

Having referred to some of the canons of the Councils of Nicea and Antioch dealing with episcopal jurisdiction as limited to their own districts, Foxe mentions a threefold ministry of bishops, presbyters, and deacons.[17] Discussing the religious situation after the reign of Constantine, he praises the work of bishops and pastors: "During this time, while the church was in this mediocre state, praise was due to the bishops and pastors who presided over the church."[18] In the Middle Ages when bishops and popes changed the image of the church, Foxe refers to the work of faithful bishops. At the same time he emphasizes the significance of their office when he states that "in them the universal church was constituted."[19]

In his commentary on the Seven Churches of Revelation,

---

[13] Cartwright, *op. cit.*, p. dcxxxiii.
[14] Whitgift, *op. cit.*, pp. 125, 128, 137, 148–150, 170, 219.
[15] Cartwright, *op. cit.*, pp. cccclxxii, cccclxxxvii.
[16] *Exc.*, sig. E7v.   [17] *Apoc.*, p. 140.
[18] *Apoc.*, p. 126.   [19] *Apoc.*, p. 209.

where the Son of God is depicted as walking in the midst of the churches, Foxe writes: "In like manner walk the other bishops, zealously through their own churches."[20] He also asserts: "O truly sublime is the emperor, but not less indeed than the emperor is the worthy bishop."[21] In his sermon *Christ Crucified* Foxe refers to the "learned bishop" of London and "his grave archdeacons;" in his benediction he prays for God's "spiritual ministers, bishops, and pastors of thy church."[22]

In Foxe's book *Of Free Justification*, in which he most clearly sets forth the main tenet of the Reformation, he also points out a threefold ministry: "Did not Paul a Servant of Jesus Christ, a proclaimer of the gospel, a teacher of the Gentiles, a chosen Vessel; did not he in writing to Timothy and Titus, prescribe a Law to you Bishops, Presbyters, Deacons, shewing in a Compendious Speech how ye ought to behave your selves in the Church of God, and what manner of Men it becomes those to be, who are overseers in the House of God."[23]

Foxe's attitude in the struggle between the two parties represented by Whitgift and Cartwright is further illustrated in a newly discovered letter from John Foxe to John Whitgift after he became archbishop.[24] The letter expresses the high regard and esteem Foxe had for Whitgift personally, as well as Foxe's respect for the chair he occupied. Furthermore, it substantiates that Whitgift and not Cartwright was correct in his evaluation of Foxe. Foxe writes: "To you first is this so outstanding honourable dignity, which you occupy by divine calling, in the State, and you hold it by virtue of your distinguished merits."[25] On the same note with which Foxe begins his letter he closes it: "I have written thus without reserve, because the very exalted reverence [due to you] has in fact allowed me the liberty of so doing."[26]

The cordial relationship between the two men is also noticed

---

[20] *Apoc.*, p. 7.

[21] *Exc.*, sig. E6r.

[22] *CC*, pp. 88, 94.

[23] *FJ*, p. 338.

[24] *FW*. For the story and content of this collection of manuscripts in which *FW* is found, see E. G. W. Bill, "Records of the Church of England Recovered by Lambeth Palace Library," *Journal of the Society of Archivists*, Vol. III, no. 1 (1965), pp. 24–26.

[25] *FW*, fol. 117r.

[26] *FW*, fol. 121r.

by Strype: "I cannot but observe the esteem and character that Dr. Whitgift expressed of that reverend man."[27] Strype brings forth an example to illustrate this esteem:

> I insert here an instance of the particular honour and respect the Archbishop had for the reverend Mr. John Fox, the famous Martyrologist: who, as a reward from the Queen, had the lease of Shipton under Whichwood in Oxfordshire given him, being a prebend, belonging to the church of Sarum, with a manor annexed. This lease Mr. Fox gave this year (the year before his death) unto his eldest son Samuel, upon his return from his travels abroad.[28]

The bishop of Sarum writes that Whitgift was "ready . . . to the utmost of his power, to pleasure that good man Mr. Fox." Having referred to Foxe's oldest son he also mentions that the archbishop had promised to bestow "some other prebend upon his younger brother, as soon as any fell void, after he was capable of it. And in the mean season to give him some exhibition quarterly towards his maintenance in the University." Strype comments: "This was the judgment and venerable esteem the Archbishop and Churchmen in those days had of that reverend and learned Confessor, and his labours."[29] Foxe's commentary on the book of Revelation, published posthumously by his son Samuel, was dedicated to the Most Reverend Father in Christ, Lord John Whitgift, Archbishop of Canterbury, Primate of All England, Metropolitan. His doing so, Samuel states, was not by his "own counsel only, but it was joined with the wish of him who, had he been still alive, would have desired to inscribe your name to whatever studies and labours of his he left as a memorial to posterity."[30] It is most doubtful that the mutual regard which Whitgift and Foxe had for one another would have been possible if Foxe, as Cartwright suggested, was an enemy unto "archbishop and primate."

In his letter to Whitgift, Foxe makes very clear his conviction regarding superiority among the English clergy. His statement confirms Whitgift's correct use of Foxe in his debate with Cart-

[27] Strype, *Annals*, Vol. III, pt. i, p. 739.
[28] Strype, *Whitgift*, I, 485.   [29] *Ibid.*, 486.
[30] *Apoc.*, sig. 2v.

wright, and leaves no doubt regarding Foxe's personal conviction. Foxe writes: "I would like to learn why the present status of the church, which is now governed through Archbishops, Bishops, Archdeacons, and Deacons, should not be preferred."[31]

Foxe not only expresses his positive view regarding the office of the bishop, but he also makes clear his opinion about Cartwright and his followers. In terms which leave no doubt of his disapproval, Foxe calls them "opposing factions, inconsiderate petitions coming from youthful minds who would advance their own judgments and postulates, tending to what they want."[32] Foxe wishes that "these restless innovators and troublesome reformers would restrain themselves."[33]

Foxe's attitude to extreme Puritans is also illustrated by his reaction to his son Samuel's dismissal from Magdalen College in 1581, initiated by the Puritans. A certain bishop had expressed his sympathy, and in his reply to the bishop, Foxe shows his personal indignation with a high degree of sarcasm seldom found in his writings:

> I marvel the more what turbulent genius has so inspired these factius puritans, that violating the laws of gratitude, scorning my letters and prayer to them, despising the intercession of the president himself, they practice this monstrous tyranny against me and my son, without warning or reason given. I grant my son is not so pure and free of all blemish as are those thrice pure puritans; nevertheless in these blemishes of his I have not yet found any mote so great as the greater beams which one may perceive in their characters.[34]

Foxe further states: "The fact is, the puritans are seeking to overthrow the president, and because my son supports him, he is disinherited from the society." Foxe suggests still another reason for Samuel's dismissal, expressing at the same time his personal stand in the conflict: "If I were a man to rage with them against bishops and archbishops, they would never have sharp-

---

[31] *FW*, fol. 120*r*.   [32] *FW*, fol. 118*r*.
[33] *FW*, fol. 118*v*.
[34] J. F. Mozley, *John Foxe and His Book* (London, 1940), pp. 111–112; *Pratt*, App. XV, p. 33; Harleian MS, no. 416, fol. 152.

ened these arrows against me. They hate me because I prefer to follow moderation and public tranquillity." Foxe may have anticipated the accusation that his outburst against the extreme Puritans at Magdalen College was caused by wounded fatherly pride. He makes it clear that for him it is more than just a question of his son's relationship to the college. "My private wrongs I can bear; it is the church's danger that moves me. This kind of men, if they gather strength, will throw all into confusion. They are worse than the old monks, and would reduce all to Judaean servitude."[35]

Fuller's comment on Foxe's letter to the bishop confirms the veracity of Foxe's belief that, in dismissing his son, the extreme Puritans were aiming at Humphrey and Foxe himself.

> We may plainly perceive, by this letter, how powerful the party of nonconformists was grown at this time, and to what violences and extravagancies some went in their practices; insomuch that Dr. Humphry, then President of Magdalen's, and Mr. Fox himself (both which scrupled subscription in some particulars) were deserted by them as lukewarm and remiss in the cause.[36]

While Foxe on the one hand makes clear his opinion about the office of bishop and expresses his dislike for the extreme Puritans, he on the other hand does not fully concur with the opponents of Cartwright, and agrees not at all with the methods used against the Puritans. He makes this evident in his letter to Archbishop Whitgift.

Foxe takes upon himself the role of mediator: "But I would strive, as I ought to, and as far as I am able, for public peace on either side in the community."[37] From his own middle-of-the-road position he points out the two extreme attitudes: "One party holds on to authority and tradition and its right, like grim death; the other side opposes them, claiming that conscience alone should be obeyed, and they are determined to yield to no one."[38] Accordingly he appeals: "We should ardently strive

---

[35] Mozley, op. cit., p. 112.
[36] Thomas Fuller, The Church History of Britain (Oxford, 1845), IV, 395.
[37] FW, fol. 120r.　　　　　　　　　　[38] FW, fol. 117r.

for peace, and together aim for the glory of Christ and loving concord in Him; not zealous for the victory of our party, but consulting the common good of the public church."[39]

Foxe opposes punishments and compulsions exercised by the High Commission against the extreme Puritans. He asks: "Should the situation be made harder for them, at the present time, by asserting authority after the Roman manner?"[40] His following opinion should also be noticed: "But my judgment is, that the matter be dealt with, in regard to those who would contravene fit and proper religious teaching, by persuasion rather than by rigid austerity."[41]

Foxe sincerely hopes that both sides will manifest moderation, and that the extreme Puritans will "contain themselves within modest lines, and consider, in the first place, that if the common vessel in which they are sailing be wrecked, they themselves also may perish."[42] Foxe further reminds them "that the concord of the church is preserved when weaknesses are tolerated, when the people consult concerning certain irregularities in practices of the teachers and when the Bishops condone certain weaknesses of the people."[43] Foxe, who himself had a sensitive nature and kind disposition, addresses Whitgift in the following way: "Then, if the Lord so will, let Him influence your most gentle mind to the counsel of moderation, that you do not exact from them all that you might rightly enforce."[44]

That Whitgift's sermon preached on the twenty-fifth anniversary of Queen Elizabeth's accession, November 17, 1583, was intended as a warning to the Puritans, there is no doubt. His choice of text indicates that he himself was going to work for conformity according to the Queen's laws: "Put them in remembrance to be subject unto principalities and powers, to obey magistrates, etc."[45] On the other hand it should not be overlooked that Foxe's hope for moderation or toleration might have had some possibility of fulfillment. Whitgift's dealing with some of the ministers from the diocese of Chichester, who re-

---

[39] *FW*, fol. 117r.
[41] *FW*, fol. 118v.
[43] *FW*, fol. 119v.
[45] Whitgift, *Works*, III, 586–596.

[40] *FW*, fol. 120r.
[42] *FW*, fol. 119v.
[44] *FW*, fol. 120.

fused to subscribe, may serve as an example,[46] even though the case did not set a precedent.

On becoming archbishop, Whitgift drafted a series of articles for the purpose of securing conformity.[47] None was permitted to "exercise any ecclesiastical function, unless he first subscribed to the following articles." They are listed as three, and only subscribers would receive license to preach. The articles are:

(1) That the Queen has supreme authority—ecclesiastical as temporal.

(2) That the Book of Common Prayer and of Ordering contains nothing contrary to the Word of God; that it may be lawfully used; and that he will use it in public prayer, and none other.

(3) That he allows the Articles agreed on in the Convocation of 1562, and believes them to be agreeable to the Word of God.[48]

On December 5, 1583, a deputation representing the recusants from the diocese of Chichester had a conversation with the archbishop in Lambeth. While they could subscribe to the first and third articles, to the Book of Common Prayer they could not conscientiously subscribe in "every particulare." Among the particulars mentioned were the omission of the Black Rubrics, "the massinge apparell, as cope, albe, vestments, tunicle etc.,"[49] private baptism, and communion. The deputation expressed their willingness to subscribe, if "a protestation might be added to the subscription," but the archbishop would not hear of this. However, he made the suggestion: "Consider of the matter, perhaps you are ashamed to subscribe before us all, come to me to morrow apart if you will, but you can never do yt in better tyme. Here be so manye of us togeather that you maye be sure your subscriptions shall not be urged otherwise than you meant them, because we are all witnesses of them." Even with this concession the men asked if they could have opportunity to seek further counsel; and the archbishop gra-

[46] *The Second Parte of a Register*, ed. Albert Peel (Cambridge 1915), I, 209–220.

[47] *Ibid.*, pp. 172–174.   [48] *Ibid.*, pp. 173–174.

[49] *Ibid.*, pp. 210, 211, 212.

ciously gave them this, saying: "Goo your wayes, and walke in the garden, or consider elsewhere of this matter, and returne againe."[50] The next day the men came to receive their licenses. In the meantime Whitgift had heard the rumor circulating that he had allowed them to subscribe by protestation. He, however, kept his promise and gave them the licenses in harmony with the words already spoken.

Theologically, Foxe would no doubt have been in sympathy with some of the objections raised by the recusants. As will be noticed later, he disapproved of the vestments and the like. He most likely had in mind points similar to those they raised when he noted "that perchance some things have crept into the customs and ceremonies of men which calls for the refinement of reformation."[51] On the other hand, he expressed his own attitude and the one he wished Cartwright's followers to adopt when he asked: "Has there ever been any kind of Reformation in the Church in which there was not spot or wrinkle? What, indeed, in human affairs has been absolutely perfect, or has there ever been a time so felicitous that there has been nothing to condone?"[52]

Foxe was deeply grieved by the contentions that disturbed the believers to the point that there was scarcely any harmony among them. This was most regrettable since they lived "under one faith, under the same sacraments, under one Head, members of one Body."[53] Foxe therefore asked Whitgift to exercise moderation and thus foster "the tranquillity of our public church, and its composure, in these troublous times which for so long have distressed our miserable native land."[54] In the 1583 edition of the *Acts and Monuments* Foxe also bemoans "the contentions and vnbrotherly diuision amongest vs most lamentable to see, but more lamentable, if all were seene which may or is like to follow."[55]

Foxe appeals for peace between the two groups fighting each other as enemies, because a third enemy appears, namely Rome. For that reason, if for none other, they ought to leave off con-

---

50 *Ibid.*, p. 217.
52 *FW*, fol. 119v.
54 *FW*, fol. 118r.

51 *FW*, fol. 119v.
53 *FW*, fol. 117r.
55 *FCCP*, sig. iiv.

tention, which bodes no good.[56] Accordingly he appeals for the bond of unity to be fostered: "For if indeed the enemies band together in an indissoluble confederacy against the gospel, it behooves us the more to determine in the strength of Christ to uphold the common cause of the gospel."[57]

Foxe's keen awareness of the danger of "a third enemy" was fully shared by Whitgift. In his conversations with the ministers of the diocese of Chichester, Whitgift says: "But since this diversitie hath beene in the church, religion hath gon backwarde, and popery hath so encreased that now it seemeth it will not be satisfied but by the Princes bloude, whom God longe preserve." Referring to Cartwright he states: "I love the man, and if he would returne and live in the peace of the church, he should not find a better frend than my self. But this strife amongst ourselves doth drive men from us, even to popery."[58]

In Whitgift's and Cartwright's references to Foxe after the presentation of the *Admonition to the Parliament*, it has been noticed that Cartwright rather owes Whitgift an answer for his use of Foxe. However on one point it is Whitgift who avoids answering Cartwright. This is when Cartwright refers to Foxe's dislike of the surplice. In his *Reply to the Answer* Cartwright argues: "You make me suspect that your praise is not hearty, but pretended, because you do so often and so bitterly speak against all those that will not receive the cap and surplice and other ceremonies, whereof M. Fox declareth his great misliking."[59] In his *Defence of the Answer to the Admonition* Whitgift avoids replying to this statement, no doubt because on this point it was Cartwright who evaluated Foxe correctly.

In his writing Foxe does not enter into any direct discussion regarding the cap and the surplice. This does not mean, however, that he agrees with their use, but that he prefers to preserve the peace of the church rather than to make it a public issue. In other words, he tries to exemplify that moderation and restraint which he later asks Whitgift to practice. We have a few statements from the pen of Foxe indicating his opinion regarding

---

[56] *FW*, fol. 117v. [57] *FW*, fol. 119r.
[58] *The Second Part of Register*, I, 216.
[59] Whitgift, *Works*, II, 335.

the vestment. He includes clerical garments in his list of many innovations that invaded the church about A.D. 1000; for example, at the time of Hildebrand was found "diuercity of apparell, which were not yet receiued in the churche, many hundred yeares after Christe." Foxe uses a historical incident to illustrate "both what we ought to do now, and to know what than was don, and used in the church." In A.D. 876 the clergy of Ravenna gave the French king the following advice: "We oughte to differ from the people and others, by doctryne: not by apparell in conversation, not in vesture, in purenesse of minde, not in garment."[60] In view of these statements it is understandable that Foxe, during the Vestiarian Controversy, could not agree with Archbishop Parker.

On March 20, 1565, a group of advanced Protestants made a petition to Archbishop Parker requesting forbearance and respect for their conscientious refusal to wear vestments. Among the twenty who signed this petition were not only Thomas Sampson and Laurence Humphrey but also John Foxe.[61] Patrick Collinson comments: "The most remarkable feature of this supplication was its conciliatory tone. The subscribers begged to be excused from conforming in the use of the vestments, but their appeal was to fraternal loyalties, and they implied that their resistance would be short-lived if the bishops should prove so ungracious as to refuse their moderate requests."[62] This evaluation of the subscribers appears to be true also of Foxe. For the more detailed story of Foxe's refusal to subscribe, we are indebted to Fuller, who first refers to the fact that the bishops

---

[60] AM (1563), p. 6. In his lengthy comparison of the early church of Rome with the latter church of Rome in the 1570 edition, he does not discuss the question of clerical garments.

[61] Strype has printed the supplication, but only signed by Thomas Sampson and Laurence Humphrey. See John Strype, The Life and Acts of Matthew Parker (Oxford, 1821), I, 322–326; III, 95–97. The original petition was among St. Paul's Cathedral MS, Add. I, "Epistolae virorum doctorum de rebus Ecclesiasticis tempore Elizabethae Reginae," no. 119. These manuscripts were bought by the Lambeth Palace Library. However, the petition to Parker was in the hands of an American collector and not obtainable. Patrick Collinson had opportunity to examine this manuscript and found twenty signatures, one of which was that of John Foxe. See Patrick Collinson, The Elizabethan Puritan Movement, p. 74.

[62] Collinson, op. cit., p. 33.

began to urge "the clergy of their diocese to subscribe to the liturgy, ceremonies and discipline of the church; and such as refused the same were branded with the odious name of puritans."[63] He then, as noticed earlier, describes two types of Puritans: ". . . some mild and moderate, contented only to enjoy their own conscience; others fierce and fiery, to the disturbance of church and state." He places Foxe among the former. It appears that Archbishop Parker was especially interested in getting Foxe to subscribe, that "the general reputation of his piety might give greater countenance to conformity." When Foxe was asked to subscribe we are told that he "produced the New Testament in Greek: 'To this,' (saith he,) 'will I subscribe.' " He further said: " 'I have nothing in the church save a prebend at Salisbury, and much good may it do you if you will take it away from me.' " (The prebend was not taken away from Foxe.) Fuller further states that though Foxe was "no friend to the ceremonies . . . he never entered any church without expressing solemn reverence therein."[64]

In the early Vestiarian Controversy, beginning in the latter part of 1565, Whitgift himself, both as a fellow of Peterhouse and as Lady Margaret's professor of divinity in the University of Cambridge, had pleaded on behalf of tender consciences. He endeavored to impede the preparation of Archbishop Parker's *Advertisements* in the University, and he himself was nearly labeled as a "Puritan" in a warning sent to the archbishop by Andrew Perne, the master of Peterhouse.[65] In this light Foxe's appeal to Whitgift after he became archbishop becomes more understandable.

Foxe's record of the life of John Hooper gives another example of his attitude toward clerical dress. Hooper had great scruples concerning the wearing of priestly garments and made a petition to King Edward asking for permission not to wear them. Foxe's comments leave no doubt of his personal sympathies:

> But I cannot tell what sinister and unlucky contention concerning the ordering and consecration of bishops, and of their apparel,

---

[63] Fuller, *op. cit.*, IV, 327.   [64] *Ibid.*, pp. 328–329.
[65] Patrick Collinson, "The 'nott conformytye' of the young John Whitgift," *The Journal of Ecclesiastical History*, Vol. XV, no. 2, pp. 192–200. Patrick Collinson, *The Elizabethan Puritan Movement*, p. 123.

with such other like trifles, began to disturb the good and lucky beginning of the godly bishop. For notwithstanding that godly reformation of religion then begun in the church of England, besides other ceremonies more ambitious than profitable, or tending to edification, they used to wear such garments and apparel as the popish bishops were want to do: first a chimere, and under that a white rochet: then, a mathematical cap with four angles, dividing the whole world into four parts. These trifles, tending more to superstition than otherwise, as he could never abide, so in no wise could he be persuaded to wear them.[66]

The King granted Hooper his request, but "the bishops still stood earnestly in the defence of the aforesaid ceremonies; saying it was but a small matter, and that the fault was in the abuse of the things, and not in the things themselves: adding moreover, that he ought not to be so stubborn in so light a matter; and that his wilfulness therein was not to be suffered." While Foxe's sympathy was with Hooper, he disliked the strife: "To be short, whilst both parties thus contended about this matter more than reason would, in the mean time occasion was given, as to the true Christians to lament,[67] so to the adversaries to rejoice."[68]

When Hooper preached before King Edward he wore the clerical gown. Foxe's comment is somewhat sarcastic: "Wherefore, appointed to preach before the king, as a new player in strange apparel, he cometh forth on the stage." Describing the cap, Foxe's irony should be noticed: "Upon his head he had a geometrical, that is, a four-squared cap, albeit that his head was round." Foxe continues: "But this private contumely and reproach, in respect of the public profit of the church, which he only sought, he bare and suffered patiently." On the other hand Foxe "would to God, in like manner, they, who took upon them the other part of that tragedy, had yielded their private cause, whatsoever it was, to the public concord and edifying of the church." However, Foxe closes his account, ". . . no man in all the city was one hair the better for that hot contention."[69]

Foxe did not want to make a great issue of the question re-

---

[66] *AM*, VI, 640.

[67] *AM*, (1563), p. 1051, reads "as they gaue to the true church of Christ occasion of muche lamentacion."

[68] *AM*, VI, 641.   [69] *AM*, VI, 641.

garding the clerical gown, yet his dislike of its use no doubt remained with him throughout his life. As late as 1583 he made this observation: "... what would they [the martyrs] haue cared how simply they walked in their attire, without any such monstrous pomp in pranckyng vp themselues, as we Englishmen in these reformed dayes walke now, more like plaiers in a stage, then gods children in his Church."[70]

The true succession for the church and its ministry, according to Foxe, is one of purity of faith and nobility of concord. He quotes Jerome: "Spiritual succession is not in the place where each one sits, but in the imitation of the principles and life of Christ who said: 'He who does the will of God, the same is my brother, sister and mother.' "[71] The ordinary succession profits nothing in the sight of God, maintains Foxe; it is the good life that makes a man apostolic. In another connection Foxe remarks: "Those who preside in the churches should not hold dignity on account of place and order, but on account of nobility of conduct; not the fame of cities, but the purity of faith, should be noted."[72]

In some notes on election and faith Foxe points out that true "succession of chair" depends upon God's free mercy and grace, which are not bound "to any ordinary place, or to any succession of chair, nor to state and dignity of person, nor to worthiness of blood, etc.; but all goeth by the mere will of his own purpose."[73] Further, "the administration of the spiritual kingdom comes by heavenly virtue and the grace of divine election; the succession is made not by the office but by the life, the doctrine, and the corresponding conduct."[74] The Christian religion is "spirituall, and not a corporall Religion."[75] This fact plays an important role in Foxe's concept of the ministry. The Catholics are not "spiritual pastors of Christ's flock."[76] Furthermore "the said Romish bishops have no less altered, both from the rule of scripture, and from the steps of the true church of Rome; which government as it hath been, and ought to be, only spiritual."[77]

---

[70] FCCP, sig. iiv.
[72] Foxe, The Pope Confvted, pp. 36–39; Apoc., p. 261.
[71] Apoc., pp. 259–260.   [73] AM, VII, 269.
[74] Apoc., p. 138.   [75] FQP, sig. iiiiv.
[76] AM, I, 58.   [77] AM, I, 57.

Having referred to the Christian armour of the apostle Paul, Foxe writes: "As we read in the apostles' time, all the armour of Christ's ministers was spiritual, and full of godly power against the spiritual enemies of our salvation, governing the church then with peace, patience, humility, true knowledge of God, the sword of the spirit, the shield of faith, the breastplate of righteousness, hearty charity, sincere faith, and a good conscience."[78] Foxe continues the same line of thought when he says, "Furthermore, by St. Paul's doctrine, the ministers and superintendents of Christ's church have their authority and armour likewise to them limited; which armour is only spiritual and not carnal."[79] Foxe refers to the "ministers of Christ's gospel" as those who as "spiritual physicians of the soul, minister to the weak conscience of man." In a public prayer Foxe beseeches the "Lord, Prince of all pastors" that the "spiritual ministers, bishops and pastors" may be "quickened daily by the Holy Spirit, whereby thy flock by them may be preserved."[80] Thus the bishop and minister were to prove themselves true servants of God.

Foxe lays emphasis on the practical and spiritual sides of the chair and the office. Only these justified the title and the office, and in turn the status of the church as a true or false church depended upon them. Foxe writes that "the excellency of the church or place doth not always argue the excellency of the minister or bishop, nor yet necessarily doth cause the same. For, in matters of the church which are spiritual, all pre-eminence standeth upon spiritual and inward gifts: ... as faith, piety, learning and godly knowledge, zeal and fervency in the Holy Ghost, unity of doctrine, etc."[81]

John Foxe's doctrine of the church implied a high conception of the ministry. "I know that there is nothing in human affairs more excellent than the sacred function of those who are dedicated by the Lord to the propagation of the Word, so long as they perform their duty faithfully."[82] In view of the high calling of the minister, his personal life and its effects, whether good or bad, are of great importance. Accordingly, Foxe writes: "I do not know how it is, but the people always respond to habits of

[78] *AM*, I, 60.   [79] *AM*, I, 64.
[80] *CC*, pp. 34, 33, 94, 95.   [81] *AM*, I, 49–50.
[82] *Apoc.*, p. 18.

the pastors."[83] The pastor should "be so grave, so learned, so temperate, so sober and chaste in look, and in walk, with all actions of life under self-control, that no one may reproach him, but all may imitate."[84]

Examining the state and doctrine of the early church, Foxe mentions that the rule of the bishop and the minister was based "on doctrine, in worship, faith, virtue, on inner pastoral gifts, the gifts of the Spirit, spiritual gifts, the example of his life and habits."[85] Foxe holds the widespread ignorance and low moral standards among the clergy partly responsible for the corruption of his own time. Foxe expresses himself publicly regarding the state of the ministry: While he is thankful that the Gospel is being preached, he cannot condone the worldly motives many have for entering the ranks of the clergy.[86]

In his letter to Archbishop Whitgift, Foxe also touches on the significance of the personality of the individual minister, as well as the responsibility of the leaders in the church to ordain only suitable men. Foxe advises that there "should be placed in authority only those who are truly trained to rule their portion and province of the flock of the Lord, and also are exercised in righteousness, in the gifts of teaching these things, consoling and confirming the flock, and refuting error." Foxe pleads: "Oh, that the bishops would ordain fewer, but more worthy ministers."[87] With this Whitgift was in full sympathy, and he achieved considerable success in improving the standard of the ministry.[88] Foxe's appeal and personal influence may have had a share in this.

Foxe emphasizes preaching as the primary ministerial function. This of course was inherited from the Reformation, since one of the significant marks of the true church was "the Gospel rightly taught."[89] Foxe clearly states "that the principal office of the ministers of the new testament is, to labour in the word and doctrine."[90] A minister was not to be a priest finding his first

---

[83] *Exc.*, sig. D1v.
[84] *Exc.*, sig. C8v.
[85] *Apoc.*, pp. 392, 393.
[86] *CC*, p. 12.
[87] *FW*, fol. 120.
[88] P. M. Dawley, *John Whitgift and the Reformation* (London, 1955), pp. 195–205.
[89] See chapter iii, "The Marks of the Church."
[90] *CC*, p. 12.

responsibility at the altar administering the sacraments, but was to be a preacher of the Gospel. The word "proclaim" may convey the idea of his work even better than "preach," for the minister was a messenger. In one of his own sermons Foxe said that God had raised up "messengers of his holy grace and gospel to his church, which so constantly accord and tune in one string together, to set forth the lively message and truth of Christ's gospel."[91] But behind them Christ, the "supreme Prince," is "the sender of this message."[92] The words of the prophet Isaiah, "How beautiful upon the mountains are the feet of him that bringeth good tidings,"[93] are verified by the fact that God from time to time stirs "up in his church . . . messengers and legates apostolical." Foxe includes himself among them "who [are] now coming to you also, Londoners."[94]

A definite similarity has been noted between the godly Puritan preachers and the medieval friars,[95] arising from such common religious aspirations as the renewal of spiritual religion, the practical application of Christian principles in helping others, and the proclamation of Christ leading to the conversion of men and women. Foxe, we have noticed, opposed ceremonial or corporal religion, but advocated spiritual religion. He was not a pastor in residence, but preached wherever opportunity was given. It may therefore not be a coincidence, as already noticed, that, in a letter to Laurence Humphrey, Foxe lists himself as a member of the mendicant order or the Preaching Friars.[96]

Along with preaching, pastoral care is one of the preeminent duties of the minister. As "spiritual men" and "true gospellers" they should "join works to works, faith to faith, faith to works, and good works to faith, as did Paul and James, and so to join St. Paul and St. James together."[97] Foxe mentions the prevalent

---

[91] CC, p. 11.   [92] CC, p. 9.
[93] Isaiah 52:7.   [94] CC, p. 18.
[95] Gerald R. Owst, *Preaching in Medieval England* (Cambridge, 1926), p. 94; G. G. Coulton, *Ten Medieval Studies* (Boston, 1959), chap. 4; M. M. Knappen, *Tudor Puritanism* (Chicago, 1965), p. ix; Irvonwy Morgan. *The Godly Preachers of the Elizabethan Church* (London, 1965).
[96] Harleian MS, no. 416, fol. 140; Mozley, *op. cit.*, p. 66.
[97] CC, p. 89.

lack of interest in "clothing the naked, visiting the sick and prisoners, comforting those who perish with cold in the open air, caring for orphans and other similar deeds of charity. It is amazing how these loving deeds are neglected by Christians nowadays." Foxe asks: "What then should the wise pastor do?" He answers: "I would wish that each should comply with the will of the Lord, not to disparage the feeble."[98] A minister should "comfort troubled consciences, with the rich grace of the gospel," "instruct the ignorant," "comfort such as be afflicted," share "with tears and compassion on other men's griefs," and manifest "humility toward the poor and miserable."[99] He should "pastor his own flock and gather the lambs in his arms."[100]

The significance of the pastor's personal interest in and sympathy for the individual, as well as the influence of his own personality, Foxe illustrates by recounting an incident in the life of Hooper. A certain person came to Hooper's house for counsel, "but being abashed at his austere look, durst not come in, but departed seeking remedy of his troubled mind at other men's hands." Foxe adds, "... which he afterward, by the help of Almighty God, did find and obtain." Foxe himself may have helped the man, for he begins the story by saying that the person under discussion was "to me not unknown." Foxe then admonishes the Christian ministry:

> Therefore, in my judgment, such as are appointed and made governors over the flock of Christ, to teach and instruct them, ought so to frame their life, manners, countenance, and external behaviour, as neither they show themselves too familiar and light, whereby to be brought into contempt, nor, on the other side again, that they appear more lofty and austere, than appertaineth to the edifying of the simple flock of Christ.[101]

Foxe's kind and sympathetic disposition, as well as his personal touch with the common people, are no doubt reflected in his disapproving remark about Hooper: "He bare in countenance and talk always a certain severe and grave grace, which

[98] *Exc.*, sig. D7v.
[99] *AM*, I, 26, 57, 58.
[100] *Apoc.*, p. 37.
[101] *AM*, VI, 639.

might, peradventure, be wished sometimes to have been a little more popular and vulgar-like in him."[102]

Patrick Collinson has pointed out that often it has "been implied that the puritans discovered this practical divinity only in the early seventeenth century, when their attempts to reform the externals of worship and church government were finally defeated," but he asserts: "I have no doubt that 'mere religion' had always been the first concern of the majority of the godly preachers of the Elizabethan Church."[103] Foxe's practical and spiritual concept of the ministry testifies to the truth of this statement. Furthermore, Foxe himself was a good example of his ideal pastor, even though he was not a residing minister. He would not have fallen short of George Herbert's and Richard Baxter's ideal of pastoral care.[104] Foxe was ordained priest in 1560 by Edmund Grindal, then bishop of London. His prebend of Shipton in the cathedral of Salisbury he may have visited once a year. The other in Durham he held only for a year.[105] However, he was known as a preacher and one who exercised pastoral care.

When, in the summer of 1563, a devastating plague broke out in the city of London, Foxe wrote a little tract "to suche as be Sicke, where the Ministers do lacke, or otherwise cannot be present to comfort them." It closes with "a prayer to be sayd ouer children, visited by Gods hand with sicknesse, in this sorrowful tyme of Gods visitation."[106] He also makes a most moving appeal to the wealthy merchants of London, asking them to extend their tender and Christian compassion upon the suffering.[107] In his sermon at St. Paul's Cross, Foxe makes a plea for the poor: "My suit is for the poor, not for one poor man or two, but for all the whole poverty in general of this city."[108] Foxe

[102] *AM*, VI, 639.

[103] Patrick Collinson, *A Mirror of Elizabethan Puritanism*, p. 28.

[104] George Herbert, *A Priest to the Temple, or the Countrey Parson, His Character and Rule of Holy Life* (London, 1652); Richard Baxter, *The Reformed Pastor* (London, 1656).

[105] Mozley, *op. cit.*, pp. 63–64, 67, 69, 84; *Pratt*, pp. 35, 87.

[106] John Foxe, *A Brief Exhortation* (London, 1563?).

[107] Harleian MS, no. 417, fol. 131v.

[108] CC, p. 87.

practiced what he preached. Fuller testifies that Foxe "in his lifetime was so large a reliever of poor people, to and above his estate, that no wonder if at his death, with some charitable churls, he bequeathed no legacies unto them."[109]

Foxe's pastoral care for the individual is illustrated in his sermon preached at the baptism of a converted Jew, which he repeated for Sir Francis Walsingham in his chamber. Being sick he had not been able to attend the service, but Foxe took time to preach for him privately.[110] His sympathetic interest in helping those in need is manifested toward foe as well as friend. When Anabaptists and even Catholics were condemned to be executed, Foxe pleaded for them.[111]

The many letters to and from Foxe throw further light on his genuine pastoral interest in all classes of people. He sends a letter to three gentlemen on behalf of a poor man who has been wronged. He introduces the letter, "Beati Pacifici."[112] For a young man applying for a position as schoolmaster in Ipswich, Foxe writes a recommendation.[113] Another young man asks for his help to obtain a scholarship at Christ's Church, Oxford.[114] A "preacher of the same word of truth" writes to Foxe asking for his help in placing a boy in the house of the dean of St. Paul's.[115] To the bishop of York Foxe inquires about work for a man named William Henkey.[116] Foxe, together with Nowell, receives a letter from a prisoner in Hartford jail asking if money could be collected for his release.[117] Two learned and godly refugees must have sought Foxe's aid, for he asks Grindal and the other bishops to help the men.[118] One who is in spiritual difficulties and temptations asks for his prayers and counsel.[119] Another seeks his advice concerning baptism with godfathers and godmothers.[120] A letter is sent to Foxe from one who has been a Christian for twenty years but feels more sinful than

[109] Fuller, *op. cit.*, V, 116.   [110] *OT*, p. 288.
[111] See chapter vi, "The Church and Toleration."
[112] Harleian MS, no. 416, fols. 147–149.
[113] *Ibid.*, fol. 135.   [114] *Ibid.*, fols. 189–190.
[115] *Ibid.*, fol. 202.   [116] *Ibid.*, fol. 142.
[117] *Ibid.*, fol. 165.   [118] *Ibid.*, fol. 137.
[119] *Ibid.*, fols. 116–117.   [120] *Ibid.*, fol. 191.

ever.[121] A person who is burdened with the temptation to blaspheme asks his help.[122]

Foxe's advice is also sought on matrimonial matters. One by the name of Barthe Clerk asks his counsel concerning the courting of a widow,[123] and in another case Foxe recommends one of his friends to a certain woman.[124] A nobleman whose wife has left him is asked to take her back again, because Foxe believes she will now be a faithful wife.[125] The oldest son of the Duke of Norfolk has fallen into evil company and neglected his wife, with the result that the wife has left him. Foxe labors hard to reconcile them, with no success; and the old Duke advises him "not to trouble himself comeing there any more about that business, there being so little hope, for the present, of doing any good therein."[126]

That women were among Foxe's spiritual patients was to be expected. When Lady Ann Hennage was lying sick unto death, "Master Fox was called to be present at her ending, whose counsell and fidelity she had often made use of, in matters appertaining to her soules health."[127] After Foxe, as a minister, had done what he could to prepare her for death, he said: ". . . know this from me, that of this sicknesse you shall not dye." The Lady's son-in-law blamed Fox for making such a statement, but to this "Master Fox smiling made answer, That for his part he hindered not any man to think of him, as he pleased; but concerning the sick Lady, it had so seemed unto God, that she should recover of that disease; and that he had said no more then was commanded him. The Lady recovered: nor can I in this tell an untruth, there being many yet living, who could reprove me."[128]

Mrs. Honywood's story is similar. After having consulted "the gravest Divines, and best Physitianes," she sent for Foxe. Having had prayer with the lady, Foxe told her "that she should not only grow well of that consumption, but also live to an

---

[121] *Ibid.*, fols. 120–121.
[122] *Ibid.*, fol. 131.
[123] *Ibid.*, fol. 108.
[124] *Ibid.*, fol. 143.
[125] *Ibid.*, fol. 158.
[126] M. A. Tierney, *The History and Antiquities of the Castle and Town of Arundel* (London, 1834), p. 371.
[127] *LJF*, sig. B3*r*.
[128] *LJF*, sig. B3*r*.

exceeding great age."[129] When the woman heard this prediction, she reacted very angrily:

> At which words the sick Gentlewoman a little moved, and earnestly beholding Master Foxe: As well might you have said (quoth she) that if I should throw this glasse against the wall, I might beleeve it would not break to pieces; and holding a glasse in her hand, out of which she had newly drunk, she threw it forth; neither did the glasse, first by chance lighting on a little Chest standing by the Bed side, and afterward falling upon the ground, either break, or crack in any place about it: And the event fell out accordingly. For the Gentlewoman, being then threescore yeers of age, lived afterward for all example of felicity, seldome seen in the off-spring of any family, being able before the 90 yeer of her age (for she lived longer) to reckon three hundred and three-score of her childrens children, and grandchildren.[130]

Edward Dering, one of the divines whom Mrs. Honywood had consulted and one whose pastoral care was highly esteemed and sought, confirms Foxe's story.[131]

Foxe's own record of his high concept and personal exercise of pastoral duties is substantiated by his two sons. Samuel tells that his father "never ceased to declare that whenever an occasion offered, he would snatch them from grievous fate."[132] In his biography of the father, Simeon writes:

> But modesty will not allow me by way of Iournall, to rehearse the voluntary paines he took upon him: in generall to say something of it will not be amisse; and how, either by good advise, comfortable perswasions, or a charitable hand, he either relieved the wants, or satisfied the desires of innumerable persons; whereupon no mans house was in those times thronged with more clients then his. These repaired to him, both Citizens, and strangers, Noblemen and Common-people of all degrees, and almost all for the same cause; to seek some salve for a wounded conscience.[133]

---

[129] *LJF*, sig. B3v.

[130] *LJF*, sig. B3v. For the same story, see Samuel Clarke, *A Mirrour or Looking-Glasse both for Saints and Sinners* (London, 1646), pp. 10–11; Thomas Fuller, *The History of the Worthies of England* (London, 1662), II, 85–86.

[131] Collinson, *A Mirror of Elizabethan Puritanism*, pp. 28–30.

[132] *Apoc.*, sig. 2v.   [133] *LJF*, sig. B2r.

Simeon closes, as previously noticed, his father's life story by reporting how the whole city lamented at the news of his death and that the large crowd at his funeral mourned as if "each man had buried his own father, or his own brother."[134] It would be reasonable to think that many who paid their last respects to John Foxe did so not only because he was the renowned historiographer but also because he had been their beloved minister giving them his sympathetic pastoral care.

[134] *LJF*, sig. B6v.

V. Church and State

*I*N HIS CONCEPT of church and state as a homogeneous Christian society within national units, Foxe was one with his time.[1] Richard Hooker, the architect of Anglican church polity, expresses the common view of the Anglican Fathers regarding the Christian commonwealth:

> We hold, that seeing there is not any man of the Church of England, but the same man is also a member of the commonwealth; nor any man a member of the commonwealth, which is not also of the Church of England, therefore as in a figure triangular the base doth differ from the sides thereof, and yet one and the selfsame line is both a base and also a side; a side simply, a base if it chance to be the bottom and underlie the rest: so, albeit properties and actions of one kind do cause the name of a commonwealth, qualities and functions of another sort the name of a Church to be given unto a multitude, yet one and the selfsame multitude may in such sort be both, and is so with us, that no person appertaining to the one can be denied to be also of the other.[2]

[1] Stephen Gardiner, *Obedience in Church and State, Three Political Tracts* (Cambridge, 1930), pp. 93, 95; J. Hooper, *Later Writings*, Parker Society (Cambridge, 1852), p. 54; John Jewel, *Works* (Cambridge, 1845–1850), III, 74; Edmund Sandys, *Sermons*, Parker Society (Cambridge, 1842), pp. 46–48, 52; John Whitgift, *Works*, I, 21–22; III, 181–182, 486; Richard Hooker, *Of the Laws of Ecclesiastical Polity* (Oxford, 1885), Vol. VIII, pt. ii, p. 3, pt. iii, p. 6, pt. vi, p. 11.

[2] Hooker, *op. cit.*, Vol. VIII, pt. i, p. 2.

Foxe shows the same belief in an appeal to his own country-
men: "No man lyueth in that common wealth where nothyng
is amisse. But yet because God so placed vs Englishmen here in
one common wealth, also in one Church as in one shippe together: let vs not mangle or diuide the shippe, which beyng
deuided perisheth: but euery man serue in hys order with diligence, wherin he is called."[3] Refering to the prophet Isaiah,
Foxe speaks about Mount Sion as "the hill of his holines" and
describes a peaceful condition where "the wolfe shall dwell with
the Lambe, and ye Leopard with the Kid: The Calfe, the Lyon,
and the Sheepe shall feede together, and a young childe shall
rule them," stating that it "beareth in the Scripture an vndoubted
type of the spiritual Church of Christ." He further mentions
"this peaceable Mount of Sion (which comprehendeth both
the states as well Ecclesiasticall as temporall)."[4]

In his preface to *Reformatio Legvm Ecclesiasticarvm* Foxe
points out the importance to the state that right religious doctrines be retained and to religion that the best laws be added.
He emphasizes the unity of church and state: "These two
matters are joined for the best administration of every state, that
they may help one another."[5] Foxe also sees a homogeneous
Christian society when the European nations, as a larger unity,
are designated as the commonwealth of Christ, or the Christian
commonwealth.[6]

Foxe's political thought is understandable only in the light of
the rise of the church as a temporal power and the struggle between the ecclesiastical and secular rulers for political sovereignty. The breakdown of the Roman Empire and the rapid spread
of Christianity led to a situation in which the bishop of Rome
had at times more power than the kings of Europe. Foxe states
the problem of papal supremacy very clearly when he writes
that one of the abuses "of the pope's jurisdiction standeth in
this; that as in spiritual jurisdiction they have vehemently ex-
ceeded the bounds of Scripture, so they have impudently inter-
meddled themselves in temporal jurisdiction, wherein they have
nothing to do."[7] Foxe considers the papal claim of universal

---

[3] *Cong.*, sig. iiiiv.   [4] Isaiah 11:9, 65:25; *FQP*, sig. iiiv.
[5] *Reformatio Legvm Ecclesiasticarvm*, p. xix.
[6] *AM*, II, 463, 487; IV, 4.   [7] *AM*, I, 19.

supremacy a strange element within the church itself, as well as within church and state as one Christian society. According to Foxe's periodization of church history, Antichrist ruled during the centuries when such popes as Gregory VII, Innocent III, and Boniface VIII claimed both spiritual and temporal supremacy.

Foxe calls Gregory VII "the first and principal cause of all this perturbation that is now, and hath been since his time, in the church," mainly because he usurped more power and authority than the emperor had.[8] Temporal supremacy was also believed to be a right by Pope Innocent III; to illustrate this, we need only refer to King John of England.[9]

The struggle over the boundary between sacerdotium and regnum and the papal claim for universal supremacy reached its climax during the pontificate of Boniface VIII. In his famous bull *Unam Sanctam*, used against Philip IV of France, Boniface VIII asserts that both the spiritual and material swords are in the power of the church and that temporal authority is subject to spiritual.[10] Accordingly Foxe states that by him "the pope's power was brought now to its full pride and perfection."[11]

Political theories that disentangled the state from the church or substituted civil for ecclesiastical authority were borne against such claims as those expressed in the *Unam Sanctum*.[12] When Foxe discusses the early beginnings of the Reformation, he goes back to the fourteenth century and pays tribute to the men who, for religious and political reasons, opposed the Papacy. Among the names he enumerates are Dante Alighieri, Marsilius of Padua, William of Ockham, and John Wycliffe.[13] In his periodization of church history, Foxe counts the reforming time from about A.D. 1300. For an understanding of Foxe's view of the early beginnings of the Reformation, especially as related to the question of church and state, it is illuminating to note that in

[8] *AM*, II, 115. For the life of Gregory VII, see *AM*, II, 115–133.

[9] *AM*, II, 324–333.

[10] Ernest F. Henderson, *Select Historical Documents of the Middle Ages* (London, 1896), pp. 435–437.

[11] *AM*, I, 7; See also pp. 10, 19, 25.

[12] T. M. Parker, *Christianity and the State in the Light of History* (New York, 1955), pp. 120–142.

[13] *AM*, II, 661, 705–707, 727, 791.

A.D. 1324, the same year in which his thousand year period expired and a reformation should begin, Marsilius of Padua finished his work *Defensor Pacis*.[14]

The work of Marsilius has been said to contain most of the ideas that "were to become the creative forces of the modern era." He has been characterized as "a precursor of the Reformation, a theorist of a popular sovereignty and constitutional systems, a herald of the modern sovereign state."[15] R. L. Poole states that "Marsiglio had arrived at the fully matured principle of religious toleration."[16] He has been called "the boldest thinker of an age when many thinkers had been provoked to erastianism by the excessive claims of Boniface VIII."[17]

Defensor Pacis, published partially in an English translation in 1535,[18] seems to have been known to the learned men at the court of Henry VIII. Thomas Starkey, chaplain to Henry VIII, was greatly influenced by Marsilius,[19] and there are similarities between Marsilius and Cranmer.[20] There are also internal evidences in the *Laws of Ecclesiastical Polity* that Hooker was indebted to Marsilius.[21]

The aim of *Defensor Pacis* is to explain "the principal causes whereby civil peace and tranquillity exists and is preserved, and whereby the opposed strife arises and is checked and destroyed."[22] The singular cause that Marsilius sets forth as the root of strife and a hindrance to peace is "the belief, desire and undertaking whereby the Roman bishop and his clerical coterie, in particular, are aiming to seize secular rulerships."[23] Marsilius

---

[14] Marsilius of Padua, *The Defender of Peace* (New York, 1956), II, 432.

[15] A. P. D'Entrèves, *The Medieval Contribution to Political Thought* (New York, 1959), p. 44.

[16] Reginald L. Poole, *Illustration of the History of Medieval Thought* (London, 1884), p. 272.

[17] A. G. Dickens, *The English Reformation*, p. 85.

[18] Marsilius of Padua, *The Defence of Peace* ([London], 1535).

[19] Franklin Le Van Baumer, "Thomas Starkey and Marsilius of Padua," *Politica*, Vol. II, no. 6, pp. 188–205.

[20] C. W. Previte-Orton, "Marsilius of Padua," *Proceedings of the British Academy* (1935), XXI, 164–165.

[21] *Ibid.*, 165–166.

[22] Marsilius, *The Defender of Peace*, II, 431.

[23] *Ibid.*, II, 425.

aims "therefore, with God's help, to expose only this singular cause of strife."[24] About this work Foxe comments that "the controversy of the pope's unlawful jurisdiction in things temporal is largely disputed, and the usurped authority of that see set forth to the uttermost."[25] Four hundred years later, A. G. Dickens confirms Foxe's evaluation: "The *Defensor* was the most able, audacious and elaborate attack ever made upon the pretensions of the medieval Church."[26] It is thus significant that Foxe traces the early beginnings of the Reformation back to A.D. 1324, when ideas were promulgated and forces let loose which led to disentanglement from papal jurisdiction both in church and state. As Marsilius points out the papal claim for secular and spiritual supremacy as the main cause for strife and lack of peace in both church and state, so does Foxe.

Foxe's tribute to Marsilius is in connection with the latter's attack upon the usurped authority of the Papacy. The two differ, however, on methods of establishing a kingly monarchy. Marsilius and Starkey prefer a ruler chosen by free election rather than by hereditary succession. They do not use scriptural references to substantiate their position.[27]

Foxe opposes the theory of ecclesiastical supremacy on the grounds that political society is of divine origin, and that kings as agents of the divine purpose, are responsible to God directly. He quotes scriptural authority to support this claim. Like the Anglican Divines in general, he illustrates the supremacy of the Christian king with examples from the Old Testament.[28] Having referred to a number of kings from Old Testament times, Foxe observes:

> By these and many other examples it is to be seen, that kings and princes in old time, as well when priests were born priests, as when they were made by election, had the dealing also in

---

[24] *Ibid.*, II, 7.   [25] *AM*, II, 661.

[26] Dickens, *op. cit.*, p. 84.

[27] Marsilius, *The Defender of Peace*, II, 28–34; Thomas Starkey, *A Dialogue Between Reginald Pole and Thomas Lupset* (London, 1948), pp. 99–108.

[28] Gardiner, *op. cit.*, pp. 107–111, 129; Jewel, *Works*, III, 97–98; Sandys, *Sermons*, pp. 41–43; Thomas Becon, *Catechism*, Parker Society (Cambridge, 1844), p. 304; Hooker, *op. cit.*, Vol. VIII, pt. i, p. 1.

ecclesiastical matters; as, in calling the people to God's service, in cutting down groves, in destroying images, in gathering tithes into the Lord's house, in dedicating the temple, in blessing the people, in casting down the brazen serpent within the temple, in correcting and deposing priests, in constituting the order and offices of priests, in commanding such things as pertained to the service and worship of God, and in punishing the contrary.[29]

Foxe, in his commendation of King Edward, compares him to King Josias of the Old Testament, calling him "this evangelical Josias."[30] One of the woodcuts in the *Acts and Monuments* depicts the young King Edward as Josias, purging the temples, burning the images, sending all popish idolatry back to Rome, restoring the Bible, and encouraging the preaching of the Word.[31]

Turning from the Old Testament to the New, Foxe mentions the example of Christ who both taught and practiced "tribute to be given to Ceasar; to Ceasar, I say, and not to the high-priest." Foxe asks, "What meaneth his [Christ's] words to Pilate, not denying power to be given to him from above? And again, declaring the kings of nations to have dominion over them, and willing his disciples not so to do, giving us to understand the difference between the regiment of his spiritual kingdom, and of the kingdoms of this world, willing all worldly states to be subject under the superior rulers and magistrates, in whose regiment are dominion and subjection, and not in the other." He also quotes the well-known words of Paul, " 'Let every soul be subject to the higher powers,' " commenting, "... from whose authority, neither pope, cardinal, patriarch, bishop, priest, friar nor monk is excepted nor exempted." Paraphrasing Peter, " 'Be you subject,' saith he, 'to every human creature, whether it be to the king as most preeminent, or to others set over you,' " Foxe concludes his biblical proof by stating: "It is sufficiently hitherto proved by God's law, that all ecclesiastical persons owe their due subjection to their lawful princes, in matters as well temporal as spiritual: so no less evidences may also be inferred out of man's law, and examples of the oldest fathers to prove the same."[32]

[29] *AM*, I, 20.
[31] *AM* (1570), II, 1483.
[30] *AM*, V, 698.
[32] *AM*, I, 20–21; see also I, 84.

Foxe's argument against the Papacy, that according to divine and human law the bishops of the ancient church acknowledged and obeyed their emperor and king in causes spiritual as well as civil, was the basic argument used by most writers who adhered to the principal of the supremacy of the monarch. They used it not only against the Papacy but also against the extreme Puritans.[33] With them Foxe enumerated a number of cases where the bishops received and "also required of the emperors, laws and constitutions to be made, touching not only such causes, but also such persons as were ecclesiastical."[34] He makes special reference to the laws and constitution of Emperor Justinian.[35]

Constantine stands out among the emperors as a true example of a Christian king. Foxe describes how the ten major persecutions of the early church were ended by God's sending "his meek Moses (gentle Constantine, I mean), by whom it hath so pleased the Lord to work deliverance to his captive people, to set his servants at liberty, to turn their mourning into joy, to magnify the church of his Son, to destroy the idols of all the world, to grant life and liberty ... unto them which before were the abjects of all the world, and all by the means of godly Constantine, the meek and most christian emperor."[36] Foxe discusses at some length the work of Constantine, thus intimating the duties and prerogatives of the godly prince.[37] Constantine acknowledged that " 'an empire was given by the determinate purpose of God; and that he to whom it was given, should so employ his diligence, as that he might be thought worthy of the same at the hands of the Giver.' " Constantine not only had delivered the church "from outward vexation of foreign tyrants and persecutors" but he had also quieted "the inward dissensions and disturbance within the church, among the christian bishops themselves." Foxe notes letters written by the emperor to vari-

[33] Gardiner, *op. cit.*, pp. 117–119; Cranmer, *Writngs and Letters*, Parker Society (Cambridge, 1846), p. 222; Hooper, *Later Writings*, p. 54; Jewel, *Works*, III, 98–99; Becon, *Catechism*, p. 303; Whitgift, *Works*, III, 306–310.

[34] *AM*, I, 22; Gardiner, *op. cit.*, p. 117; Jewel, *Works*, III, 98–99; Whitgift, *Works*, III, 306–311; Hooker, *op. cit.*, Vol. VII, pt. xviii, p. 2.

[35] *AM*, I, 23. For similar references to Justinian, see Gardiner, *op. cit.*, p. 117; Jewel, *Works*, I, 284–287; Hooker, *op. cit.*, Vol. VII, pt. xviii, pt. 2.

[36] *AM*, I, 292.   [37] *AM*, I, 292–301.

ous bishops telling them what to do for the churches and the clergy. The Council of Nicea was summoned by Constantine, grieved by the division of the church. Foxe's general wish for concord and peace in the church is reflected in his discussion of Constantine's dealing with the disagreements at Nicea. He also refers to Constantine's various humanitarian laws as well as the many in favor of Christians and Christianity as a whole. Foxe notices that in "his own palace he set up a house peculiar for prayer and doctrine, using also to pray and sing with his people." To the emperor's interest in schools and education, as well as to his making available the Scriptures, Foxe pays tribute: "In viewing, perusing, and writing this story, and in considering the christian zeal of the emperor, I wish that either this our printing and plenty of books had been in his days, or that this so heroical heart toward Christ's religion, as was in this so excellent monarch, might something appear in inferior princes reigning in these our printing days." In view of all that Foxe has said about Constantine, it is not surprising that he appeals to the godly prince: "Thus much I thought summarily to comprehend, whereby the divine disposition and singular gentle nature of this meek and religious Constantine might more notoriously appear to all princes, for them to learn by his example what zeal and care they ought to bear toward the church of Christ, and how gently to govern, and how to be beneficial to the same."[38]

According to Foxe the golden age of the church began with the Constantine church-state relationship. The Christian commonwealth then created remained as the ideal for Foxe, but confined within national units. Foxe emphasizes that Constantine was from Britain. In *Christus Triumphans* Foxe says through Ecclesia: "From the day when Constantine of Britain became ruler of the State we have enjoyed peace for a long time."[39] In the *Acts and Monuments*, as well as in his dedicatory preface to Queen Elizabeth, Foxe points out that not only was Constantine born in Britain, but his mother, Helena, was a daughter of an English king.[40] Thus the principles manifested in the creation of the Christian society by Constantine belonged in a special

---

[38] *AM*, I, 293, 296, 299, 300, 298.   [39] *CT*, 62.
[40] *AM*, I, 312; *QE*, ed. (1563), sig. Bir.

sense to Britain. Foxe strongly encouraged her monarch to manifest the same principles.

Foxe deals in detail with the function of the Christian magistrate, and it may be advantageous to quote him at length even though some of the points mentioned have already been noticed or will be considered separately. Having mentioned the duties of the bishop, he writes:

> And as these properly belong to the function of the ecclesiastical sort, so hath the civil governor or magistrate again his proper charge and office to him assigned, which is, to see the administration of justice and judgment, to defend with power the right of the weak that suffer wrong, to defend from oppression the poor oppressed, to minister with equity that which is right and equal to every man, to provide laws and good and godly, to see the execution of the same as cause moveth: especially to see the law of God maintained, to promote Christ's glory and gospel in setting up and sending out good preachers; in maintaining the same; in providing bishops to be elected that be faithful; in removing or else correcting the same being faulty or negligent; in congregating the clergy, when need is of any counsel or election, to hear their learning in causes propounded; and, according to the truth learned, to direct his judgment in disposing such rites and ordinances for the church as make to edification, not to the destruction thereof, in conserving the discipline of the church, and setting all things in a congruous order. Briefly, the office of the civil ruler and magistrate extendeth to minister justice and judgment in all courts, as well ecclesiastical as temporal; to have correction over all transgressors, whether they be laymen or persons ecclesiastical. And finally, all such things as belong to the moving of the sword whatsoever, (that is to say, all outward punishment) are referred to the jurisdiction of the secular magistrate, under whose subjection the ordinance of God hath subjected all orders and states of men.[41]

While Foxe emphasizes the supremacy of the monarch, he also stresses the importance of the Council. To ascertain his view of its power and authority, it may be profitable to consider it in the light of the writings of his contemporaries and close associates. During the Marian persecution Foxe spent some time

[41] *AM*, I, 26.

in Frankfurt and took part in the liturgical discussions among the English refugees. One group wanted to follow the liturgy established during the reign of Edward VI, but a more radical group insisted upon a Genevan form of worship. Foxe was found among the radicals together with John Knox, Anthony Gilby, and others;[42] however, he was greatly distressed with the disagreement between the two groups.[43] Foxe left Frankfurt with the Knoxians when no agreement could be reached, although later he departed from some of the views advocated by Knox. The attack of John Knox upon the legality of female rulers[44] was not shared by Foxe. A letter written by Knox to Foxe from Geneva, dated May 18, 1558, reveals that Foxe must have reproached Knox for his book.[45] Foxe's regard for Queen Elizabeth indicates that he was in sympathy with Aylmer's attack upon Knox.[46] Furthermore Strype tells us about the close association and friendship between Foxe and Aylmer while Foxe lived in Basel.[47]

When John Knox and Anthony Gilby left Frankfurt they settled in Geneva. In 1558 each published a book[48] with the same objective, to prove that it was not only a right but a duty, not merely of the nobles, but also of the common people, to rebel against an ungodly, tyrannical ruler. Christopher Goodman wrote a book on the same subject, also published in Geneva in

[42] J. F. Mozley, *John Foxe and His Book* (London, 1940), pp. 45–46. For a historical record of the Frankfurt dispute, see William Whittingham, *A Brief Discourse of the Troubles at Frankfort, 1554–1558 A.D.* (London, 1907).

[43] See chapter vi, "The Church and Toleration."

[44] [John Knox], *The First Blast of the Trumpet Against the Monstrvovs Regiment of Women* (n.p., 1558).

[45] Strype, *Annals*, Vol. I, pt. ii, pp. 487–488, App. xvii.

[46] John Aylmer, *An Harborowe For Faithfvll and Trewe Subiectes* (Strassburg, 1559).

[47]Strype, *Historical Collections of the Life and Acts of ... John Ayler* (Oxford 1821), pp. 7–10.

[48] John Knox, *The Appellation of Iohn Knoxe from the cruell and most iniust sentence pronounced against him by the false bishoppes and clergie of Scotland* (Geneva, 1558); Anthony Gilby, *An Admonition to England and Scotland to call them to repentance* (Geneva, 1558).

1558.[49] Two years earlier the doctrine of tyrannicide had been advocated by John Ponet in his book on political power.[50]

At the time these writings were published Foxe wrote his address to the English nobility. Not a political theorist, his main burden in this small treatise is an appeal to the nobility to persuade Queen Mary to end the persecution; however, Foxe makes a few statements that indicate his political ideas. Regarding the best form of government he writes: "I believe that there is no constitution more fit or suitable for ruling the state than the monarchy, provided that the Prince administers the laws with moderation and virtue and rules himself as well as others. But I notice that if the monarch is a tyrant he can often stir up grave disturbances in the state."[51] Foxe's ideal monarchy has definite limits: "And I think it was very wisely done by the ancient philosophers and astute law-giver who divided the state (and the senatorial power) into three parts: the rulers, the nobles and the commoners, and joined the public assembly and the senatorial nobility with the monarchy."[52] Foxe does not preach tyrannicide; neither does he try to stir the people to rebellion, but he relies upon the influence of the nobility. The fact that the power of the monarch is joined with that of the nobility "makes for pacification against those two greatest inconveniences and trouble-makers in the state, namely tyranny and sedition."[53] Foxe therefore appeals to the nobility: "I call on you, eminent leaders, who follow in the second place of authority: be present now with your Counsels."[54] Even in the case of an ungodly monarch God overrules for "the government and constitution of times, and states of monarchies and policies, fall not to us by blind chance, but be administered and allotted unto us from above."[55] Because the English nation had not properly

---

[49] Christopher Goodman, *How Svperior Powers Oght to be Obeyd of their subiects* (Geneva, 1558).

[50] John Ponet, *A Short Treatise of Politike Pouuer* (n.p., 1556). A summary of the political theories of Ponet, Knox and Goodman is found in J. W. Allen, *A History of Political Thought in the Sixteenth Century* (London, 1928), pp. 106–120.

[51] *Nob.*, pp. 58–59.

[52] *Nob.*, p. 59.

[53] *Nob.*, p. 60.

[54] *Nob.*, p. 63.

[55] *AM*, IV, 93.

responded to the light of the Gospel during Edward's reign, the oppressive rule of Mary followed.[56]

Laurence Humphrey also wrote a book to the nobility, first printed in Latin in 1560, and later in English in 1563.[57] While Foxe deviated from Ponet, Knox, and Goodman, he was in sympathy with Humphrey.[58] Foxe, like Humphrey, seeking the cooperation of the Protestant nobility in the work of the Reformation, appealed for unity among the nobles.[59] Both were opposed to rebellion against the monarch,[60] but hoped that the nobility through its influence would bridle any tyranny.[61] Knox, Goodman, and Digby in their theory of political resistance deviated from Calvin, while Foxe was more faithful to Calvin's teaching of obedience to rulers, good or bad.[62]

Although the king and the parliament had God-given power and the duty, as chief rulers in a Christian commonwealth, to see that the clergy performed their ministerial functions, yet they could not themselves assume priestly functions. The Bishops Book of 1537 reads that "we may not think that it doth appertain unto the office of kings and princes to preach and teach, to administer the sacraments, to absoyle, to excommunicate, and such other things belonging to the office and administration of bishops and priests."[63] Jewel, Whitgift, and Hooker make similar statements.[64] The latter affirms that there is "a manifest difference acknowledged between the power of Ecclesiastical Order, and the power of Jurisdiction ecclesiastical."[65]

[56] *AM*, VI, 350.

[57] Lawrence Humfrey, *Optimates, sive de Nobilitate* (Basel, 1560); Lawrence Humfrey, *The Nobles or of Nobilitye* (London, 1563).

[58] J. W. Allen deals with Knox, Goodman, and Ponet, but not with Foxe, Aylmer, or Humphrey. The political theories of the latter two are discussed by M. M. Knappen in *Tudor Puritanism: A Chapter in the History of Idealism* (Chicago, 1965), pp. 173–178.

[59] Humfrey (1563), *op. cit.*, sig. Oiiiir.

[60] *Ibid.*, sig. Dir.   [61] *Ibid.*, sig. Div.

[62] John Calvin, *Institutes*, Vol. IV, pt. xx, pp. 25–29.

[63] Charles Lloyd, *Formularies of Faith Put Forth by Authority during the Reign of Henry VIII* (Oxford, 1825), p. 121.

[64] Jewel, *Works*, IV, 976–1145; Whitgift, *Works*, I, 22; III, 592; Hooker, *op. cit.*, Vol. VI, pt. ii, Vol. VIII, pt. ii, p. 16.

[65] Hooker, *op. cit.*, Vol. VI, pt. ii, p. 1.

These writers and Foxe enumerate the same priestly functions and fully agree on the difference between kingly and priestly functions. Foxe believes "that ecclesiastical ministers and servitors have their power also committed unto them, after their sort, of the Lord, yet it becometh every man to know his own place and standing, and there to keep him, wherein his own precinct doth pale him; and not rashly to break out into other men's walks." Furthermore, as "it is not lawful for a civil magistrate to intermeddle with a bishop's or preacher's function, so unseemly and unorderly it is again," that the Roman bishop should take upon himself temporal supremacy. Therefore, "let every man consider the compass and limitation of his charge, and exceed no further."[66]

Concerning the election of the priests and bishops Foxe writes that "by the holy Scriptures, and by decrees of councils, as also by ancient custom of the primitive church, it may easily be proved, that in the first age of the church the chief care and power of distributing ecclesiastical offices were vested in the christian people, regard, however, being had to the counsels of the administrators of ecclesiastical concerns." Later on, "when kings and princes began to embrace Christ's religion, both for honour and order's sake it was granted, that when the people desired such ministers as were by them thought meet, the princes should either confirm such as were so nominated, or else themselves should place fit men over the churches; who should then be presented for consecration to those who were chiefest in ecclesiastical function and authority."[67] By a series of examples from the time of Constantine up to the twelfth century, Foxe tries to show that the emperor nominated or elected the bishops.[68] Up to the time of Hildebrand "the church of Rome was in some order, and bishops quietly governed under christian emperors, and also were defended by the same.[69] One of the various functions of the Christian magistrate enumerated by Foxe is "to promote Christ's glory, and gospel in setting up and sending out good preachers; in maintaining the same." Another is "in pro-

---

[66] *AM*, I, 25–26.
[67] *AM*, II, 460. See also *AM*, I, 14.
[68] *AM*, II, 460–463.　　　　　　[69] *AM*, II, 115.

viding bishops to be elected that be faithful; in removing or else correcting the same being faulty or negligent."[70]

Foxe, along with Cranmer, Whitgift, and Hooker, brings out the point that in the early church the people elected the bishop because they did not have a Christian magistrate. Where there is a Christian commonwealth with a Christian magistrate, it is his prerogative to elect the bishop. This argument was used against the Papists by Cranmer, against the extreme Puritans by Whitgift, and against both by Hooker.[71] Foxe no doubt would agree with Hooker's explanation:

> For as much as, if we speak properly, we cannot say kings do make, but that they only do place, bishops. For in a bishop there are these three things to be considered; the power whereby he is distinguished from other pastors; the special portion of the clergy and people over whom he is to exercise that bishoply power; and the place of his seat or throne, together with the profits, preeminences, honours thereunto belonging. The first every bishop hath by consecration; the second his election investeth him with; the third he receiveth of the king alone.[72]

Hooker does not say that the king is alone in the election. Foxe evidently agrees, for while he says that the king should provide "bishops to be elected," he also affirms that one of the duties of the Christian magistrate is "in congregating the clergy, when need is of any counsel or election."[73] No doubt Hooker stressed the point that was of basic importance when he wrote that "we cannot say kings do make, but that they only do place, bishops."

When Foxe speaks about royal supremacy and the power of the Parliament, he takes it for granted that the secular rulers are members of a Christian church in a Christian commonwealth. These Christian princes and magistrates should be governed by God in order to fulfill their God-given functions. Foxe emphasizes these points in his closing prayer "for the church and all the states thereof" in his sermon preached at St. Paul's Cross in A.D. *1570*. Foxe first refers to "a large church, a universal

---

[70] *AM*, I, 26.
[71] Cranmer, *Writings and Letters*, p. 116; Whitgift, *Works*, I, 394, 398; Hooker, *op. cit.*, Vol. VIII, pt. vii, pp. 2, 3.
[72] Hooker, *op. cit.*, Vol. VIII, pt. vii, p. 1.
[73] *AM*, I, 26.

church, spread far and wide," but "now driven into a narrow corner of the world," namely Western Europe. Outside are the Turks, but inside are the Papists and even the Protestants who do not agree among themselves. However, Christendom is confined within its borders, and church and state are one society. Thanking God for the Queen, he petitions: "In this her government, be her governor, we beseech thee; so shall her majesty well govern us, if first she be governed by thee."[74]

In the dedicatory preface to the *Acts and Monuments* (1563), Foxe tells the readers that the Queen is the "defendour of the faith, and supreme governour . . . as well in causes ecclesiasticall, as also to the temporall state appertaining," but "next vnder the Lorde."[75] In the 1570 edition the first paragraph conveys the same idea more emphatically with a slight change of wording. Foxe calls her not only the defender of the faith but "defendour of Christes Fayth and Gospel." He changes the words supreme governor to "principall gouernour both of the Realme and also ouer the sayd Church of England and Ireland," and he emphasizes her subservience to God by saying that she should rule "vnder Christ the supreme head."[76]

In his sermon at St. Paul's Cross, Foxe points out the significance and importance of the Parliament when he says that "no government can long stand without good counsel," but, as with the Queen, "neither can any counsel be good except it be prospered" by God. Foxe therefore asks God to bless "both her majesty and her honourable council, that they both rightly may understand what is to be done, and she accordingly may accomplish that which they do counsel, to thy glory, and furtherance of thy gospel, and public wealth of this realm." In his prayer for the nobility of England he also includes "other christian realms; so, as they, christianly agreeing among themselves, may submit their nobility to serve thee; or else let them feel, O Lord, what a frivolous thing is that nobility which is without thee." For "all magistrates" Foxe asks that through them be "God's glory maintained, and the commonwealth truly served." For the people in general he asks that God "give to all the people,

---

[74] *CC*, pp. 91, 94.   [75] *QE* (1563), sig. Bir.
[76] *QE* (1570), sig. ir.

and the whole state of this realm such brotherly unity in knowledge of thy truth, and such obedience to their superiors, that they neither provoke the scourge of God against them, nor their prince's sword to be drawn against her will. . . . Especially, give thy gospel long continuance amongst us."[77]

In emphasizing that the Queen and the government should be governed by God, Foxe established the right of the priest to admonish them. Therefore, among the functions of "a bishop or servitor ecclesiastical" is the one "to admonish also the magistrates erring or transgressing in their office."[78] Foxe's close friend Edmund Grindal illustrates this principle. In 1567 a Londoner, who was examined before the ecclesiastical commissioners, stated "that the Prince and people both should obey the word of God"; to this Grindal, then bishop of London, "gravely answered, that it was true in effect, that the Prince should and must obey the word of God only."[79] Ten years later in 1576, after having become archbishop, Grindal addressed the Queen concerning the suppression of prophesying:

> Take heed, that ye never once think of declining from God. . . . Ye have done many things well; but except ye persevere to the end ye cannot be blessed. For if ye turn from God, then God will turn away his merciful countenance from you. And what remaineth then to be looked for, but only a terrible expectation of God's judgments, and an heaping up of wrath against the day of wrath?[80]

Grindal felt the tension inherent in the principle: on the one hand, the bishop must render obedience to the monarch, the supreme governor in things civil and ecclesiastical; and on the other, as servitor ecclesiastical he must admonish the monarch who should first of all be governed by God. In a letter to the Privy Council, nearly a year after his message to the Queen, he expressed his reverence and respect for her. He longed to regain her favor, but at the same time his heart and conscience, bound by the word of God, compelled him, as archbishop, to admonish her.[81] When Hooker discusses the priestly functions that are

---

[77] *CC*, pp. 94, 95.   [78] *AM*, I, 26.

[79] John Strype, *The History of the Life and Acts of . . . Edmund Grindal* (Oxford, 1821), p. 172.

[80] Edmund Grindal, *Remains*, Parker Society (Cambridge, 1843), p. 390.

[81] *Ibid.*, pp. 392–394.

denied to the king, such as "power to administer the word and sacraments, power to ordain, ... to bind and loose, to excommunicate, and such like," he may have had in mind the above-mentioned tension. He closes his statement by saying:

> ... even in these very actions which are proper unto dominion, there must be some certain rule, whereunto kings in all their proceedings ought to be strictly tied; which rule for proceedings in ecclesiastical affairs and causes by regal power, hath not hitherto been agreed upon, with so uniform consent and certainty as might be wished.[82]

Another illustration of the expectation that the king be a Christian king governed by God is the fact that those who acknowledge the monarch as the supreme head or governor of the church also emphasized, as did Foxe to Queen Elizabeth, that "Christ is the supreme Head of the same." He expresses the same point when he writes that Christ is "the one Head of the church" or "the Head of the universal church and supreme Lord."[83] That Christ was also the only Head seemed, first to the Papists and later to the extreme Puritans, contradictory; and those who accepted the monarch as the supreme governor of the church had to deal with this question. They emphasize that the king is head not of the universal church or of the church of Christ but of the Church of England.[84] Whitgift writes: "The church may be established without the magistrate, touching true faith, and the spiritual government of it by Christ in the heart and conscience of man, but not touching the visible society and the external government."[85] In other words the headship given to the king is one of the "principal instruments for the Church's outward government."[86] Even in that headship he does not have ultimate power, as has already been noticed. Hooker states: "If magistrates be heads of the Church, they are of necessity Christians; if Christians, then is the Head Christ."[87] This is no doubt

---

[82] Hooker, *op. cit.*, Vol. VIII, pt. ii, p. 16.
[83] *Apoc.*, pp. 230–231, 274.
[84] Cranmer, *Writings and Letters*, p. 219; Jewel, *Works*, IV, 976.
[85] Whitgift, *Works*, I, 392; III, 198.
[86] Hooker, *op. cit.*, Vol. VIII, pt. iv, p. 9. See also pp. 1, 4, 5, 7.
[87] *Ibid.*, Vol. VIII, pt. iv, p. 7.

what Foxe meant when he said that Christ should be the governor of Queen Elizabeth.

Although head of the church, the monarch should not issue laws and make major decisions without counsel. Foxe states that one of his duties is fulfilled "in congregating the clergy, when need is of any counsel or election, to hear their learning in causes propounded; and, according to the truth learned, to direct his judgment in disposing such rites and ordinances for the church as make to edification, not to the destruction thereof."[88] Jewel says that if controversy arises on spiritual matters, the Queen "commendeth and giveth to her learned divines the due consideration thereof."[89] Whitgift too is in line with Foxe when he writes: ". . . the queen's majesty, being supreme governor in all causes, both ecclesiastical and temporal, committeth the hearing and judging of ecclesiastical matters to the archbishops and bishops, and temporal matters to the lord chancellor and other judges."[90] He further writes: "No godly princes having godly bishops and ministers of the church will alter or change, determine or appoint anything in matters of religion, without their advice and counsel."[91] Hooker, with Foxe and the other writers, emphasizes that the council, which includes the monarch and the convocation, has the final authority, not any one of them separately.[92]

We have noticed that Foxe considers Constantine the ideal Christian ruler. He points out that the emperor, in his relationship to the bishop Eusebius, "aske of him what so euer he thought expedient or necessary for the state and commoditie of his Churche, promising to graunt vnto him the same, whatsoeuer he should aske." The emperor listened to and granted Eusebius's petitions. Foxe makes known to Elizabeth the importance of the bishops and how she, as supreme governor, should relate herself to them. Taking upon himself the role of her ecclesiastical adviser he writes:

> In whiche Historie (most excellent and noble Queene) twoo thynges put me in a variable doubt, whether of these two rather

[88] *AM*, I, 26.　　　　　　　　[89] Jewel, *Works*, IV, 1145.
[90] Whitgift, *Works*, III, 302–303.
[91] *Ibid.*, p. 311.
[92] Hooker, *op. cit.*, Vol. VIII, pt. ii, pp. 1–5, 16–17.

to commend or extolle: the good Emperour, or the godly Byshoppe: the one for his Princely proferre, the other for his godly
and syncere peticion. The Emperour for his rare and syngular
affection in fauouring and furtherynge the Lordes churche, or
the Byshoppe in zealying the publique busines of the Lord, before
the priuate lucre of hym selfe. Certes in bothe together may to
vs appeare, what all maner estates may learne to knowe: not
onelye what in those dayes was done, but also what ought nowe
to be followed.[93]

The various estates we have been discussing are harmoniously
combined in the closing prayer of Foxe's sermon, *Christ Crucified*. He concludes his sermon: "And now let us pray as we
began, making our earnest invocation to almighty God for the
universal state of Christ's church, and all other estates and degrees in order particularly, as custom, and also duty, requireth."
First of all, Foxe prays for the universal church, that it may be
saved from the manifold dangers of the latter days, especially
the dangers from the bishop of Rome. Having offered a special
petition for the Church of England, Foxe prays for Queen Elizabeth I, at the same time praising her: "thy singular goodness hath
given them a queen so calm, so patient, so merciful, more like a
natural mother than a princess, to govern over them, such as
neither they nor their ancestors ever read of in the histories of
this land before." He then emphasizes that she should be
governed by God, and next mentions the importance of the
"honourable council." For the Christian ministry he prays: "But
especially to thy spiritual ministers, bishops, and pastors of thy
church, we beseech thee." For the English people as a nation he
asks: "In general, give to all people, and the whole state of this
realm such brotherly unity in knowledge of thy truth, and such
obedience to their superiors, that they neither provoke the
scourge of God against them, nor their prince's sword to be
drawn against her will." He refers to the pope, who on Good
Friday used "to accurse us as damned heretics, we here curse
not him, but we pray for him, that he, with all his partakers
either may be turned to a better truth; or else, we pray thee,
gracious Lord, that we never agree with him in doctrine." Final-

---

[93] *QE* (1563), sig. Bir–v.

ly he touches the elect and his eschatological concept when he prays: "And forasmuch as thy poor little flock can scarcely have any place or rest in this world, come Lord, we beseech thee, with thy, It is finished, and make an end, that this world may have no more time nor place here, and that thy church may have rest for ever."[94] Foxe, in this prayer, brings into a proper relationship his concept of the nature of the church, his apocalyptic expectations, and the various ruling groups which should be considered in connection with his ideas of church-state relationships.

[94] CC, pp. 91–95. See also "A Book of Christian Prayers," 1578, printed in *Private Prayers, Put forth by Authority during the Reign of Queen Elizabeth*, Parker Society (Cambridge, 1851), pp. 462–467.

VI. The Church and Toleration

THE CONCEPT of religious toleration was revived during the
sixteenth century by the Reformers who in the early period of the Reformation advocated freedom of conscience, as
well as obedience to God, as man's primary duty. Belief in the
Bible as the sole authority in matters of faith, the truth of justification by faith, the doctrine of the priesthood of all believers, the
participation of Christian laity in church government, as well as
the Protestant concept of Christ as the sole head of the church,
created a platform on which the cause of religious toleration
could be furthered. On the other hand, the Reformers' alliance
with the state, the doctrine of the sovereignty of God, and the
spirit of Protestant orthodoxy and scholasticism led to intol-
erance. The Reformers required freedom of conscience and
religious liberty for themselves, but generally they were not
ready to grant this to others. In marked contrast to this incon-
sistent attitude stand the life, preaching, and writing of John
Foxe.

To the 1583 edition of the *Acts and Monuments* Foxe adds a
new preface with "Four Considerations Geuen out to Christian
Protestantes, Professours of the Gospell." In it Foxe again brings
to the reader's attention the blessings of the reign of Queen Elizabeth. He makes a special reference to "the peacable libertie"
bestowed upon England and the Gospel which was "so freely
preached, with such libertie of conscience without daunger pro-

fessed."[1] Josiah Pratt suggests that the expression "liberty of conscience" here "appears to have been first used in its modern sense."[2] However, Pratt does not enter into any discussion of the subject in order to substantiate his assertion. Furthermore, one standard work on toleration in England refers only briefly to one of Foxe's numerous pleas for toleration,[3] and a recent work on the same subject does not mention his position at all.[4] Thus Foxe's concept of toleration calls for an examination, particularly because it has a direct bearing upon his concept of the church, and an evaluation of the latter cannot be complete without a study of the former.

Foxe's sensitive, kind, and gentle nature, which has already been noticed on a number of occasions, made him well-disposed to toleration. In his plea of 1575 to Queen Elizabeth on behalf of some Anabaptists condemned to death by burning, he says: "I befriend the lives of men since I myself am a man. And I speak for them, not that they may continue in error, but that they may come to their senses. Not for men only. Would that I might be able to help the very beasts!" He even confesses that the slaughtering of animals in the marketplace brings him feelings of pain.

The latter brings to mind one of the details in Thomas More's description of the marketplace in his *Utopia*. The animals are slaughtered and cleansed by the slaves outside the city in order that the citizens may not "accustom themselves to the butchering of animals, by the practice of which they think that mercy, the finest feeling of our human nature, is gradually killed off."[5] Foxe also expresses his admiration and veneration for "the clemency of God himself in ordaining that those brute and lowly creatures which were formerly made ready for sacrifice should not be committed to the flames before their blood was poured

[1] *FCCP*, sig. iiv.

[2] *Pratt*, p. 87.

[3] W. K. Jordan, *The Development of Religious Toleration in England* (London, 1932), pp. 181–182.

[4] Joseph Lecler, *Toleration and the Reformation* (London, 1960).

[5] Thomas More, *Utopia*, in *The Complete Works of St. Thomas More*, Vol. IV., ed. Edward Surtz and J. H. Hexter (New Haven and London, 1965), p. 139.

out at the foot of the altar." From this example Foxe concludes that "in exacting punishments, no matter how just, rigour should not bear sole sway, but clemency should temper the harshness of rigour."[6]

Foxe's concept of toleration did not have its roots just in his own character, but resulted from Gospel teaching and the ideals of the Christian Humanists. There are manifest echoes of the latter throughout his writings, as when he writes to the English nobility that ". . . among all human affections none is so fitting to men as clemency, which we all trace back to the image of the Divine nature."[7] Foxe also expresses the hope that toleration would "shortly come to pass, by the most prosperous success of learning, which daily flourisheth more and more in England: and as it is to be hoped, foreign examples, and greater experience of things, will bring a more civility to this, which is already obtained by learning."[8]

Many of Foxe's thoughts on toleration are specifically reminiscent of Erasmus. He also shares Erasmus's hatred of dissension and aversion to contention, and he adheres closely to Erasmus's exclamation: "I do not deny that I seek peace whenever possible. . . . I love liberty. I do not wish to serve any faction, neither can I."[9] These words were written to Ulrich von Hutten, who, as the German Demosthenes at the Diet of Worms, had exerted all his power of violent denunciation against Rome and for the Lutheran cause. After an unsuccessful military attack on the archbishop of Trier, von Hutten sought refuge in Basel. Erasmus's apparent cautiousness in not being willing to let von Hutten pay him a visit caused, among other things, the latter to write the *Expostulatio cum Erasmo.* Erasmus replied with the *Spongia Erasmi adversvs Adspergines Ulrici Hvtteni,* which reveals his personal attitude toward the Lutheran-Roman struggle. He writes:

> The one to whom the Spirit of Jesus imparts the gift of abstruse erudition, let him impart it with candor, with clemency,

---

[6] *Pratt,* App. X, p. 28; Harleian MS, no. 416, fol. 151r–v.

[7] *Nob.,* pp. 70–71. [8] *AM,* V, 226.

[9] Desiderius Erasmus, *Desiderii Erasmi Opervm Omnivm* (Lugduni Batavorum, 1703), X, 1643F, 1650D.

sustaining and tolerating those who cannot follow at once what is given, as the Lord Jesus for long a time has born with the infirmity of his own as they grow. . . . Is it not more conducible for them to lead men to a knowledge of truth than to exasperate them by wrangling? . . . Let private cupidity be put away and let peace loving Spirit be implored, lest by mutual differences the Christian state, now less happy, be inwardly destroyed, and lest we furnish to Satan and the enemies of the name of Christ a spectacle of mutual tearing each other in turn as do wild beasts and fishes. . . . Yielding will prepare for friendship, obstinacy will bring tumult. What will the end be if one part has nothing but tumult, strifes and insults, and the other censures, Bulls, articles and burning? It is not a great deed to throw a weak mortal man into flames. It is a great accomplishment to teach and persuade him.[10]

Erasmus expressed a similar sentiment to Duke George of Saxony, who during his reign, 1500 to 1539, held the course of the Reformation back within his own territory. Erasmus understood the Duke's worry regarding the religious disputes, but suggests that the matters be tried by a serious council composed of calm minds with the attitude of moderation. He regrets the atrocious hatred manifested on both sides, but exclaims: "Oh, that the matters might be effected with gentleness and solicitude, as is becoming to all most holy negotiations!"[11]

After Adrian VI had ascended the papal chair in 1522, he twice invited Erasmus to come to Rome. Erasmus declined but in several letters conveyed privately to the pontiff his proposals for dealing with the Lutheran trouble. The proposals he describes as an "exhortation to Christian concord" (*cohortatiuncula . . . ad Christianam concordiam*).[12] He realizes "that to many it seems right, that evil should be healed by austerity, but [I fear] indeed the outcome of the matters once this imprudent council be accepted." Accordingly he states: "Certainly, if the right method to destroy this evil is by prisons, scourgings, confiscations, exiles, censures, deaths, there will be no need for my counsel, but I know that your most gentle nature would be

---

[10] *Ibid.*, 1672D.

[11] P. S. and H. M. Allen, eds., *Opvs Epistolarvm Des. Erasmi Roterodami* (Oxford, 1906–1958), Vol. V, epist. 1313, p. 126.

[12] *Ibid.*, Vol. V, epist. 1358, pp. 276–277; epist. 1329, pp. 155–156; epist. 1376, p. 308; epist. 1408, p. 381.

pleased with a different counsel, which would heal rather than punish. . . . If God daily forgives the contrite sinner, should the vicar of God do less?"[13] In another connection Erasmus writes:

> The sum of our religion is peace and unanimity, but this will scarcely be obtained, unless we can define as little as possible and in many matters leave each to follow his own judgment. . . . At length the matter leads to sophisticated disputes causing a myriad of discourses to burst forth. Hence it leads to terror and threats. Where our life is destitute, whose faith is in the mouth rather than in the heart, when the sound understanding of sacred Scriptures fails us, nevertheless by terrorization we drive men to believe what they do not believe, to love what they do not love, to know what they do not know. That which is coerced cannot be sincere, and that which is not sincere cannot please Christ.[14]

Finally two further statements from the pen of Erasmus should be noticed. To John Botzheim he writes: "While truth is efficacious and unconquerable, Evangelical prudence should be manifested everywhere. I hate dissension, but love concord."[15] In a letter to a certain Marcus Laurinus he reiterates: "I hate discord, not only because it is evil, or on account of the teaching and precepts of Christ, but also because of a certain hidden force of nature."[16]

In evaluating the influences and motives that formulated Foxe's concept of toleration, it seems significant that he went to Basel, not Geneva, where other of his friends went after the split among the members of the English Church in Frankfurt. In Basel, Erasmus had left behind him a circle of Erasmians. Durin the 1540s and until the 1570s many Italian Humanists found their homes here. Among them was Sebastien Castellio. He was first occupied as proofreader for Oporinus, and during this period he wrote the preface to his Latin Bible which was a plea for religious liberty. It was dedicated to King Edward VI. In the year Servetus was burned, 1553, Castellio began a teaching post at the University of Basel and became a leader in the protests against the burning of heretics. Bernardino Ochino had lived

---

[13] *Ibid.*, Vol. V, epist. 1352, pp. 260–261.
[14] *Ibid.*, Vol. V, epist. 1334, pp. 177, 181.
[15] *Ibid.*, Vol. V, epist. 1331, p. 159.
[16] *Ibid.*, Vol. V, epist. 1342, p. 220.

twice in Basel prior to his stay in England during the reign of Edward VI. He returned at the time Servetus was executed. He lived for a short while in Basel again and joined Castellio in disapproval of the execution of Servetus. They were joined by another citizen of Basel, David Joris, a Dutchman and secret Anabaptist who wrote his own tract in remonstrance.

However significant the influence of the Christian Humanists is in the life of Foxe, his concept of toleration can be fully appreciated only if seen in the light of the Reformers' evangelical message of God's forgiving grace in Christ Jesus. It appears that "the precepts of Christ" and "a certain hidden force of nature" were rather equal factors in Erasmus's plea for toleration, but in Foxe's case the first was more prominent.

In the Gospel is found his basic motivation for advocating religious toleration. In view of the fact that "God Himself daily forgives those who fail, how much more should mortals judge one another leniently."[17] Gentleness, meekness, consideration, and the like are virtues ultimately connected with true Christian living; thus the Gospel, rightly preached and accepted, leads to a manifestation of tolerance. Foxe's writings richly illustrate this point. Referring to Christ as the example to be followed by the church, Foxe writes: "He forced no one against his will. He sought the life of none, nor their fortune, nor did he take men's bodies. He instilled into their minds only the doctrine of peace. ... Only that meek spirit, and the practice of the gospel of lowliness did he proclaim."[18] Examining Foxe's many pleas for toleration, we see that he is not a mere academic theorist, but a Christian pragmatist who is devoted to his Master in service for his fellow men.

In 1555 during the liturgical discussions among the English exiles in Frankfurt, Foxe wrote a letter to Peter Martyr in which he expressed his great sorrow over the hatred, quarrels, and divisions among the expatriated Christians. He would like "to bring healing to these wounds," and states: "So far as I am concerned, I shall everywhere be a promoter of concord."[19] Foxe's conciliatory attitude in the Vestiarian Controversy during the

---

[17] *Adul.*, sig. Aiiv–Aiiir.   [18] *Apoc.*, p. 61.
[19] Strype, *Ecclesiastical Memorials* (Oxford, 1821), Vol. III, pt. ii, p. 310.

early years of Elizabeth's reign has already been noticed, and his appeal to moderation and toleration in the debate between Whitgift and Thomas Cartwright has also been considered.[20] Likewise his search for peace in the controversy over the doctrine of the Eucharist has been mentioned.[21] Discussing various possibilities of biblical interpretation, Foxe points out that in the church there must be some freedom of opinions: "When we reflect upon the church, in the plans for which we equally share, there always have been free investigation and declaration of truth."[22] In regard to undecided or debatable points, Foxe believes: "Surely a church ought not to be deprived of that liberty, which Christ always wanted to remain inviolate."[23] In another connection he states that "in a free church freedom to express one's personal opinion should be allowed."[24]

Foxe expressed strong disapproval of the death penalty for religious reasons; and, where he had opportunity, he did all that he possibly could to intervene on behalf of the condemned. During the reign of Edward VI only two were put to death on account of their religion. One, Joan of Kent, seems to have been an Anabaptist; and the other, George,[25] or George the German,[26] an Arian. Since both were liable to capital punishment according to old Roman law, it is significant that Foxe pleaded on their behalf.

Emperor Justinian I (A.D. 527–565) codified the Roman laws and incorporated ecclesiastical laws in the Corpus Juris Romani. In this way the ecclesiastical laws had the enforcement of the civil power. Justinian issued severe laws against heretics, who, he decreed, "might not hold public office, engage in the liberal professions, hold meetings, or maintain churches of their own, or even enjoy all the civil rights of the Roman citizen: for them, said Justinian, 'to exist is sufficient.' "[27] The law of Justinian also decreed the death penalty on those who denied the

---

[20] See chapter iv, "The Church and its Ministry."
[21] See chapter iii, "The Marks of the Church."
[22] *Apoc.*, sig. 4v.
[23] *Apoc.*, p. 21.
[24] *Apoc.*, p. 26.
[25] *AM*, V, 704.
[26] *AM* (1559), p. 202.
[27] Margaret Deanesly, *A History of the Medieval Church*, 590–1500 (London, 1954), p. 9.

doctrine of the Trinity or repeated baptism. During the Reformation this law of Justinian was used by the leading Reformers against Anabaptists and Anti-Trinitarians.[28]

In the 1559 Latin edition of the *Acts and Monuments*, a description is given of one who pleaded with John Rogers on behalf of Joan of Kent.[29] The story sounds suspiciously autobiographical. Josiah Pratt notices this point and asks: "Was this Foxe himself?"[30] Mozley believes it was.[31] The present study confirms Mozley's conviction. The appeal is similar to the one on behalf of the Anabaptists in 1575, and the whole story reflects the general sentiment of Foxe in regard to capital punishment for heretics.

In connection with the death of Joan of Kent, Foxe also makes some comments relative to the martyrdom of George, who was burned a year later in 1551. Foxe tells us that George's accusers had to admit that he was "an upright and blameless person." Foxe exclaims. "Oh, that a person of such a life had not held such a view, or that by some other means than by death he could have been dealt with."[32]

In October 1553, Michael Servetus was burned as a heretic. Hardly a year later Foxe dedicated his small 1554 Latin edition of the *Acts and Monuments* to Duke Christopher of Würtemberg. His preface reflects the animosity among Christians of which the burning of Servetus was an example. To the Duke, Foxe writes: "But these contentions of minds . . . are taking away private liberty. . . . Where indeed has not zeal for parties today spread among Christians?"[33] Foxe appeals for a "community of brotherly love" with "mutual forbearance and forgiveness."[34] Throughout the preface Foxe calls for a unity of Christian concord in which hatred of errors should be joined with love of persons. Mozley points out that Thomas Sampson of Lausanne, in his copy of the 1554 edition, has added some comments which clearly indicate that Foxe must have had Servetus in mind. There

---

[28] Roland H. Bainton, *The Travail of Religious Liberty* (New York, 1958), p. 18.

[29] *Ibid.*, pp. 202–203.   [30] *AM*, V, 860 n. 1.

[31] J. F. Mozley, *John Foxe and His Book* (London, 1940), p. 35.

[32] *AM* (1559), p. 202.   [33] *AM* (1554), sig. iiv.

[34] *AM* (1554), sig. iiiv.

is good reason to believe that Sampson is correct. Mozley's suggestion that Foxe may have openly condemned burning seems very plausible.[35]

In 1575 the fire of persecution was kindled anew in Smithfield as two Dutch Anabaptists were burned for their religious views.[36] An earnest plea had been made on their behalf by the Dutch Reformed congregation in London, one of the Strangers' Churches which had been organized by Archbishop Cranmer during the reign of Edward VI. Perhaps it was hoped that these churches, composed of foreigners, would become models of the reformed church and thus in turn advance the Reformation of the English Church; although the reign of Mary and the conservatism of Elizabeth made their influence insignificant.[37] However the Dutch church, which greatly opposed the teaching of the Anabaptists, showed itself as a model church in regard to religious toleration. The congregation tried in every possible way to prevent the burning of the Anabaptists, to the point that they were themselves in danger of being accused of Anabaptism.[38] Jacques de Somere, a Reformed layman, made a supplication to Queen Elizabeth; and Thomas Bodley, the endower of the Bodleian Library, Oxford, conferred with the bishop of London.[39] Foxe, too, exerted all his influence in trying to avert the execution. We have already mentioned his plea to the Queen, and in his letter to Chief Justice Monson he appeals for clemency by pointing out that "the nearer each approaches the sweet spirit of the Gospel, so much farther he is from the hard decision of burning and torturing.[40] Foxe little doubts the clemency of the Chief Justice because of his "extreme prudence" and "sincere

---

[35] Mozley, *op. cit.*, pp. 47–48.

[36] Strype, *Annals*, Vol. II, pt. ii, p. 564.

[37] Frederick A. Norwood, "The Strangers' Model Churches in Sixteenth-Century England," printed in *Reformation Studies, Essays in Honor of Roland H. Bainton*, ed. Franklin H. Littel (Richmond, Va., 1962), pp. 181–196.

[38] J. H. Hessels, ed., *Ecclesiae Londino-Batavae Archivum* (Cambridge, 1889), II, 700–708.

[39] Thieleman J. van Braght, *The Bloody Theater or Martyrs Mirror* (Scottsdale, Pa., 1951), pp. 1008–1024.

[40] *Pratt*, App. XI, p. 28; Harleian MS, no. 417, fol. 111r.

religion."[41] Foxe also writes a letter to the condemned Anabaptists in which he appeals to them not to fight against the will and Word of God. He mainly deals with their obstinate contention concerning the humanity of Christ.[42] The Anabaptists answer Foxe most cordially, thanking him for the "admonition, which notwithstanding it seems to us to be written somewhat severely, we are nevertheless assured proceeds from love and from good zeal which you have for the truth and the welfare of your neighbour." In the letter they seek to give an account of their faith, and they conclude, "... thanking you for the trouble to which you have been pleased to go for us, and requesting you that you will do the best in our cause, with the council, and especially before her royal majesty."[43]

In connection with this plea for mercy toward the Anabaptists, Foxe lays down the principle that toleration is necessary for the Gospel to have opportunity to make its influence felt. Foxe asks the chief justice to consider "their souls, lest they perish eternally. Often there occur sicknesses in which piety accomplishes more than asperity and time more than the hand of the physician. I speak of those sicknesses, now, which are more in need of spiritual medicine than corporal."[44] Foxe also writes to the Lord Treasurer concerning the same condemned Anabaptists, and appeals for the use of "the mercy of the Gospel."[45] On still another occasion Foxe writes: "It is tyrannical to constrain by faggots. Consciences love to be taught, and religion wants to teach. Moreover the most effective master teacher is love. Where this is absent, there is never anyone who can teach aright nor can anyone learn properly."[46]

As a proclaimer of the Gospel and its bearing upon toleration, Foxe felt the importance of the question of the right relationship between the Mosaic law and grace. The Calvin-Beza theology had considerable influence in England. According to Calvin, God's precepts for right ethical living are found in the Deca-

[41] *Ibid.*
[42] *Pratt*, App. XII, pp. 29–30; Harleian MS, no. 417, fol. 111v.
[43] Van Braght, *op. cit.*, pp. 1023, 1024.
[44] *Pratt*, App. XI, p. 29; Harleian MS, no. 417, fol. 111r.
[45] *Pratt*, App. XIII, p. 31; Harleian MS, no. 417, fol. 110v.
[46] *Nob.*, pp. 52–53.

logue; all levitical laws are but interpretations of its meanings. It is an error to think that "Christ was only a second Moses," to supplement the limitations of the Mosaic law.[47] Calvin believed that the Gospel had abolished the ceremonial requirements of the laws of Moses, but not their moral and judicial injunctions. Therefore, much of Calvin's justification for the execution of heretics is based on Deuteronomy 13.[48] In his fifth sermon on Deuteronomy 22, dealing with the stoning of those taken in adultery, Calvin strongly suggests that adultery ought to be punished by death.[49] The same was believed by the Protestant Reformers in general.[50]

The Roman Catholics, on account of their Thomistic sacramental concept of marriage, held that the marriage tie was indissoluble; thus the sin of adultery could only separate the partners from board and bed (*divortium a mensa et thoro*) with no allowance made for remarrying. The Protestant Reformers, who taught that remarriage is justified in the event of adultery, used as one of their scriptural "proofs" the teaching of the Mosaic law that the guilty party should be stoned. Although this punishment was no longer exercised, the guilty party was still considered dead in his relationship to the former spouse, and the latter was free to marry again. While both Luther and Calvin agree to this interpretation, there is a basic theological difference between them which should be noticed.

Luther's doctrine of the two kingdoms was of basic importance in his consideration of matrimonial matters. Marriage was not only a *res sacra* but also a secular matter. The secular aspect of marriage is shown by the fact that the only means of punishment given to the church is excommunication, while to the magistrate is given the authority to declare a divorce legal and the power of the sword to punish the guilty party. Secular so-

[47] John Calvin, *Institutes*, Vol. II, pt. viii, p. 7.

[48] John Calvin, *The Sermons of M. John Calvin vpon the Fifth Booke of Moses called Deuteronomie* (London, 1583), pp. 539–546.

[49] *Ibid.*, pp. 791–796.

[50] For a detailed discussion of the question of divorce during the Reformation era see V. Norskov Olsen, *The New Testament Logia on Divorce: A Study of Their Interpretation from Erasmus to Milton* (Tübingen, 1971).

ciety is governed by laws different from those operating in the kingdom of God. It is true that the nearer the magistrate ruled according to the law of God, the nearer he was to the ideal government, but as Moses himself among the Israelites (as in the case of the letter of divorce), so also the magistrate had to do his best under the given circumstances. The laws of the Christian emperors illustrated this point.

Calvin sought to make the administration of Geneva "bibliocratic," which meant that the secular society ought to be governed by a "thus saith the Lord." His hermeneutical principle was that God is ever the same and does not contradict himself; accordingly, laws and regulations, including those governing discipline and punishment, which should guide the magistrate in matrimonial matters had to be in harmony with the teaching of Christ. Calvin and Beza contended that both the Old and New Testaments had made adultery the one exception for divorce only because the stoning had been neglected. Calvin's theological reasons and arguments on this point, as on others, were further sharpened and brought to their logical conclusion by Beza, who declared that the same law should still be applied: "then there would be no place for the question of divorce among Christians."[51]

Having stated that the laws of divorce must be sought in the word of God alone,[52] Beza asks two questions whose answers are implicit in his previous statements. First, "But I ask whether, if at the universal forum of conscience, there can by human laws be any excuse for straying one iota outside the word of God." Next, "Whether in fact it can be right for the magistrates in anything to go beyond the law of Moses?"[53] Beza realizes that bishops of old did not oppose the imperial laws, and that many during his own time favored these laws, but in the light of his exegesis his own opinion is: "It is not a question as to what was done, but what should be done."[54]

It was the Calvin-Beza theology of divorce that Cartwright

[51] Theodore Beza, *Nouum Testamentum ... Annotationes* (n.p., 1582), pt. 1, p. 283 (Luke 16:18).
[52] Beza, *De Divortiis*, p. 245.
[53] *Ibid.*, p. 246.
[54] *Ibid.*, p. 247.

perpetuated in his discussion with Whitgift.[55] He clearly states: "I affirmed that there are certen lawes amongest the Judicialles, which can not be chaunged. And hereof I gaue example, in the lawes which command, that a stubbern Idolater, blasphemer, murtherer, incestuous person, and suche like, should be put to death."[56] Referring to Deuteronomy 13 he categorically affirms "that the false teacher shall die."[57] Whitgift, on the other hand, takes the position that both the ceremonial and judicial laws of Moses had been abolished.[58] In regard to the judicial laws the magistrate can therefore "add to it or take from it, or to alter and change it, as shall be thought most fit for the time, manner of the country, and condition of the people."[59] Whitgift states that Christ abolished the death penalty for adultery.[60]

It has been stated that the embryo of the Anglican-Puritan conflict is found in their different concepts of law and grace, or their diverse views of the relationship between the Old and New Testaments.[61] Foxe's view of law and grace is revealed in his concept of toleration; this puts a basic theological difference between himself and Cartwright, as well as those seventeenth-century Puritans who would agree with the Calvin-Beza view of the judicial laws of Moses. It should be noticed that Cartwright's concept of the laws of Moses, especially as related to capital punishment and the question of toleration, was published by the Puritans in a booklet in 1648.[62]

The significance of John Foxe's appeal to Thomas Picton against death sentences on adultery can be fully appreciated only when it is seen in the light of Calvin's theology. In the appeal he states: If I might set forth my opinion freely, in a free church of Christians, for my part, I would judge that it is neither practicable nor necessary to sentence the adulterer to death."[63] Thus

---

[55] Thomas Cartwright, *The Second Replie*, pp. xcii–cxviii.

[56] *Ibid.*, p. xcv.   [57] *Ibid.*, p. cxii.

[58] Whitgift, *Works*, I, 270–278.   [59] *Ibid.*, 278.

[60] *Ibid.*, 273–274.

[61] John F. H. New, *Anglican and Puritan: The Basis of Their Opposition*, 1558–1640 (London, 1964).

[62] Thomas Cartwright, *Helpes for the Discovery of Truth in the point of Toleration* (London, 1648).

[63] *Adul.*, sig. Aiiiir.

Foxe opposes the philosophy behind the harsh Mosaic character of the theocratic administration at Geneva. He even derogates Moses, supporting himself on the contention that the Gospel made null the Law.[64] For Foxe the problem of the death sentence becomes a question of whether we are under grace or law. The Gospel itself is at stake. He closes his appeal against the death sentence for adultery: "I am only appealing to evangelical liberty against those who appear to want to bring us back to the necessity of the Mosaic Law."[65] In another connection Foxe speaks of the "sovereign grace of the Gospel," and "that mild trumpet of the Gospel." He further states:

> But in my opinion, they who are admitted to the ministry and function of the word of God ought to hold and follow that way of teaching whereby Christ, rather than Moses, may be imprinted in the people's hearts. And whereby the riches of God's mercy may be so laid open before their eyes, out of the wonderful treasures of Christ Jesus, that, like true christians, they may at last begin to know and acknowledge their good gifts and blessings.[66]

One of the marks of the true church is that the Gospel is rightly preached.[67] Since the concept of toleration is rooted in the Gospel, and since toleration is needed for the Gospel to make its influence felt, then it is only logical that, in Foxe's opinion, toleration is a mark of the true church, and persecution a sign of an apostate church. At the close of *Christus Triumphans* the suggestion is made to the true church of God that she use the methods of the pontiff. Ecclesia answers: "That must not be: nor will I allow force to be used." The question is asked, "Why not?" Ecclesia replies: "Because I will give a better and more upright counsel. Dismiss all force; let us exchange threats for patience and turn violence into prayers."[68]

Foxe's great work, the *Acts and Monuments*, especially the editions with woodcuts, could not but impress its readers with the fact that a persecuting church could not be the true church.

[64] *Ibid.* [65] *Adul.*, sig. Cviiv.

[66] John Foxe, *Christ Jesus Triumphant* (London, 1831), pp. 118–119. Originally printed in Latin in the latter part of *Christus Trivmphans*, as *De Christo Trivmphante, Eivsdem authoris Panegyricon.*

[67] See chapter iii, "The Marks of the Church."

[68] *CT*, p. 106.

In its closing pages Foxe refers to a number of persons who did persecute, and how God's punishment came upon them. He also points out a number of persons who had shown toleration and consequently through the providence of God received due reward.[69] In light of these examples it is not without significance that a marginal note reads: "The nature of the church is not to persecute with blood."[70] Referring to the Papists, Foxe says that they extinguished the light of the Evangelical faith, abolished the grace of the Gospel, and took away liberty of conscience;[71] furthermore, they sought "to dominate the consciences of men."[72] That a persecuting church is a false church Foxe expresses in the following way:

> And thus the church of Rome, pretending only the name of Christ and of his religion, is so far altered from the truth of that which it pretendeth, that, under the name of Christ, it persecuteth both Christ and his religion; working more harm to the church of Christ, than ever did the open tyrants and persecuting emperors among the heathen: not much unlike herein to the old synagogue of the scribes and pharisees.[73]

In his preface, "A Declaration Concerning the Utilitie and Profite of Thys History," Foxe appeals:

> Let vs geue no cause of offense to any man. And if any be geuen to vs, let vs ouercom it with patience, forgeuing and not reuenging the same. And let vs not onely keepe our handes from shedding of bloud, but our tonges also from hurting the fame of others. Besides, let vs not shrinke or make much a doo, if the case require martirdome, or losse of our lyues, but according to their example let vs yelde vp the same in the defense of the Lords flock. Which thing if we would do, much lesse contention and business would be in the worlde then there is.[74]

The peaceful picture of Mount Sion, where the people "shall not hurt nor destroy in my holy mountain" (Isaiah 11:9), is in "the Scripture an vndoubted type of the spirituall Church of

---

[69] *AM*, VIII, 628–671.
[70] *AM*, VIII, 671.
[71] *Apoc.*, p. 249.
[72] *Apoc.*, p. 234.
[73] *AM*, I, 70.
[74] *UPH*, sig. Bviv. See also *AM*, I, 60.

Christ."[75] True, this peaceful condition was not the state of the church as Foxe knew her; therefore he found it necessary "to write such a long history . . . of the suffering of so many Martyrs."[76]

Having noticed that Foxe believed in toleration as a mark of the true church, and that "the nature of the church is not to persecute with blood," then we may wonder about Foxe's attitude toward Roman Catholics.[77] In our discussion of Foxe's concept of the nature of the church, we pointed out his pacifistic attitude toward the Catholics. All this was not mere theory, for in 1581 Foxe pleaded on behalf of the Jesuit Edmund Campion who was sentenced to be burned. This is still more significant in view of the facts that the Catholics were plotting against Elizabeth, and that Foxe's own name was on the blacklist in Rome.[78] In his loyalty to the Queen, he also fully realized her political difficulties. His son Simeon, speaking about his father's attitude to the Catholics, writes: "I will speak a word or two of his moderation towards them. I could produce letters of his, wherein he perswadeth the Lords, and others, who then held the places of chiefest authority, not to suffer Edmund Campion, and his fellow conspirators to be put to death, nor to let that custome continue longer in the Kingdome, that death rather then some other punishment should be inflicted on the Papist offendors."[79] It appears that Robert Beale, an extreme Puritan, also disagreed with Campion's execution.[80]

---

[75] *FQP*, sig. iiiv.　　　　　[76] *FQP*, sig. iiiv.

[77] The strange answer is that he, who stirred up anti-Catholic feelings through the *Acts and Monuments* and who abhorred with his whole soul Roman Catholic doctrines, manifested a conciliatory attitude toward the Catholics.

[78] Anthony Munday, *The English Romayne Lyfe* (London, 1582), p. 16; Strype, *Annals*, Vol. II, pt. ii, pp. 355–357. A certain Anthony Munday, while attending the English College in Rome, had seen a list with the names of many of the prominent ministers who would be executed when the Catholic plot had succeeded against Elizabeth. Among the names listed was that of Foxe. When Munday came to England he turned Protestant.

[79] *LJF*, sig. B4v.

[80] James McMullen Rigg, "Robert Beale," *Dictionary of National Biography*, II, 3–7.

Foxe's concept of toleration did not in the least lead to a spineless compromise of basic evangelical truths and moral standards, as we can see from his treatise on excommunication. Here Foxe also advocates that no stronger means than excommunication be used in dealing with heretics and sinners. It is true that Foxe keeps the door open for handing the person over to the civil authority "whose duty it always will be to see that the Christian state suffers no detriment from such evils."[81] While he states that "many are the kinds of wrong-doing which come under the administration of the external laws,"[82] he does not enumerate any. While Foxe states that the magistrate has been given powers of life and death, he does not designate when capital punishment could be used. That Foxe would not sanction its use for religious reasons seems obvious from that which already has been noticed regarding his teaching on this point. Foxe's opinion regarding capital punishment is perhaps best reflected in his comment on the eight kinds of punishment used by the Romans: ". . . with the early Romans death was seldom inflicted unless on patricides, traitors, murderers and those who fought duels."[83]

Though he was against executing the Anabaptists he would agree to exiling them: "Many have been exiled, which I think is just treatment."[84] In this connection it should be noticed that the question of the death penalty and its bearing on religious toleration, was brought up at the time of the passing of the Act of Supremacy. On this occasion one member of Parliament, Robert Atkinson, asserted that "the greatest punishment that hath been taught by the apostles in case of religion hath been by excommunication."[85]

We should also mention the work *Reformatio Legvm Ecclesiasticarvm*. Among its injunctions are regulations regarding heretics and adulterers. This book does not provide for a punishment of heretics beyond excommunication. While the ex-

[81] *Exc.*, sig. E3*v*.   [82] *Exc.*, sig. E4*r*.
[83] *Exc.*, sig. E3*r*.
[84] *Pratt*, App. X, p. 27; Harleian MS, no. 416, fol. 151*r*.
[85] Strype, *Annals*, Vol. II, pt. i, pp. 446–455; J. E. Neale, *Elizabeth I and her Parliaments*, 1559–1581 (London, 1953), pp. 118–120; Jordan, *op. cit.*, p. 90.

communicated could be handed over to the state, as previously noticed in Foxe's tract to the archbishop and bishops, yet the death penalty is not mentioned. In the section dealing with adultery, no Calvin-Beza argument is found for capital punishment. If a minister or a layman is found guilty "he should be exiled permanently or put into the eternal darkness of the prison."[86] Concerning obstinate heretics it is said: "When the error has penetrated so deeply and the roots are so deep that the guilty cannot be led to the truth even with the sentence of excommunication, having exhausted all the other remedies, let him finally be committed to the civil magistrates to be punished."[87]

Some argue that by handing the defiant offender over to the state, the *Reformatio Legvm Ecclesiasticarvm* still kept the door open for capital punishment. Among older historians, Jeremy Collier and J. Lingard held this view, as do the more recent Philip Hughes and Joseph Lecler. Commenting on Collier's and Lingard's viewpoint, Henry Hallam points out the bias of the first two men; however, though inclined to the opposite opinion, he hesitates to give a final answer. A. G. Dickens, in his recent work, *The English Reformation*, refers to the statement under discussion, but makes no comment regarding what sort of punishment could be envisaged. Gilbert Burnet asserts that the authors of *Reformatio Legvm Ecclesiasticarvm* intended to discontinue the old penal laws.[88] Foxe's personal abhorrence for the death penalty and his own involvement in the editing of the new laws speak in favor of this conclusion.

J. F. Mozley indicates that Foxe, when editing the new regulations, had a manuscript copy which had belonged to Archbishop Cranmer. Where the injunction appears regarding hand-

---

[86] *Reformatio Legvm Ecclesiasticarvm*, p. 50.

[87] *Ibid.*, p. 25.

[88] Jeremy Collier, *An Ecclesiastical History of Great Britain* (London, 1708), II, 326; John Lingard, *A History of England*, 1819–1830, IV, 462; Henry Hallam commenting on Collier and Lingard points out the bias of these two men. He himself is not ready to give a final answer. See H. Hallam, *The Constitutional History of England* (London, 1827), I, 109–110. For A. G. Dickens's discussion see: *The English Reformation*, pp. 250–251; Gilbert Burnet, *The History of the Reformation of the Church of England* (London, 1679–1715), II, 197–198.

ing over the contemptuously offensive religious offender to the state, Foxe suggests ". . . either that he be exiled for ever, or condemned to the darkness of perpetual prison, or otherwise punished, as the wisdom of the magistrate shall think most conclusive to his conversion."[89] This recommendation was not added in the published book. No doubt it was felt that it was not the prerogative of ecclesiastical injunctions to tell the state what to do or not to do. Since the injunctions did not mention capital punishment, certain scholars have inferred that the editors purposely left the door open for its use. Joseph Lecler asserts that "Thomas Cranmer had laid down the most severe penalties for heretics." Furthermore, some have insinuated that the editors were actually secretly advocating the death penalty, as when Hughes declares that "where others may see uncertainty, I can only see the traditional hypocrisy of the medieval which leaves the nasty word unsaid but thoroughly understood. We sometimes find continuity where we would rather have found a new departure. Not only Arians and Anabaptists, but intractable Romanists and intractable Lutherans would have been burnable under the reformed law of the reformed church of England."[90]

But to charge these editors with deceitful motives in order to perpetuate rigorous medieval policies seems indeed doubtful and contrary to the spirit of Foxe and the other men who formulated these laws and encouraged their advancement. Foxe's preface to this collection of ecclesiastical laws makes this evident. He writes: "I propose that in constructing laws prudence should be used in their selection, so that they may be recommended to the State, not rash or tyrannical, but as much as possible approximating the archtype in honesty, equity and the rule of perfect reason." Furthermore, they should not "breathe out cruelty," as do the laws of Draco and Phalaris, and, he adds, "the Bishop of Rome."[91]

Even when allowance is made for the fact that Foxe may not have agreed with all the details in the new laws, it would seem strange that he would go so far as to edit and write a preface to

[89] Mozley, *op. cit.*, p. 80.
[90] Lecler, *op. cit.*, II, 348; Philip Hughes, *The Reformation in England* (London, 1954), II, 132.
[91] *Reformatio Legvm Ecclesiasticarvm*, p. xx.

a work containing regulations and laws that could lead to execution for religious reasons. Foxe's personal attitude appears certain beyond any shadow of doubt. While it cannot be proven explicitly that all who advanced the new ecclesiastical laws shared his view, they at least did not oppose it and may rather have been sympathetic toward it; their thinking and motivation by no means fall within the description made by Philip Hughes and Joseph Lecler.

Foxe's idea of toleration is further elaborated in his story of the Tudor sovereigns. Having described the burning of a number of persons at the close of Henry VII's reign, Foxe points out the principle: "Where the church is quietly and moderately governed, and the flock of Christ defended by godly princes in peace and safety, from devouring and violence of bloody wolves," there the state will flourish and the ruler long continue to govern. If the church or its members are persecuted, then the opposite will be true for both the state and the rulers.[92] Foxe expresses the wish that the otherwise "prudent and temperate" Henry VII had not permitted the burning of "the poor flock of Christ." Had it not been for "this defect" he would have "been inferior but to a few."[93]

Foxe's evaluation of the tolerance shown in the reign of Henry VIII is illustrated by his comments on the burning of John Lambert in 1538. Foxe laments the burnings and persecutions and expresses the hope that he himself "might engrave more meekness in the hearts of our men."[94] He greatly regrets that Henry VIII had not seen fit to manifest pity to "the miserable, to relieve the oppressed, to rescue the wrongs of the poor, and to tender and respect the weaker part." If the king had done this in the opinion of Foxe, "it would have redounded to the immortal renown of his princely estate to all posterity."[95]

Edward VI is called the "evangelical Josias" and "this christian young Josias"; Foxe praises his reign and "excellent virtues and singular graces. He especially mentions that by nature and disposition Edward was "meek and much inclined to clemency." Furthermore, he "always spared and favoured the life of man,"

---

[92] *AM*, IV, 129.
[94] *AM*, V, 226.

[93] *AM*, IV, 132.
[95] *AM*, V, 234.

even "the life of heretics." Foxe therefore points out most emphatically that the two burned at Smithfield during the reign of Edward VI suffered this punishment against the will of the king:

> ... when Joan Butcher should be burned, all the council could not move him to put to his hand, but were fain to get Dr. Cranmer to persuade with him, and yet neither could he, with much labour, induce the king so to do: saying 'What, my Lord? will ye have to send her quick to the devil in her error?' So that Dr. Cranmer himself confessed, that he had never so much to do in all his life, as to cause the king to put to his hand, saying that he would lay all the charge thereof upon Cranmer before God.[96]

According to Foxe the unhappy reign of Queen Mary should be an admonition to all Christian rulers not "to stir up persecution in Christ's church, to the effusion of christian blood."[97] He writes "A Brief Declaration, Showing the Unprosperous Success of Queen Mary in Persecuting God's People, And How Mightily God Wrought Against Her in All Her Affairs."[98]

Foxe praised Queen Elizabeth and the success of her reign, but in view of the fact that Queen Elizabeth executed Anabaptists as well as Catholics and was very harsh toward the extreme Puritans, Foxe may have painted too rosy a picture. In evaluating this, we must bear in mind that Elizabeth was no doubt motivated politically and not religiously in this matter, and that it was not until these persons, in her opinion, became politically dangerous that she used capital punishment.[99] Furthermore, it seems certain that for Foxe, "liberty of conscience" includes more than simple disapproval of burning heretics; thus the scope of Foxe's religious toleration is wider than suggested by William Haller.[100] A few references, in addition to what we have already read from Foxe's pen on this subject, suggest that Foxe's concept of toleration was advanced for his time. In addition to adding a new preface to the 1583 edition of the *Acts and Monuments*, he brings into his conclusion of the same edition the story of the horrible massacre of the Protestants in France on Bartholomew's

---

[96] *AM*, V, 698, 699.
[98] *AM*, VIII, 625–628.
[100] Haller, *op. cit.*, p. 45.
[97] *AM*, VIII, 628.
[99] Jordan, *op. cit.*, pp. 233–238.

Day, 1572.[101] Thus he contrasts the peaceable liberty of conscience in England with the persecution in France. Foxe refers to Queen Elizabeth:

> Under whom you see how gently you are suffered, what mercy is shewed vnto you: how quietly ye liue. What lacke you, that you woulde haue, hauyng almost the best rowmes and offices in all the Realme, not onely without any losse of life, but also without any feare of death. And though a fewe of your Archclerkes be in custody: yet in that custody so shreudely are they hurt, that many a good Protestant in the Realme woulde be glad with all their hartes to chaung rowmes and dyett with them if they might. ... For what Papist haue you seene in all this lande to lose eyther life or lymme for Papistry duryng all these xii yeares hetherto since this Queenes reigne? And yet all this notwithstandyng, hauyng no cause to complayne, so many causes to geue God thankes, ye are not yet content ... ye haue conspired, and rise vp in open rebellion agaynst your Prince, whom the Lord hath set vp to be your gouernour.[102]

We have already referred to Foxe's address to the nobility of England during the persecution of Mary, while he himself was in exile. It is most interesting to notice Foxe's appeal for toleration among Christians, both Catholic and Protestant. Foxe writes: "What is to hinder the token of Christian friendship's remaining unharmed and unbroken, when it is permitted to differ in minor matters? It is a great step towards restoring concord to have wished it."[103] Notice also the following statement: "The most serene King Edward was able to reign and control with the greatest moderation two most opposite parties. And what less may be effected by you, with similar temperament? Why was it necessary for this cord of Ecclesiastical contention to be stretched on both sides so bitterly and tightly that now neither party can live in the State with the other?"[104]

These sentiments expressed by Foxe during the reign of Mary were not advocated just because the Protestants were in difficulty and would have had all the advantages of toleration, for

---

[101] *AM* (1583), II, 2152–2154; *AM*, VIII, 748–753.

[102] *FQP*, sig. iiiv. The validity of Foxe's description of the Catholic position has been confirmed by Jordan, *op. cit.*, pp. 112–131.

[103] *Nob.*, p. 53.   [104] *Nob.*, p. 64.

during the reign of Elizabeth, Foxe was indeed ready to beg the monarch to grant the same to the Catholics. In evaluating the Tudor sovereigns, it would be fair to say that Foxe counted their success in direct proportion to the toleration manifested by them.

Foxe was in advance of his time in advocating religious toleration; yet he was still a son of his own time in that full religious toleration as we see it today, not mentioning complete liberty for the exercise of all religions, did not enter his mind. This was probably too much to expect. Foxe was not a sixteenth-century John Locke; but the admonition he gave to both church and state, as well as the Gospel principles and humanistic ideals on which his concept of toleration was built, created a platform from which religious toleration could further be promoted.

Appendix

A Table declaring divers and sundry respects how the holy real body of Christ our Saviour, both in the Sacrament and beside the Sacrament is present, eaten, and united to us.

REALLY

Present:

So was the body of Christ once present here on earth with us, and shall be again at the day of his coming. Otherwise it is not here really present but only to our faith, really apprehending his body in heaven, and here feeding upon the same in earth. And thus is he present only to good men, whether with the symbols or without the symbols.

Eaten:

Really, not with our bodily mouth, but with the mouth of faith, apprehending the real body of Christ, which suffered for us, and worketh to us nourishment of life and grace, &c.

United:

Really and corporally the body of Christ is united to us by his incarnation, and the partaking of our flesh.

SPIRITUALLY

Present:

Spiritually we say his body to be present, when either the body of Christ is present to our spirit and faith, or when the virtue of his body is present and redoundeth to our bodies and spirits by grace: and this differeth from the other real presence above in this, that the one hath respect to the body apprehended: the other to the thing that doth apprehend.

Eaten:

Spiritually, we eat the body and blood of Christ, not with mouth and teeth, but with faith only, whensoever we believe on the passion of Christ, being the true bread of life and the only food of man's soul. And thus is he eaten, but only of good men, as well besides the sacrament, as with the sacrament. And of this eating speaketh the 6th of John. And so was he eaten in the time also of the old law.

United:

Spiritually he is united unto us, when the properties of his holy body: as his innocency, power, glorification, eternity, beatitude, &c. are united to our bodies and spirits, which cometh by our faith in him, according to his words John xvii. Ego in eis, et tu in me, &c. And this uniting standing by grace, cometh as well besides the sacrament, as with the sacrament, only to the Godly.

SACRAMENTALLY

Present:

Sacramentally his body is present by representation of another thing, which beareth a similitude or a memorial of his body: and this sacramental presence, pertaining to the outward mouth of the receiver, is common as well to the good, as to the evil. And this sacramental presence ought not to be alone, but to be joined with the spiritual presence, &c.

Eaten:

Sacramentally, we eat with our bodily mouth the mysteries of bread and wine, not being the real body in deed, but representing the real body in deed. i.e. Non panem dominum, sed panem domini: and this eating, if it be not joined with the other two above it profiteth nothing, and so is eaten only of the evil. If it be adjoined, then is it eaten of the good, and them it profiteth.

United:

The sacrament, as it is not the real body itself of the Lord: so it causeth not itself any real conjunction betwixt Christ's real body and ours, but representeth the same, declaring, that as the material bread digested in our bodies is united to the same, so the body of Christ being received by faith changeth our spirits and bodies to the nature of him.

In considering "sacramentally uniting, eating and presence of Christ," Foxe expresses the need of explaining two other points: "Mutation and Operation." Mutation is defined as substantial or accidental. The latter has to be viewed from "three points: that is, when the use, the name, and the honour of the sacramental elements be changed." Concerning Operation, two aspects are mentioned, namely in and of the sacraments. "To the sacramental presence and eating of Christ, pertaineth two things chiefly to be considered," and this is expressed in Foxe's second table:

MUTATION

Substantial:

Whereby one substance is changed into another: as, water into wine, the rod of Aaron into a serpent, &c. And this mutation (which they call transubstantiation) belongeth nothing to the sacrament. For then accidents of bread should also be changed, as the accidents of Aaron's rod were changed with the substance into a serpent.

Accidental:

(And of this mutation speak the doctors, meaning not of the change of substance, but of accidencies, which standeth in three things)

1. In the use:

As when the use of common bread is changed into a mystical and heavenly use.

2. In name:

When the name of bread and wine pass away, and are changed into the name of the body and blood of the Lord, and so is the name changed.

3. In honour:

As when the bread and wine which before were received not with honour, are now received with honour and reverence: not that we honour the bread and wine, but the things represented in them. As in a king's letters and seal, we honour the king and not the seal.

OPERATION

In the Sacraments:

The operation of the word in the sacraments is this, to change not the substance of the sacrament, but that the substance thereof remaining, may be made the body of Christ: that is, the sacrament of the body of Christ. And this operation can not come but by the Holy Ghost. Whereof August. lib. iii. cap. 4, de Trinitate, saith: Panis non sanctificatur in sacramentum tam magnum, nisi operante invisibiliter Spiritu Dei.

Of the Sacraments:

The operaton of Sacraments is thought of the Papists to give grace, which in very deed give not grace of their own work: but only serve as instruments and means of that grace and life, which cometh from God. So Peter calleth verbum vitae, the word of life: and St. Paul calleth the Gospel of Christ the power of God to salvation: not that they themselves give life and salvation, but that they are certain means and instruments of that life and salvation, which cometh to us from God.

—AM, VI, 523–525

Bibliography

I. PRIMARY SOURCES

A. WORKS OF JOHN FOXE

i. *Acts and Monuments*

Commentarii Rervm in Ecclesia Gestarum, maximarumque, per totam Europam, persecutionum, a Vuicleui temporibus ad hanc usque aetatem descriptio. Liber primus. Strassburg, 1554.

Rervm in Ecclesia Gestarum quae postremis et periculosis his temporibus euenerunt, maximarumque; per Europam persecutionum, ac Sanctorum Dei Martyrum, caeterarumque; rerumque; rerum si quae insignioris exempli sint, digesti per Regna et nationes Commentarij. Pars Prima. Basel, 1559.

Actes and Monuments of these latter and perillous dayes, touching matters of the Church, wherein ar comprehended and described the great persecutions and horrible troubles . . . Gathered and collected according to the true copies and wrytinges certificatorie, as wel of the parties them selues that suffered, as also out of the Bishops Registers, which wer the doers therof. London, 1563.

The Ecclesiasticall History, Contaynyng the Actes and Monumentes of Thynges passed in euery Kynges tyme in this Realme especially in the Church of England principally to be noted . . . from the primitiue tyme till the reigne of K. Henry VIII. 2d ed. London, 1570. 2 vols.

Ecclesiasticall History, Contayning the Actes and Monumentes of thinges passed in euery Kinges time, in this Realme, especially in the Churche of England principally to be noted . . . from the primitiue time, till the raigne of King Henry the Eyght. 3rd ed. London, 1576. 2 vols.

Actes and Monuments of matters most speciall and memorable, happenyng in the Church, with an Vniuersall history of the same, wherein is set forth at large the whole race and course of the Church, from the primitiue age to these latter tymes of ours . . . especially in this Realme of England and Scotland. 4th ed. London, 1583. 2 vols.

Actes and Monuments of matters most speciall and memorable, happening in the Church, with an vniversall history of the same. Wherein is set forth at large the whole race and course of the Church, from the primitiue age to these latter times of ours . . . especially in this Realme of England and Scotland. 5th ed. London, 1596. 2 vols.

Actes and Monuments of Matters most speciall and memorable, happening in the Church, with an vniuersall historie of the same. Wherein is set forth at large the whole race and course of the Church, from the primitiue age to these latter times of ours . . . especially in this Realme of England and Scotland. 6th ed. London, 1610. 3 vols.

Acts and Monuments of Matters most speciall and memorable, happening in the Church, with an vniuersall Historie of the same. Wherein is set forth at large the whole race and course of the Church from the primitiue age to these latter times of ours . . . especially in this Realme of England and Scotland. 7th ed. London, 1632. 3 vols.

Acts and Monuments of Matters most speciall and memorable, happening in the Church, with an universall Historie of the same. Wherein is set forth at large, the whole Race and Course of the Church, from the Primitive age to these times of ours . . . especially in this Realme of England and Scotland. 8th ed. London, 1641. 3 vols.

Acts and Monuments of Matters most Special and Memorable, Happening in the Church: with an Universal History of the same. Wherein is set forth at Large, the whole Race and Course of the Church, from the Primitive Age to these later

Times of Ours . . . especially in this Realme of England and Scotland. 9th ed. London, 1684. 3 vols.

The Acts and Monuments of John Foxe in *The Church Historians of England.* Ed. Josiah Pratt. London, 1853–1870. 8 vols.

The benefit and invention of printing; by J. F., that famous martyrologist. Extracted out of his "Acts and Monuments." London, 1704.

ii. Prefaces to *Acts and Monuments*
"A Declaration Concerning the Utilitie and Profite of Thys History," *AM* (1563).

"To the Persecutors of Gods Truth, Commonlye called Papistes," *AM* (1563).

"To the Qvenes Moste Excellent Maiestie Quene Elizabeth," *AM* (1563).

"To the Right Vertvovs, Most Excellent, and Noble Princesse, Quene Elizabeth," *AM* (1570).

"To the True and Faithful Congregation, of Christes Vniuersall Church, with all and singular the members thereof, wheresoeuer congregated, or dispersed through the Realme of England," *AM* (1570).

"To All the Professed Frendes and Folowers of the Popes Proceedinges, Foure Questions Propounded," *AM* (1576).

"Foure Considerations Geuen out to Christian Protestantes, Professours of the Gospell with a brief exhortation inducing to reformation of life," *AM* (1583).

"Prefaces to the Acts and Monuments," ed. Josiah Pratt. *The Life and Defence of John Foxe.* London, 1870. Printed in *The Acts and Monuments of John Foxe* (London, 1853–1870), Vol. I, pt. 1, pp. i–xxxvi.

iii. Minor Works
De non Plectendis Morte Adulteris Consultatio. London, 1548.

De Censvra sive Excommvnicatione Ecclesiastica. London, 1551.

Christus Trivmphans, Comoedia Apocalyptica. Basel, 1556.

Le Triomphe de Iesus Christ: Comedie Apocalyptique, traduite du Latin de Iean Foxus Anglois, en rithme Francoise, &

augmentee d'vn petit discours de la maladie de la Messe, Par Iaques Biennenu citoyen de Geneue. Geneva, 1562.

Christus Triumphans. Comoedia Apocalyptica. Ed. T[homas] C[omber]. London, 1672.

Christ Jesus Triumphant. Reprinted in *British Reformers*, Vol. XII. London, 1831. (First printed in Latin in *Christus Trivmphans* as "De Christo Trivmphante, Eivsdem authoris Panegyricon." First printed in English, 1579.)

Ad Inclytos ac Praepotentes Angliae Proceres, Ordines, & Status, totamque eius gentis Nobilitatem, pro Afflictis Fratribus Svpplicatio. Basel, 1557.

Syllogisticon. London, 1560–1564?

A Brief Exhortation, Fruitfull and Meete to be Read, in this heauy tyme of Gods visitation in London, to suche as be Sicke, where the Ministers to lacke, or otherwise cannot be present to comfort them. London, 1563?

A Sermon of Christ Crucified, preached at Paules Crosse the Friday before Easter, commonly called Goodfryday. Written and dedicated to all such as labour and be heauy laden in conscience, to be read for their spirituall comfort. London, 1570.

A Sermon of Christ Crucified, preached at Paul's Cross, the Friday before Easter, commonly called Good Friday. A. D. 1570. Written and dedicated to all such as labour and are heavy laden in conscience, to be read for their spiritual comfort. Reprinted in *British Reformers*, Vol. XII. London, 1831.

A Sermon of Christ Crucified; preached at Paul's Cross the Friday before Easter, commonly called Good Friday. Written and dedicated to all such as labour and be heavy laden in conscience, to be read for their spiritual comfort. 3rd ed. Printed 1570 and, republished with a Recommendatory Preface, by the Rev. Mr. Whitefield, 1759. Reprinted in London, 1838.

Notes Appertayning to the Matter of Election. Printed in *The Treasvre of Trueth* by Theodore Beza. N. p., 1576.

And W. Haddon. *Contra Hieron Osorium, euisq; odiosas insectationes pro Euangelicae veritatis necessaria Defensione, Responsio Apologetica. Per clariss, virum, Gualt. Haddonum inchoata; Deinde suscepta & continuata per Ioan Foxum.* London, 1577.

And W. Haddon. *Against Ierome Osorivs, Byshopp of Siluane*

in Portingall and against his slaunderous Inuectiues. An Aunswere Apologeticall: For the necessary defence of the Euangelicall doctrine and veritie. First taken in hand by M. Walter Haddon, then undertaken and continued by M. Iohn Foxe, now Englished by Iames Bell. London, 1581.

De Oliva Evangelica. Concio, in Baptismo Iudaei habita Londini, primo mens, April. Cum enarratione capitis vndecimi D. Pauli ad Romanos. London, 1578.

A Sermon Preached at the Christening of a certaine Iew, at London, by Iohn Foxe. Conteining an exposition of the xi Chapter of S. Paul to the Romanes. Trans. James Bell. London, 1578.

De Oliva Evangelica, The True and Gladsome Olive Tree. A Sermon preached at the Christening of a certain Jew, at London, by John Fox. Containing an Exposition of the eleventh chapter of St. Paul to the Romans. Trans. James Bell. London, 1578. Reprinted in *British Reformers*, Vol. XII (London, 1831).

Anon. *The Pope Confvted. The holy and Apostolique Church confuting the Pope.* Trans. James Bell. London, 1580.

De Christo gratis iustificante. Contra Osorianam iustitiam ... Iesuiticam. London, 1583.

Of Free Justification by Christ. Written first in Latine by John Foxe, Author of the Book of Martyrs, Against Osorius, &c. And now translated into English, for the Benefit of those who love their own Souls, and would not be mistaken in so great a point. London, 1694.

Eicasmi sev Meditationes in Sacram Apocalypsin. London, 1587.

Some Minor Works and Letters. Ed. Josiah Pratt. *The Life and Defence of John Foxe.* London, 1870. Printed in *The Acts and Monuments of John Foxe*, Vol. I. pt. 1, pp. i–xxxvi. London, 1853–1870.

iv. Manuscripts

"Papa Confutatus." Lansdowne MS, no. 353 (2), fols. 112–191. 1580.

A Letter of John Foxe to Archbishop Whitgift. Lambeth Palace Library MS, no. 2010, fols. 117–121v. N.d.

Letters to and from John Foxe. Harleian MSS, nos. 416 and 417.

v. Works Edited and Prefaced by Foxe

Luther, Martin. *A Frutfull Sermon of the moost Euangelicall wryter M. Luther, made of the Angelles vpon the xviii Chapt. of Mathew.* Translated and prefaced by John Foxe. London, 1547?

———. *A Commentarie vpon the Fiftene Psalmes, called Psalmi Graduum, that is Psalmes of Degrees: Faithfully copied out of the lectures of D. Martin Luther, very frutefull and comfortable for all Christian afflicted consciences to read.* Trans. Henry Bull. Edited and prefaced by John Foxe. London, 1577.

Regius, Urbanus. *An Instruccyon of Christen fayth howe to be bolde vp on the promyse of God and not to doubte of Our Saluacyon.* Translated and prefaced by John Foxe. London, 1548?

———. *Reformatio Legvm Ecclesiasticarvm, Ex Avthoritate primum Regis Henrici. 8. inchoata: Deinde per Regem Edouardum 6. prouecta, adauctaq; in hunc modum, atq; nunc ad pleniorem ipsarum reformationem in lucem aedita.* London, 1571. (Reprinted Oxford, 1850, ed. Edward Cardwell.)

B. OTHER PRINTED SOURCES

Alsted, Johann Heinrich. *Diatribe de mille annis Apocalypticis. Christliches . . . Bericht von der künfftigen Tausand-Jährigen Glückseligkeit der Kirchen Gottes auff dieser Erden, nach der Weissagung des . . . Propheten Daniels; vnd . . . Apostel Johannis . . . Verdeutschet durch Sebastianum Francum.* [With a table] 1630. English translation, *The Beloved City or, the Saints Reign on Earth a Thovsand Yeares, Asserted, and . .Illustrated from LXV. places of Holy Scripture; Besides the judgement of Holy Learned men, both at home and abroad: and also Reason it selfe.* London, 1643.

The Ante-Nicene Fathers: Translations of the Writings of the Fathers Down to A.D. 325. American reprint of the Edinburgh edition of Alexander Roberts and James Donaldson, revised and annotated, with supplements, by A. Cleveland Coxe. New York, 1899–1900. 10 vols.

Archer, John. *The Personall Reign of Christ vpon Earth. In a Treatise Wherein is fully and largely laid open and proved, That Jesus Christ, together with the Saints, shall visibly possesse a Monarchicall State and Kingdome in this World.* London, 1642.

Aylmer, John. *An Harborowe for Faithfvll and Trewe Subiectes, agaynst the late blowne Blaste, concerninge the Gouernment of Wemen, wherin be confuted all such reasons as a straunger of late made in that behalfe with a briefe exhortation to Obedience.* Strassburg, 1559.

Baillie, Robert. *A Dissvasive from the Errours of the Time: Wherein the Tenets of the principall Sects, especially of the Independents, are drawn together in one Map, for the most part, in the words of their own Authours, and their maine principles are examined by the Touchstone of the Holy Scriptures.* London, 1645.

Baronius, Caesare. *Annales Ecclesiastici.* Antwerp, 1593.

Baxter, Richard. *The Reformed Pastor. Shewing the nature of the Pastoral work; Especially in Private Instruction and Catechizing. With an open Confession of our too open Sins.* London, 1656.

Bede, the Venerable. *Baedae opera historica.* Trans. J. E. King. London and New York, 1930.

———. *The Explanation of the Apocalypse by Venerable Beda.* Trans. Edward Marshall. Oxford and London, 1878.

Beza, Theodore. *Iesv Christi D.N. Nouum Testamentum, siue Nouum foedus. Cuius Graeco contextui respondent interpretationes duae: vna, vetus: altera, noua, Theodori Bezae, diligenter ab eo recognita. Eivsdem Th. Bezae, Annotationes, quas itidem hac tertia editione recognouit, & accessione non parua locupletauit.* N.p., 1582.

———. *The Treasvre of Trueth, touching the grounde worke of man, his saluation, and chiefest pointes of Christian Religion: with a briefe summe of the comfortable doctrine of God his Prouidence, comprised in 38 short Aphorismes.* Trans. John Stockwood. Containing *Notes Appertayning to the Matter of Election* by John Foxe. N.p., 1576.

———. *The Treasvre of Trueth.* Another edition. London, 1581.

———. *Tractatio De Repvdiis et Divortiis: in qva pleraeqve de causis matrimonialibus (quas vocant) incidentes controuersiae ex verbo Dei deciduntur. Additur Iuris Ciuilis Romanorum, & veterum his de rebus canonum examen, ad eiusdem verbi Dei, & aequitatis normam. Ex Th. Bezae Vezelii praelectionibus in priorem ad Corinthios Epistolam.* Geneva, 1573.

Brightman, Thomas. *Apocalypsis Apocalypseos. Id est, Apocalypsis D. Ioannis Analysi et Scholiis illustrata; ubi ex scriptura sensus, rerumque praedictarumex historijs even tus discutiuntur.* Frankfurt, 1609.

———. *A Revelation of the Reuelation that is the Revelation of St. John opened clearly with a logicall Resolution and Exposition. Wherein the sense is cleared, out of the Scripture, the euent also of thinges foretold is discussed out of the Church-Historyes.* Amsterdam, 1615.

———. *The Workes of that Famous, Reverend and Learned Divine, Mr. Tho. Brightman . . . Containing an Exposition of the whole book of the Revelation of Saint John . . . Whereunto is added, a most comfortable Exposition of the last and most difficult part of the Prophesie of Daniel . . . together with a Commentary on the whole Book of Canticles, or Song of Solomon.* London, 1644.

Braght, Thieleman J. van. *The Bloody Theater or Martyrs Mirror of the Defenseless Christians who Baptized only upon Confession of Faith, and Who Suffered and Died for the Testimony of Jesus, Their Saviour, From the Time of Christ to the year A.D. 1660.* Trans. Joseph F. Sohm. Scottsdale, Pa., 1951.

Bucer, Martin. *De Regno Christi Iesu seruatoris nostri, Libri II. Ad Edvardvm VI. Angliae Regem, annis abhinc sex scripti: non solum Theologis atque Iurisperitis profuturi, uerum etiam cunctis Rempub. bene & feliciter administraturis cognitu cumprimis necessarii.* Basel, 1557.

———. *Deux Livres dv Royavme de Iesvs Christ Nostre Savvevr.* N.p., 1558.

———. *The Ivdgement of Martin Bucer, concerning Divorce, Writt'n to Edward the Sixt, in his second Book of the Kingdom of Christ. And now Englisht. Wherin a late Book restoring the Doctrine and Discipline of Divorce, is heer confirm'd and justify'd by the authoritie of Martin Bucer. To the Parlament of England.* London, 1644. Printed in *The Works of John Milton,* IV. New York, 1931.

———.*Martini Bvceri Opera Latina.* Ed. F. Wendel. Paris and Gütersloh, 1955.

———. *Vom Reich Christi vnsers Herren vnd Heilands, Wie das selbige von allen Christlichen Oberkeiten anzustellen, vnd ins werck zubringen seye.* Strassburg, 1563.

Bullinger, Henry. *A Hundred Sermons vpon the Apocalips of Jesu Christe, reueiled in dede by Thangell of the Lorde: but seen or receyued and written by thapostle and Euangelist S. John: Compiled by the famous and godly learned man, Henry Bullinger, chief Pastor of the Congregation of Zuryk.* Trans. John Daws. N.p., 1561.

Burgess, Thomas. *Tracts on the Origin and Independence of the Ancient Church.* London, 1815.

Calendar of Letters and State Papers relating to English Affairs, II (Elizabeth, 1568–1579). Ed. Martin A. S. Hume. London, 1894.

Calvin, John. *Institutes of the Christian Religion.* Trans. Henry Beveridge. Grand Rapids, Mich., 1957. 2 vols.

———. *The Sermons of M. John Calvin vpon the Fifth Booke of Moses called Deuteronomie: Faithfully gathered word for word as he preached them in open Pulpit; together with a preface of the Ministers of the Church of Geneua, and an admonishment made by the Deacons there. Also there are annexed two profitable Tables, the one containing the chiefe matters; the other the places of Scripture herein alledged.* Trans. Arthur Golding. London, 1583.

Cartwright, Thomas. *Helpes for the Discovery of Truth in the point of Toleration: Being the judgment of that eminent Scholler Tho. Cartwright . . . Wherein the power and duty of the Magistrate in relation to matters of Religion is discussed; as also whether the Judiciall Lawes given by Moses to the Jewes are abrogate by the coming of Christ. More particularly in relation to some sinnes, viz. Blasphemy, Adultery, &c. Occasionally handled in a Controversie betweene the said publicke Professor T. C. and Doctor Whitgift. Here also by the way is laid downe his judgment in the case of Divorce, and that the party innocent may marrie again.* London, 1648.

———. *The Second Replie of Thomas Cartwright: agaynst Maister Doctor Whitgiftes Second Answer touching the Churche Discipline.* London, 1575.

Charles, R[obert] H[enry], ed. *The Apocrypha and Pseudepigrapha of the Old Testament in English.* Oxford, 1913. 2 vols.

Clarke, Samuel. *A Mirrovr or Looking-Glasse both for Saints and Sinners: Wherein, by many memorable examples is set forth, as Gods exceeding great mercies to the one, so his severe judgements upon the other.* London, 1646.

Cornwell, Francis. *King Jesvs is the Beleevers Prince, Priest, and Lawgiver, in things appertaining to the Conscience, Isai. 55.4. Heb. 7. 17. Jam. 4.12. Or, the Loyall Spouse of Christ hath no Head, nor Husband, but Royall King Jesvs.* London, 1645.

Cotton, John. *The Powring ovt of the Seven Vials: or an Exposition, of the 16. Chapter of the Revelation, with an Application of it to our Times. Wherein is revealed Gods powring out the full Vials of his fierce wrath . . . .* London, 1642.

Dent, Arthur. *The Rvine of Rome: or an Exposition vpon the whole Reuelation. wherein is plainly shewed and proued, that the Popish Religion, together with all the power and authoritie of Rome, shall ebbe and decay still more and more throughout all the Churches of Europe, and come to an vtter ouerthrow euen in this life before the end of the world. Written especially for the comfort of Protestants, and the daunting of Papists, Seminary Priests, Iesuites, and all that cursed rabble.* London, 1603.

Erasmus, Desiderius. *Desiderii Erasmi Opervm Omnivm.* Lugduni Batavorum, 1703–1706 (reprinted 1963). 10 vols.

———. *Opvs Epistolarvm Des. Erasmi Roterodami.* Ed. P. S. and H. M. Allen. Oxford, 1906–1958. 12 vols.

Eusebius. *The Ecclesiastical History.* Trans. J. E. L. Oulton. Cambridge, 1953. 2 vols.

Flacius, Matthias I. *Ecclesiastica Historia . . . Per aliquot studiosos & pios uiros in urbe Magdeburgica.* Basel, 1561–1574. 13 cent.

Foxe, Simeon, "The Life of Mr. John Fox." In *AM*, Vol. II. London, 1641.

Gardiner, Stephen. *Obedience in Church and State, Three Po-*

litical Tracts. Ed. Pierre Janelle. Cambridge, 1930.

Gilby, Anthony. *An Admonition to England and Scotland to call them to repentence.* Geneva, 1558.

Goodman, Christopher. *How Svperior Powers Oght to be Obeyd of their Subiects: and Wherin they may lawfully by Gods Worde be disobeyed and resisted. Wherin also is declared the cause of all this present miserie in England, and the onely way to remedy the same.* Geneva, 1558.

Goodwin, Thomas. *The expositione of ... T. G. ... on the Book of Revelation....* London, 1843.

———. *The French Revolution foreseen in 1639. Extracts from an exposition of the Revelation, by an eminent divine of both Universities, ... (T. G.) who explains a prophecy in that book of a revolution in France, its separation from Rome ... To which are subjoined, some observations and remarks, to illustrate facts, etc.* London, 1796?

———. *A Sermon of the Fifth Monarchy, proving by invincible arguments that the saints shall have a kingdom here on earth, which is yet to come ... preached on Rev. v. 9, 10, etc.* London, 1654.

Gray, Louis Herbert, ed. *The Mythology of All Races.* Boston, 1916–1932. 13 vols.

Gyfford, George. *Sermons Vpon the Whole Booke of the Revelation.* London, 1596.

Harding, Thomas. *A Confvtation of a Booke Intitvled an Apologie of the Church of England.* Antwerp, 1565.

———. *A detection of sundrie foule errours ... by M. Jewell.* Louanii, 1568.

———. *A Reioindre to M. Jewels Replie. By perusing wherof the discrete and diligent Reader may easily see, the Answer to parte of his insolent Chalenge iustified, and his Obiections against the Masse, whereat the Priest sometime receiueth the Holy Mysteries without present companie to receiue with him, for that cause by Luthers Schoole called Priuate Masse, clearly confuted.* Antwerp, 1566.

Harpsfield, Nicholas (Alan Cope). *Dialogi Sex contra Summi Pontificatvs, Monasticae vitae, Sanctorvm, Sacrarvm Imaginvm Opovgnatores, et Psevdomartyres.* Antwerp, 1566.

Hayne, Thomas. *Christs Kingdome On Earth, Opened accord-*

ing to the Scriptures. Herein is examined, What Mr. Th. Brightman, Dr. J. Alstede, Mr. I. Mede, Mr. H. Archer, The Glympse of Sions Glory, and such as concurre in opinion with them, hold concerning the thousand years of the Saints Reign with Christ, etc. London, 1645.

Henderson, Ernest F. *Select Historical Documents of the Middle Ages.* Trans. and ed. E. F. Henderson. London, 1896.

Hessels, J. H., ed. *Ecclesiae Londino-Batavae Archivum.* Cambridge, 1887–1897. 3 vols.

Herbert, George. *A Priest to the Temple, or The Countrey Parson, His Character and Rule of Holy Life.* London, 1652.

Homes, Nathaniel. *The Nevv VVorld, or the Nevv Reformed Chvrch.* London, 1641.

Hooker, Richard. *The Works of that Learned and Judicious Divine, Mr. Richard Hooker: With an Account of His Life and Death by Isaac Walton.* Oxford, 1885. 2 vols.

Humfrey, Lawrence. *Optimates, sive de Nobilitate, eivsqve Antiqva origine, natura officijs, disciplina, & recta ac Christiana institutione Idbri tres.* Basel, 1560.

———. *The Nobles or of Nobilitye. The Original nature, dutyes, right, and Christian Institucion thereof.* London, 1563.

Joachim of Floris. *Liber Concordie Novi ac Veteris Testamenti.* Ventijs, 1519.

Kidd, B. J., ed. *Documents Illustrative of the Continental Reformation.* Oxford, 1911.

Knox, John. *The Appellation of Iohn Knoxe from the cruell and most iniust sentence pronounced against him by the false bishoppes and clergie of Scotland, with his supplication and exhortation to the nobilitie, estates, and communaltie of the same realme.* Geneva, 1558.

[Knox, John.] *The First Blast of the Trumpet Against the Monstrvovs Regiment of Women.* N.p., 1558.

Lanterne of Light, The. Ed. Lilian M. Swinburn. London, 1917.

Lloyd, Charles. *Formularies of Faith Put Forth by Authority during the Reign of Henry VIII. Articles about Religion, 1536. The Institution of a Christian Man, 1537. A Necessary Doctrine and Erudition for any Christian Man, 1543.* Oxford, 1825.

Luther, Martin. *D. Martin Luthers Werke. Kritische Gesam-*

tausgabe. Weimar, 1883–1948. 58 vols.

Marsilius of Padua. *The Defence of Peace*. Trans. William Marshall. [London], 1535.

———. *The Defender of Peace*. Trans. Alan Gewirth. New York, 1956. 2 vols.

Mede, Joseph. *The Key of the Revelation*. London, 1643.

Migne, J[acques]-P[aul]. *Patrologiae Cursus Completus*. . . . Series Latina. Parisiis, 1841–1886. 221 vols. in 222.

More, Thomas. *Utopia*, in *The Complete Works of St. Thomas More*, Vol. IV. Ed. Edward Surtz and J. H. Hexter. New Haven and London, 1965.

Munday, Anthony. *The English Romayne Lyfe. Discouering: The liues of the Englishmen at Roome: the orders of the English Seminarie . . . Therevnto is added, the cruell tiranny, vsed on an English man at Roome, his Christian suffering and notable Martirdome, for the Gospell of Iesus Christe, in Anno. 1581. Written by A. M. sometime the Popes Scholler in the Seminarie among them*. London, 1582.

Napier, John L. *A Plaine Discouery of the whole Reuelation of Saint Iohn: set downe in two treatises: the one searching and prouing the true interpretation thereof: The other applying the same paraphrastically and historically to the text*. Edinburgh, 1593.

Overall, J. *Bishop Overall's Convocation-Book, MDCVI. Concerning the Government of God's Catholick Church and the Kingdoms of the Whole World*. London, 1690.

Pantaleone, Heinrico. *Martyrvm Historia. Hoc est, Maximarvm per Evropam Persecvtionvm ac Sanctorvm Dei Martyrum, caeterarum que rerum insignium, in Ecclesia Christi postremis & periculosis his temporibus gestarum, atque certo consilio per Regno & Nationes distributarum, Commentarij*. Basel, 1563.

Parker, T. H. L., ed. *English Reformers* (The Library of Christian Classics, Vol. XXVI). London, 1966.

Parker Society. *Select Works of John Bale, D.D., Bishop of Ossory. Containing the Examinations of Lord Cobham, William Thorpe, and Anne Askewe, and the Image of Both Churches*. Ed. Henry Christmas. Cambridge, 1849.

———. *The Catechism of Thomas Becon, S.T.P., Chaplain to Archbishop Cranmer, Prebendary of Canterbury, &c. with other pieces written by him in the reign of King Edward the Sixth.* Ed. John Ayre. Cambridge, 1844.

———. *The Early Works of Thomas Becon, S.T.P., Chaplain to Archbishop Cranmer, Prebendary of Canterbury, &c. Being the Treatises published by him in the Reign of King Henry VIII.* Ed. John Ayre. Cambridge, 1843.

———. *Prayers and other Pieces of Thomas Becon, S.T.P., Chaplain to Archbishop Cranmer, Prebendary of Canterbury, etc.* Ed. John Ayre. Cambridge, 1844.

———. *The Writings of John Bradford, M.A., Fellow of Pembroke Hall, Cambridge, and Prebendary of St. Paul's Martyr, 1555. Containing Sermons, Meditations, Examinations, etc.* Ed. Aubrey Townsend. Cambridge, 1848.

———. *The Writings of John Bradford, M.A., Fellow of Pembroke Hall, Cambridge, and Prebendary of St. Paul's Martyr, 1555. Containing Letters, Treatises, Remains.* Ed. Aubrey Townsend. Cambridge, 1853.

———. *The Decades of Henry Bullinger, Minister of the Church of Zurich.* Ed. Thomas Harding. Cambridge, 1849. 3 vols.

———. *Miscellaneous Writings and Letters of Thomas Cranmer, Archbishop of Canterbury, Martyr, 1556.* Ed. J. E. Cox. Cambridge, 1846.

———. *The Two Liturgies . . . in the Reign of King Edward VI.* Ed. Joseph Ketley. Cambridge, 1844.

———. *The Remains of Edmund Grindal, D.D., successively Bishop of London, and Archbishop of York and Canterbury.* Ed. William Nicholson. Cambridge, 1843.

———. *Later Writings of Bishop Hooper together with his Letters and other Pieces.* Ed. Charles Nevinson. Cambridge, 1852.

———. *The Works of John Jewel, Bishop of Salisbury.* Ed. John Ayre. Cambridge, 1845–1850. 4 vols.

———. *Original Letters Relative to the English Reformation, written during the Reigns of King Henry VIII, King Edward VI, and Queen Mary: Chiefly from the Archives of Zurich.* Ed. Hastings Robinson. Cambridge, 1846–1847. 2 vols.

———. *Correspondence of Matthew Parker, D.D., Archbishop of Canterbury. Comprising Letters Written by and to Him, From A.D. 1535, to His Death, A.D. 1575.* Ed. John Bruce. Cambridge, 1853.

———. *The Works of Nicholas Ridley, D.D., Sometime Lord Bishop of London, Martyr, 1555.* Ed. Henry Christmas. Cambridge, 1841.

———. *The Sermons of Edwin Sandys, D.D., successively Bishop of Worcester and London and Archbishop of York; to which are added some miscellaneous Pieces by the same Author.* Ed. John Ayre. Cambridge, 1842.

———. *The Works of John Whitgift, D.D., Master of Trinity College, Dean of Lincoln, etc. afterwards successively Bishop of Worcester and Archbishop of Canterbury.* Ed. John Ayre. Cambridge, 1851–1853. 3 vols.

———. *Private Prayers, put forth by Authority during the Reign of Queen Elizabeth. The Primer of 1559. The Orarium of 1560. The Preces Privatae of 1564. The Book of Christian Prayers of 1578. With an Appendix, containing the Litany of 1544.* Ed. William Keatinge Clay. Cambridge, 1851.

———. *The Zurich Letters, Comprising the Correspondence of Several English Bishops and Others, with some of the Helvetian Reformers, during the early part of the Reign of Queen Elizabeth.* Ed. Hastings Robinson. Cambridge, 1842.

Parson, Robert. *A Treatise of Three Conversions of England from Paganiame to Christian Religion.* N.p., 1603.

A parte of a register, contayninge sundrie memorable matters, written by divers godly and learned in our time, which stande for, and desire the reformation of our church, in discipline and ceremonies, according to the pure worde of God, and the law of our lande. Middelburg, 1593.

Pauck, Wilhelm, ed. *Melanchthon and Bucer* (The Library of Christian Classics, Vol. XIX). Philadelphia, 1969.

Peel, Albert, ed. *The Second Parte of a Register, Being A Calendar of Manuscripts under the title intended for publication by the Puritans about 1593, and now in Dr. William's Library, London.* Cambridge, 1915. 2 vols.

Ponet, John. *A Shorte Treatise of Politike Pouuer, and of the true Obedience which Subiectes owe to Kynges and other ciuile Gouernours, with an Exhortacion to all true naturall Englishe men.* N.p., 1556.

Poole, Reginald Lane. *Illustrations of the History of Medieval*

Thought in the Departments of Theology and Ecclesiastical Politics. London, 1884.

The praier and complaynte of the plowmen vnto Christe: writtē not longe after the yere of oure Lorde A thousande and thre hundred. [Antwerp, 1531].

Richter, Aemilius Ludwig, ed. *Die evangelischen Kirchenordnungen des sechszehnten Jahrhunderts.* Weimar, 1846. 2 vols.

Schaff, Philip, ed. *The Creeds of Christendom, with a History and Critical Notes.* 6th ed. New York, 1931. 3 vols.

A Select Library of the Nicene and Post-Nicene Fathers of the Christian Church. 1st ser. Ed. Philip Schaff. New York, 1905–1917. 14 vols.

A Select Library of the Nicene and Post-Nicene Fathers of the Christian Church. 2d ser. Ed. Philip Schaff. New York, 1890–1900. 14 vols.

Sleidan, John. *De Statv Religionis et Reipvblicae, Carolo Qvinto, Caesare, Commentarij.* N.p., 1555.

———. *A Famouse Cronicle of Oure Time, Called Sleidanes Commentaries, Concerning the State of Religion and Common Wealth, during the Raigne of the Emperour Charles the fift.* Trans. John Daye. N.p., 1560.

———. *A Briefe, Chronicle of the Foure Principall Empyres. To witte, of Babilon, Persia, Grecia, and Rome. Wherein, is compendiouslye conteyned the whole discourse of histories.* Trans. Stephan Wythers. London, 1563.

———. *The General History of the Reformation of the Church from the Errors and Corruptions of the Church of Rome.* London, 1689.

Stapleton, Thomas. *A Fortresse of the Faith.* Antwerp, 1565.

Starkey, Thomas. *A Dialogue between Reginald Pole and Thomas Lupset.* Ed. Kathleen M. Burton. London, 1948.

Stowe, John. *Three Fifteenth-Century Chronicles, with Historical Memoranda by John Stowe, the Antiquary, and Contemporary Notes of Occurrences Written by Him in the Reign of Queen Elizabeth.* Ed. James Gairdner. Camden Society, n.s., Vol. XXVIII. London, 1880.

Thomas Aquinas. *The "Summa Theologica" of St. Thomas Aquinas.* Trans. Fathers of the English Dominican Province.

London and New York, 1920–1935. 22 vols.

Thomas, J. M. Lloyd, ed. *The Autobiography of Richard Baxter* (abridged from the *Reliquiae Baxterianae*, 1696). London, 1925.

Tichonius. *The Book of Rules of Tychonius.* Ed. F. C. Burkitt. (Vol. III in *Texts and Studies: Contributions to Biblical and Patristic literature*, ed. J. A. Robinson, 1st ser. Cambridge, 1894.

Whittingham, William. *A Brief Discourse of the Troubles at Frankfort, 1554–1558 A.D. Attributed to William Whittingham, Dean of Durham, 1575 A.D.* Ed. Edward Arber. London, 1907.

Wilkinson, Henry. *Babylons Ruine, Jerusalems Rising. Set forth in a sermon preached before the honourable House of Commons, on the 25 Octob. being the day appointed for the monthly fast, etc.* (London, 1643.

Willet, Andrew. *Hexapla in Danielem: That is, A Six-fold Commentarie vpon the most diuine prophesie of Daniel, wherein according to the method propounded in Hexapla vpon Genesis and Exodus, sixe things are obserued in euery Chapter.* Cambridge, 1610.

Wycliffe, John. *The Last Age of the Churche.* N.p., 1356.

Zwingli, Huldreich. *Huldrici Zuinglii Opera* (*Huldreich Zwingli's Werke*). Ed. M. Schuler and J. Schulthess. Zürich, 1828–1842. 8 vols.

II. SECONDARY SOURCES

A. BOOKS

Alford, Henry. *The New Testament for English Readers: Containing the Authorized Version, with marginal corrections of Readings and Renderings; marginal references; and a critical and explanatory commentary.* London, 1863.

Allen, J. W. *A History of Political Thought in the Sixteenth Century.* London, 1928.

Bainton, Roland H. *The Travail of Religious Liberty.* New York, 1951.

Bett, Henry. *Joachim of Flora.* London, 1931.

Burgh, William. *Lectures on the Second Advent of our Lord*

Jesus Christ, and Connected Events: with an Introduction on the use of unfulfilled Prophecy. Dublin, 1832.

Burnet, Gilbert. *The History of the Reformation of the Church of England.* London, 1679–1715. 3 vols.

Cohn, Norman. *The Pursuit of the Millennium. Revolutionary messianism in medieval and Reformation Europe and its bearing on modern movements.* London, 1962.

Collier, Jeremy. *An Ecclesiastical History of Great Britain, chiefly of England: from the First Planting of Christianity, to the End of the Reign of King Charles the Second. With a Brief Account of the Affairs of Religion in Ireland. Collected from the best Ancient Historians, Councils and Records.* London, 1708. 2 vols.

Collinson, Patrick. *The Elizabethan Puritan Movement.* London, 1967.

Coulton, G. G. *Ten Medieval Studies.* Boston, 1959.

Dawley, Powel Mills. *John Whitgift and the Reformation.* London, 1955.

Deanesly, Margaret. *A History of the Medieval Church, 590–1500.* London, 1954.

D'Entrèves, Alexander P. *The Medieval Contribution to Political Thought.* New York, 1959.

Dickens, A. G. *The English Reformation.* London, 1964.

Digby, William. *A Treatise on the 1260 Days of Daniel and Saint John: Being an Attempt to Establish the Conclusion that They are Years; and also to fix the Date of their Commencement and Termination.* Dublin, 1831.

Dugmore, C. W. *The Mass and the English Reformers.* London, 1958.

Elliott, E. B. *Horae Apocalypticae; or, a Commentary on the Apocalypse, Critical and Historical; including also and Examination of the chief Prophecies of Daniel . . . containing besides other matter, a sketch of the History of Apocalyptic Interpretation, critical reviews of the chief apocalyptic counter-schemes, and indices.* 5th ed. London, 1862. 4 vols.

Faber, George Stanley. *A Dissertation on the Prophecies, that have been fulfilled, are now fulfilling, or will hereafter be fulfilled, relative to the great period of 1260 years; the Papal and Mohammedan Apostasies; the Tyrannical Reign of Antichrist, or the Infidel Power; and the Restoration of the Jews.* London, 1807. 2 vols.

Fuller, Thomas. *The Church History of Britain; from the Birth of Jesus Christ until the Year MDCXLVIII.* Ed. J. S. Brewer. Oxford, 1845. 6 vols.

———. *The History of the Worthies of England.* London, 1662.

Guinness, H. Grattan. *History Unveiling Prophecy or Time as an Interpreter.* New York, 1905.

Hallam, Henry. *The Constitutional History of England from the Accession of Henry VII to the death of George II.* London, 1827.

Haller, William. *Foxe's Book of Martyrs and the Elect Nation.* London, 1963.

Hardwick, Charles. *A History of the Articles of Religion.* London, 1888.

Headley, John M. *Luther's View of Church History.* New Haven and London, 1963.

Hill, Christopher. *Intellectual Origins of the English Revolution.* Oxford, 1965.

———. *Society and Puritanism in Pre-Revolutionary England.* London, 1966.

Holl, Karl. *The Cultural Significance of the Reformation.* New York, 1959.

Hughes, Philip. *The Reformation in England.* London, 1954. 2 vols.

Jordan, W. K. *The Development of Religious Toleration in England from the Beginning of the English Reformation to the Death of Queen Elizabeth.* London, 1932.

Knappen, M. M. *Tudor Puritanism: A Chapter in the History of Idealism.* Chicago, 1965.

Köhler, Walther. *Zürcher Ehegericht und Genfer Konsistorium.* Leipzig, 1932–1942. 2 vols.

Lamont, William M. *Godly Rule: Politics and Religion, 1603–60.* London, 1969.

———. *Marginal Prynne, 1600–1669.* London, 1963.

Lechler, Gotthard. *John Wycliffe and his English Precursors.* London, 1884.

Lecler, Joseph. *Toleration and the Reformation.* Trans. T. L. Westow. London, 1960.

Lingard, John. *A History of England from the first Invasion by the Romans (to the Revolution in 1688).* London, 1819–1830. 8 vols.

Maitland, Charles. *The Apostles' School of Prophetic Interpretation: with its History down to the present time.* London, 1849.

Maitland, S. R. *Facts and Documents Illustrative of the History, Doctrine, and Rites, of the Ancient Albigenses and Waldenses.* London, 1832.

——. *Notes on the Contributions of the Rev. George Townsend, M.A., prebendary of Durham, etc., to the New Edition of Fox's Martyrology.* London, 1841–1842. 3 pts.

McLelland, Joseph C. *The Visible Words of God: An Exposition of the Sacramental Theology of Peter Martyr Vermigli, A.D. 1500–1562.* London, 1957.

Milner, Joseph. *The History of the Church of Christ.* London, 1834. 4 vols.

Morgan, Irvonwy. *The Godly Preachers of the Elizabethan Church.* London, 1965.

Mozley, J. F. *John Foxe and His Book.* London, 1940.

Neale, J. E. *Elizabeth I and her Parliaments, 1559–1581.* London, 1953.

New, John F. H. *Anglican and Puritan: The Basis of Their Opposition, 1558–1640.* London, 1964.

Norskov Olsen, V. *The New Testament Logia on Divorce: A Study of Their Interpretation from Erasmus to Milton.* Tübingen, 1971.

Owst, Gerald R. *Preaching in Medieval England: An Introduction to Sermon Manuscripts of the Period c. 1350–1450.* Cambridge, 1926.

Parker, T. M. *Christianity and the State in the Light of History.* New York, 1955.

Pauck, W. *Das Reich Gottes auf Erden.* Berlin, 1928.

Pratt, Josiah. *The Life and Defence of John Foxe.* London, 1870. Printed in *The Acts and Monuments of John Foxe,* Vol. I. pt. 1, pp. 1–162. London, 1853–1870.

Ridley, Jasper. *Thomas Cranmer.* Oxford, 1962.

Rupp, Gordon. *Six Makers of English Religion, 1500–1700.* London, 1964.

Schaff, Philip. *History of the Christian Church.* Grand Rapids, Mich., 1953–1959. 8 vols.

Simpson, Alan. *Puritanism in Old and New England.* Chicago, 1961.

Soames, Henry. *The Anglo-Saxon Church.* London, 1844.

Strype, John. *Annals of the Reformation and Establishment of Religion, and other various occurrences in the Church of England, during Queen Elizabeth's Happy Reign: together with an Appendix of original papers of state, records, and letters.* Oxford, 1824. 4 vols., 7 pts.

———. *Ecclesiastical Memorials, Relating chiefly to Religion, and the Reformation of it, and the emergencies of the Church of England, under King Henry VIII. King Edward VI. and Queen Mary I.* Oxford, 1821. 3 vols. 6 pts.

———. *Historical Collections of the Life and Acts of the Right Reverend Father in God, John Aylmer, Lord Bishop of London in the Reign of Queen Elizabeth. Wherein are explained many Transactions of the Church of England; and what Methods were then taken to preserve it, with respect to the Papist and Puritan.* New ed. Oxford, 1821.

———. *The History of the Life and Acts of the Most Reverend Father in God, Edmund Grindal, the first Bishop of London, and the second Archbishop of York and Canterbury successively, in the Reign of Queen Elizabeth.* Oxford, 1821.

———. *The Life and Acts of Matthew Parker, the first Archbishop of Canterbury, in the Reign of Queen Elizabeth. To which is added, an Appendix, containing various Transcripts of Records, Letters, Instruments, and other Papers, for the asserting or illustrating the foregoing History.* Oxford, 1821. 3 vols.

———. *The Life and Acts of John Whitgift, D.D. the third and last Lord Archbishop of Canterbury in the Reign of Queen Elizabeth. The whole digested, compiled, and attested from Records, Registers, original Letters, and other authentic MSS, taken from the choicest Libraries and Collections of the Kingdom. Together with a large appendix of the said papers.* Oxford, 1822. 3 vols.

———. *Memorials of Archbishop Cranmer.* Oxford, 1848–1854. 3 vols.

Tanner, Joseph. *Daniel and the Revelation: the Chart of Prophecy, and our place in it. A study of the historical and futurist interpretation.* London, 1898.

Tierney, M. A. *The History and Antiquities of the Castle and Town of Arundel; including the Biography of its Earls, from the Conquest to the Present Time.* London, 1834.

Todd, James Henthorn. *Discourses on the Prophecies Relating to Antichrist in the Writings of Daniel and St. Paul; preached before the University of Dublin, at the Donnellan Lecture, MDCCCXXXVIII.* Dublin, 1840.

Trinterud, Leonard J., ed. *Elizabethan Puritanism.* New York, 1971.

Weber, Alfred. *Heinrich Bullingers "Christlicher Ehestand", seine zeitgenössischen Quellen und die Anfänge des Familienbuches in England.* Leipzig, 1929.

Williams, George Huntston. *The Radical Reformation.* London, 1962.

Williams, Glanmor. *Reformation Views of Church History.* London, 1970.

Woodhouse, H. F. *The Doctrine of the Church in Anglican Theology, 1547–1603.* London, 1954.

B. ARTICLES AND ESSAYS

Baumer, Franklin Le Van. "Thomas Starkey and Marsilius of Padua," *Politica*, II (Nov. 1936), 188–205.

Bill, E. G. W. "Records of the Church Recovered by Lambeth Palace Library," *Journal of the Society of Archivists*, Vol. III, no. 1 (1965), pp. 24–26.

Clebsch, William A. "The Elizabethans on Luther," in *Interpreters of Luther: Essays in Honor of Wilhelm Pauck*, ed. Jaroslav Pelikan (Philadelphia, 1968).

Cohen, Alfred. "Two Roads to the Puritan Millennium: William Erbury and Vavasor Powell," *Church History*, XXXII (Sept. 1963), 322–338.

Collinson, Patrick. *A Mirror of Elizabethan Puritanism, The Life and Letters of 'Godly Master Dering.'* London, 1964.

———. "The 'nott conformytye' of the young John Whitgift," *The Journal of Ecclesiastical History*, Vol XV, no. 2, pp. 192–200.

Cuninghame, William. *On the Jubilean Chronology of the Seventh Trumpet of the Apocalypse, and the judgment of the Ancient of Days, Daniel vii. 9. With a brief account of the discoveries of Mons de Chesaux as to the great astronomical cycles of 2300 and 1260 years, and their difference 1040 years.* Glasgow, 1834.

Dickens, A. G. From *The English Historical Review*, No. CCCXVI (July, 1965), pp. 589–91.

Dowling, John Goulter. *A Letter to the Rev. S. R. Maitland on the Opinions of the Paulicians.* London, 1835.

Hall, Basil. "Puritanism: the Problem of Definition," in *Studies in Church History*, Vol. II, ed. G. J. Cuming (London, 1965), pp. 283–296.

Haller, William. "John Foxe and the Puritan Revolution," in *The Seventeenth Century: Studies in the History of English Thought and Literature from Bacon to Pope*, ed. Richard F. Jones (Stanford, 1951).

King, John. *Examination of Milner's History of the Fourth Century and of certain Strictures on that History, contained in the Second Letter of the Rev. S. R. Maitland to the Rev. H. J. Rose: To which is prefixed a letter to the Rev. S. R. Maitland.* London, 1836.

———. *Maitland not Authorized to Censure Milner.* London, 1835.

Lee, Sidney. "John Foxe," in *The Dictionary of National Biography*, Vol. VII (London, 1949–1950), pp. 581–590.

MacCulloch, J. A. "Eschatology," in *Encyclopaedia of Religion and Ethics*, ed. James Hastings (New York, 1925), Vol. V, pp. 373–391.

Maitland, S. R. *An Attempt to Elucidate the Prophecies Concerning Antichrist.* London, 1830.

———. *The Dark Ages: A Series of Essays Intended to Illustrate the State of Religion and Literature in the Ninth, Tenth, Eleventh, and Twelfth Centuries.* Reprinted from *The British Magazine*, with corrections and some additions. London, 1844.

———. *An Enquiry into the Grounds on which the Prophetic Period of Daniel and St. John has been Supposed to Consist of 1260 Years.* London, 1826.

———. *A Letter to the Rev. William Digby, A.M., Occasioned*

by his Treatise on the 1260 Days. London, 1831.

———. *A Letter to the Rev. John King, M.A., incumbent of Christ's Church, Hull; Occasioned by His Pamphlet entitled "Maitland not Authorized to Censure Milner."* London, 1835.

———. *A Letter to the Rev. W. H. Mill, D.D., late principal of Bishop's College, Calcutta; Containing some Strictures on Mr. Faber's Recent Work, entitled "The Ancient Vallenses and Albigenses."* London, 1839.

———. *A Letter to the Rev. Hugh James Rose, B.D., Chaplain to His Grace the Archbishop of Canterbury; with Strictures on Milner's Church History.* London, 1834.

———. "On the Personal History of Foxe the Martyrologist," *The British Magazine,* XXIII (May 1843), 493–500; XXIV (Nov. 1843), 477–489.

———. *Remarks on that part of the Rev. J. King's pamphlet, entitled "Maitland not Authorized to Censure Milner," which relates to the Waldenses, including a reply to the Rev. G. S. Faber's supplement, entitled "Reinerius and Maitland."* London, 1836.

———. "Remarks on the New Edition of Foxe's Work, and on the Work Itself," *The British Magazine,* XI (June 1837), 620–625; XII (July 1837), 6–13; XII (Aug. 1837), 137–144; XII (Sept. 1837), 253–259; XII (Oct. 1837), 376–381; XII (Nov. 1837), 496–502; XII (Dec. 1837), 620–627; XIII (Jan. 1838), 12–20; XIII (Feb. 1838), 122–129; XIII (Mar. 1838), 254–263; XIII (April 1838), 385–389; XIII (June 1838), 613–619.

———. *A Review of Fox the Martyrologist's History of the Waldenses.* London, 1837.

———. *A Second Enquiry into the Grounds on which the Prophetic Period of Daniel and St. John, has been supposed to consist of 1260 years, containing an examination of the arguments of Mede-Remarks on a passage in the dialogues on prophecy,—on various reviews of the first enquiry,—and on the common interpretation of the seven heads of the beast.* London, 1829.

———. *A Second Letter to the Rev. Hugh James Rose, B.D., Chaplain to His Grace the Archbishop of Canterbury; Containing Notes on Milner's History of the Church in the Fourth Century.* London, 1835.

——. *Six Letters on Fox's Acts and Monuments, addressed to the editor of the British Magazine and re-printed from that work with notes and additions.* London, 1837.

——. *The Twelve Hundred and Sixty Days in Reply to a Review in the* Morning Watch. London, 1830.

——. *The Twelve Hundred and Sixty Days: in Reply to the Strictures of William Cuninghame, Esq.* London, 1834.

A Member of the Church of England, *Reply to an Enquiry, by the Rev. S. R. Maitland, perpetual curate of Christ Church, Gloucester, into the grounds on which the Prophetic Period of Daniel and St. John has been Supposed to Consist of 1260 Years.* London, 1828.

Newman, John Henry. "Advent Sermons on Antichrist," *Tracts for the Times,* Vol. V (London, 1840).

——. "The Protestant dea of Antichrist," in *Essays Critical and Historical* (2d ed.; London, 1872).

Norwood, Frederick A. "The Strangers' Model Churches in Sixteenth-Century England," printed in *Reformation Studies, Essays in Honor of Roland H. Bainton* (Ed. Franklin H. Littel; Richmond, Va., 1962).

Previte-Orton, C. W. "Marsilius of Padua," *Proceedings of the British Academy,* XXI (London, 1935), 137–183.

Ratcliff, E. C. "The Liturgical Work of archbishop Cranmer," *Journal of Ecclesiastical History,* Vol. VII, no. 2 (1956), pp. 189–203.

Rigg, James McMullen. "Robert Beale," *The Dictionary of National Biography* (London, 1949–1950), Vol. II, pp. 3–7.

Scott, Joseph Frederick. "John Napier," in *Encyclopaedia Britannica* (London, 1964), Vol. XVI, p. 77.

Whibley, Charles. "Chroniclers and Antiquaries," in *Cambridge History of English Literature,* ed. A. W. Ward and A. R. Waller (Cambridge, 1949–1953), Vol. III, pp. 331–334.

C. UNPUBLISHED DISSERTATIONS

Knox, Robert Buick. "The Ecclesiastical Policy of James Ussher, Archbishop of Armagh." Ph.D. dissertation, University of London, 1956.

Oliver, Leslie Mahin. "The Acts and Monuments of John Foxe: A Study of the Growth and Influence of a Book." Ph.D. Harvard dissertation, Harvard University, 1945.

Indexes

Topical Index

Name Index

Scriptural Index